COMMUNITY OF INTEREST

COMMUNITY
of
INTEREST

Oscar Newman

ANCHOR BOOKS
ANCHOR PRESS/DOUBLEDAY
Garden City, New York   1981

Community of Interest was originally published in hardcover by Anchor Press/Doubleday in 1980. Anchor Books edition: 1981.

Library of Congress Cataloging in Publication Data

Newman, Oscar.
  Community of interest.

  Bibliography: p. 331
  Includes index.
  1. Community development, Urban—United States.
2. Housing—United States. 3. Housing policy—
United States. 4. Urban renewal—United States.
I. Title.
HN90.C6N49   309.2′62′0973   77-76257
ISBN 0-385-11124-X

To my children, Paul, Jon, and Hinde, who
revealed a world to me beyond the horizons of
my architectural and planning perspectives.

CONTENTS

ACKNOWLEDGMENTS

I should first like to acknowledge the staff of the Institute for Community Design Analysis who participated in and directed the many studies which are referred to here. Allan Christianson and Max Kawer, architects, for their assistance in preparing the graphic material in chapters VII, VIII, and IX; Frank Wayno, Dean Grandin, Sanford Low, and Edward Robbins for their work on the private streets of St. Louis synopsized in Chapter VI; Imre Kohn, Karen Franck, and Sue Fox for their work on the effects of the defensible space modification to two housing projects in New York; Karen Franck, Barbara Bryan, David Nasatir. Tony Longo and our consultant Noel Dunivant for their work on the factors affecting crime and instability in federally assisted housing developments, the findings from which are referred to throughout.

Karen Franck must also be singled out for special thanks for her review of the first draft of this book and for providing me with invaluable suggestions on its reorganization. The review of the literature on racial and economic integration in housing, which appears at the conclusion of Chapter II, was also prepared by her.

The agencies that made possible the research studies mentioned above were: the National Institute for Law Enforcement and Criminal Justice, which provided most of the funding to prepare a manual entitled *Design Guidelines for Creating Defensible Space* from which some of the illustrations and text in Chapters VII and VIII are borrowed; the National Science Foundation for providing partial funding for the study of the private streets of St. Louis and the study of the effects of defensible space modifications to two housing projects; and the Department of Housing and Urban Development for funding to prepare the schematic plans for the Newark housing development discussed in Chapter IX.

The following state and local housing agencies provided additional assistance either in the form of professional service contracts or in providing access to their data and projects: the Oklahoma City Housing Authority; the Seattle Housing Authority; the City of Indianapolis Department of Metropolitan Development; the Jersey City Criminal Justice Co-ordinating Council; the St. Louis City Planning Commission; and the housing authorities and police departments of the cities of Newark, San Francisco, New York, and St. Louis.

The following professionals in the architectural and market analysis firms participated in the projects cited below: Bob Barth of the Oklahoma City University Business Center in the survey of potential applicants for public housing; Tom Flesher of Noftsger, Lawrence, Lawrence and Flesher, architects, Oklahoma City; and Dick Shavey of Shavey and Schmidt, architects, Seattle, for their assistance in preparing the plans for the modification of the housing developments in Oklahoma City and Seattle, respectively.

I should like to thank the members of the board of directors of the Institute for Community Design Analysis for their support of the Institute and for encouraging me in this effort: Saul B. Cohen; Robert E. Crew Jr.; Lloyd Kaplan; William Porter; Thomas A. Repetto; George Sternlieb; and Charles R. Work.

Finally, I should like to express special thanks to Gerald Kaplan, former director of the National Institute of Law Enforcement and Criminal Justice for his support of our institute's research activity. It is unlikely that much of the Institute's work over these past five years would have progressed so far without him.

Oscar Newman
Institute for Community Design Analysis
New York City
April 1979

Introduction

In the early 1960s our nation had a dream—that with personal commitment and government assistance we could remedy the neglect of generations, through new programs and funding we could raise the poor into the middle-class and enable different racial groups to live together. Now, some fifteen years and hundreds of billions of dollars later, the mood of the country has changed; our dream has dissipated. We see our problems still unsolved, the costs incurred larger than anticipated, and our faith in the efficacy of social intervention badly damaged.

In our expanding urban societies the communities we thought so stable they would become the backbone of our economic and racial integration efforts have proven as ephemeral as our dreams. The old concepts of communities no longer hold; they have gone with the actual communities that were used as the models to explain them. The dissolution of our older physical communities has given many social scientists and philosophers the opportunity to lament the passing of still another golden era and further fuel for their anger with this post-industrial age. But communities have not disappeared from contemporary life—they have just taken on a new form. Today's communities are as different from the communities of the turn of the century as those were different from the small-town and rural communities they, in turn, replaced.

It has also become vogue among social scientists and physical planners to disparage the concept of the physical community and to insist that it be replaced by the concept of the social, nongeographic community of common interests. This new concept, it is claimed, more accurately explains current patterns of association and identification. Fair enough. It is my conviction, though, that not only do physical communities exist today as vital organisms, but that they continue to play an essential role in people's lives. This book is an effort to formulate a new concept for geographic communities which reflect contemporary needs and political realities. My interest is not only in identifying these new, physical communities and their functions so as to learn how better to plan and design them. but also to learn enough about them to achieve societal goals larger than the simple satisfaction of each community's internal needs. The first of these larger goals is the bringing together of separate communities so as to be able to refashion urban environments, to stablize threatened neighborhoods and rehabilitate our older cities. The second societal goal is the achievement of racial and economic integration within communities rather than between them—that is, to plan integrated communities so that the social and physical environments created enable their members to transcend the economic and racial differences between them.

The concentration of our nation's population into large metropolitan areas, coupled with our increased mobility and the movement of racial groups, has created havoc in our older residential neighborhoods. People have responded to these changes by seeking stability and community through the creation of new residential areas of economic, racial, and religious uniformity. Our new suburbs are little more than an attempt to transplant old ethnic urban neighborhoods to the periphery of cities. Although these suburban developments have been somewhat successful in stemming instability, they have not always succeeded in creating a community for their inhabitants.

In a 1978 nationwide survey of their views and concerns about urban life, Americans were asked about what sort of communities they wanted to live in and whether their preferences differed from where they live now. Although three times as many Americans now live in urban concentrations than fifty years ago, 47 per cent of those interviewed said they would prefer to live in a rural area or in a small city, town, or village not located in the suburbs; 27 per cent preferred a medium-size city, small city, or town in the suburbs; while only 16 per cent said they would prefer a large city of over 250,000 population.[1] In spite of where the lure of opportunity may have brought us, we seem to pine for the communities of the old.

Our older towns and cities were composed of extended families and friendship networks. They housed many different communities, age groups, and life-styles within a few blocks of each other and contained a variety of communal and commercial institutions. Our new suburban communities house few extended families and facilitate little in the way of contact with one's neighbors or between different ethnic or income groups. They are spread over too large areas and provide little incentive to encourage residents in one group to seek out the community or institutions of another. Each suburban community is intentionally designed to be self-contained. And because of the small size of its population, each can support only the most mundane of communal and commercial facilities: a small library, a few branches of chain stores, indifferent restaurants, mediocre movie houses. There is no purpose in the members of one suburban community seeking out the institutions of another when both are identical.

Also, by not being able to find a meaning for community in contemporary society, we have been unable to come together with our neighbors to share in the creation of collective resources. As a consequence, each family unit is required to spend a large percentage of its earnings to provide the equivalent of these community amenities on its own property. In a like manner, small residential developments, unable to determine a commonality of purpose with neighboring developments, must each provide their own communal facilities, and their small size and limited resources dictate that these communal facilities be parochial and uninspired, The fact, too, that our funds are being channeled into providing resources which are restricted for the use of the few, means that the poor, who in the past at least, had access to the rich public resources produced by the society's collective wealth, are now deprived of even these.

The communities of interest I am advocating are more dense, smaller in size and scale, and more closely juxtaposed with others than are suburbs. They facilitate interaction between different ethnic and economic groups and make possible the investment in public facilities that serve a large and varied populace rather than encourage investment in private, small-scale, parochial facilities. But the creation of such communities of interest and their larger urban agglomerations require our acceptance of concepts which, although they have been with us for many years, may be viewed distastefully. But the course of action we pursued in the past involved our advocating one set of housing and urban policies while implementing another. Certain of the policies I will be advocating may appear, at first hearing, abhorrent to the democratic process. But without them we have achieved the opposite of our planned intentions—and these opposite results are far more abhorrent than those I am advocating. The solution that the more affluent members of our society adopted to solve the problem of unstable neighborhoods and rising crime was to move away from them. They put ever increasing distances between themselves and what they viewed as the source of their problems. Like much else that we do in America, this solution is not the result of a carefully formulated, collectively articulated national policy, but the consequence of millions of individuals acting independently. We have not even been able to find a community of purpose in our response to crime.

The most unsuspecting casualty of decades of massive population movements and rising crime in America has been our collective belief in the efficacy of urban culture. The urban environment, man's most important invention for facilitating the concentration and interaction of different trades, skills, cultures, philosophies, and income groups, has been abandoned in the minds of Americans as a place to live and raise a family.[2] In Western civilization the industrial city was the womb which first nurtured and then gave birth to a new economics, science, and technology. It provided the protection necessary for the establishment of new freedoms, the arena for a new politics and the societies which followed. The city was also the ladder of upward mobility for the poor and illiterate, a haven of tolerance for oppressed minorities and religious groups. In spite of the fact that most American cities compared poorly in physical splendor with their European counterparts, our cities were second to none in their function as portals to a new life for the poor and disadvantaged. They provided opportunity for self-advancement to the rural and small-town immigrant, both from abroad and from our own hinterlands. But the increasing growth of our cities and the attending crime has diminished the opportunities for interaction between different income and ethnic groups and has served to make strangers of us all. Our capacity to be open and receptive to those different from ourselves appears to have spent; suspicion and distrust are now the most frequent of attitudes that urban dwellers bring to new encounters. The cost has been the dispersal of our once proud centers of social and economic heterogeneity. With it we have lost the rich, interactive milieus with made American urban culture unique, virile, and the envy of other nations.

We have grown to accept the fact that America is no longer a country with urban environments. San Francisco, Boston, and Minneapolis are among the few remaining cities which still have neighborhoods where people feel they can walk the streets safely at night and where middle- and working-class families can raise their children within the city limits. But even in these cities rising crime rates suggest that their uniqueness may be short-lived.

In response to our fears, we have adopted a course of action which suggests that we have given up many of our society's past hopes and aspirations — we have abandoned our commitment to urban life and to the poor and dark-skinned living in inner cities. Our heterogeneous cities have been dispersed into a myriad of small suburban communities of ethnic and economic uniformity. We now content ourselves with the safe fortresses of white, middle-class suburbia. American society has become polarized into suburban, white, and wealthy versus urban, dark, and poor. The middle-class has put tens of miles between themselves and their fears and have forsaken the environments which once provided them with the nourishment essential to their own development. They have left behind the decaying remnants of a once rich urban environment to shelter the last generation of urban migrants.

It has become clear that the more divergent the interacting cultures, the greater the need for a commonly accepted decorum to provide the medium for encounter. Our inability to develop an acceptable code for dealing with aberrant and criminal behavior in the public areas of our cities has led us to abandon the use of these areas as arenas for free and unanticipated human interaction. Our public areas which were once intensively used, have been reduced to mere arteries, mechanisms to get us from one place to another. We are now determined to limit our encounters with others to those of a premeditated nature. We are no longer receptive to new ideas or faces. The development of new sociophysical mechanisms for allowing divergent racial and economic groups to live next to each other without trauma has become essential to the survival of the concept of the urban life in America in this final quarter of the twentieth century.

A response to crime that entails running from it has no termination; there is no place that is either safe or distant enough from the criminal, the poor, and the black. Our fear of crime has made what was previously unacceptable, desirable — that we might have a nation divided between the wealthy white and the dark-skinned poor, entrenched in two separate urban encampments, framed by a social contract that will not change with successive generations.

In my previous research activity, which culminated in the publication of *Defensible Space*, I was primarily concerned with how the physical form of low-income, public housing developments could assist residents in determining and controlling activities in the areas outside their homes. My purpose was to find ways, through the mechanism of physical design, of improving the security and utility of the housing environment for low-income families with children living in public housing.

In this book, I examine many different types of housing environments — middle- as well as low-income developments, those serving elderly and working couples as well as those serving families with children, detached single-family units as well as multifamily units — I also examine the ways that housing environments function as sociopolitical entities. Residential environments are examined as settings which not only answer housing needs but which also influence residents by the social milieu they offer, the life-style that can be pursued, and the capacity to influence activities within the development and the areas beyond.

This is not to say that I have set aside my interest in how physical design facilitates interaction between neighbors and enables residents better to control the areas outside their homes. Rather, I have extended my interest in the effects of physical form to the measurement of how it varies with differences in the socioeconomic makeup of residents. I am also concerned with how variations in the physical form of housing can better serve different age and life-style groups; how the vulnerability of residents to poorly designed housing varies with income group; and how the physical form of housing affects the percentage of low-income residents that can be integrated into middle-income developments while still maintaining stable, low-crime communities.

My over-all interest is in determining how the physical form of housing, in varying combinations with the social characteristics of residents, serves to help create a community among neighbors. However, people's experience of crime and their fear of crime remain the critical factors affecting the creation and stability of urban communities in America today.[3] The concepts of defensible space, therefore, appear in this volume as well — but they are further developed and enlarged upon, following upon the findings of subsequent research.

This book provides specific guidelines both for the creation of new housing developments and for the stabilization of existing developments and communities, Neither as a nation nor as individuals do we have the resources once again to contemplate the tearing down or abandonment of existing residential areas and the building of a new world in the suburbs or on the ashes of the old. The past few years have made clear to us that the most promising answer to our housing need is to find ways to make what we already have workable again. If we build new housing, it will have to be as part of an over-all plan which provides new components to accommodate inadequacies in local existing housing resources. For the past decade the solution being most advocated by planners for solving the housing and economic needs of low-income residents was an assault on the ramparts of suburbia. More recently, there has been a withdrawal from this position, first, because of the realization of the full extent of the effort required to accomplish even a small part of this goal, and second, because a more careful reassessment of the benefits which would accrue to the low-income families who would be resettled in the suburbs was found to be wanting. But for either plan—the creation of new communities or the rehabilitation of old ones—the means for achieving stable, low-crime communities are essential to this new round of community development activity.

In this book I deal not with the political mechanisms for achieving economic integration, but with the psychological ones. I project models for housing environments which are designed to serve the needs of specific types of residents, as distinguished by their age and life-style. From an examination of how different groups perceive and use their home environments, I develop a series of housing models which satisfy these needs at different densities and at costs that are comparable with standard development practice. The fundamental thesis of this book is that working- and middle-class families will accept racial and economic integration if it is carried out within a framework which provides three things: (1) the grouping of similar age and life-style groups in housing environments designed to carefully fit their life-style needs; (2) a mix of income groups that will allow the values and life-styles of the upper-income group to dominate; and (3), percentage of low-income and/or black families that is determined by the community and strictly adhered to. It is my belief that economic and racial integration is both workable and acceptable if the interests and capacities of all the parties are respected and are codified into strict housing and management policies.

We cannot refute the fact that government assistance for housing directed at achieving the integration of low-income families into middle-income communities is a form of deprivation of individual and communal rights. These policies have been justified with the argument that the poor and black are being deprived of their rights by housing policies which facilitate economic and racial segregation and that a greater social good can be accomplished through government intervention. If this argument is accepted, then we must also accept the other side of the coin: government must also intervene to guarantee that the stability of the host community not be disrupted. Government may therefore be required to set quotas on the levels of economic and racial integration to be achieved and to insure that these quotas are strictly maintained. The notion of quotas in housing may be abhorrent to our concept of freedom of action, but it should serve to accomplish three things: (1) it should make more sites available for low-and moderate-income housing developments; (2) it should attract more white, middle-income residents to racially and economically integrated developments; and (3), it should eliminate much of the trauma normal to integration processes—trauma which in the past has resulted in people feeling that their entire community would likely turn over. The institution of quotas involves restrictions on the freedeom of rich and poor alike. This limit on freedom may not be desired by either group, but I am convinced that economic and racial integration can only be achieved by requiring it of both groups.

I am certain that many will find my concept for contemporary communities as unnecessarily limiting. I am also certain that some will think that the need to define communities as intact and separate elements, defined by fences if need be, as contradictory of my stated purposes. My larger goals would suggest that people should instead be housed in large communities where everyone is of like mind and safe and where, as a consequence, no segregation by life-style, or definition by fencing, is required. But that is what the suburbs are; upper-income, economically pure, racially intact enclaves. They provide segregation at the grand scale. If we desire the noninteraction of racially and economically segregated communities, the ethnically intact suburban community is the answer. But if, instead, we prefer the richness of cultural interaction that comes with the mixing of different groups in close spatial proximity, then life-style groupings in communities of interest as I define them here is an important alternative worth consideration.

I

Community of Interest

As the economic utility of maintaining ties to the geographical areas and ethnic-group concentrations of one's youth have diminished in importance, so have many of the traditional roles of community. To compensate, the immediate family has taken on an increasingly important role for its members and a new inward focus. In the postindustrial era, the size of the family, the age distribution of its members, and the internal clock that governs the timing of its critical events have also changed, and in ways which have further affected the maintenance and meaning of community.

Residential areas, once part of an integrated amalgram with one's place of work, shopping, and entertainment, are now distantly located, unifunctional zones. They contain a mixture of unrelated, inwardly oriented, small, nuclear families, living in what often appears as self-imposed isolation. Traditional communities composed of large, extended families or of families who shared a commonality of interests and vocational pursuits and provided each other with mutual support exist now only as dying remnants of older urban neighborhoods or as portions of rural towns. From that traditional perspective today's communities are little more than a haphazard assembly of families of diverse ages and backgrounds, sharing little more than an occasional similarity in incomes, race, or religious origin.

Since World War II the size of the family has been shrinking just as the timing of the cycles in the lives of its individual members has been becoming more exact.[1] Children grow up and go off to pursue higher education and careers in a more closely timed and systematic fashion. Marriage and the raising of a family are no longer the reasons needed for young people to leave home and set up on their own, either alone or with someone else. And this has become as increasingly true for women as it has been for men. With fewer children to raise and share a home environment with — and a longer life expectancy — parents now look forward to ten to twenty years of life together after the children have grown and gone. All these changes are reflected in our increased mobility. It has become commonplace for Americans to move every few years. In the five years between 1965 and 1970, 47 per cent of Americans changed their place of residence. The rate also appears to be increasing: 18.4 per cent of those who moved did so between 1969 and 1970.[2] Much of the reason for this mobility and willingness to accept change is that for the past few decades the best opportunities for self-improvement have been perceived as being located in distant metropolitan areas. Not only are we, as a nation, moving about continually, we are concentrating ourselves in our large cities. Sixty-nine per cent of all Americans now live in urban areas, almost three times as many people as fifty years ago (see Table 1.1).

Table 1.1: U.S. Population Residing in Urban Concentrations

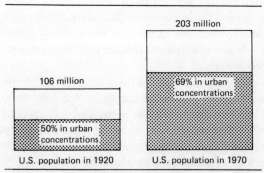

SOURCE: U. S. Bureau of the Census. Urban concentrations, defined by the Bureau of the Census as "Standard Metropolitan Statistical Areas (SMSAs)," include proximate groupings of 50,000 population or more.

The pattern of family life that seems to be emerging is one in which we share a few short years with blood relatives for limited purposes, and, when these are realized, each of us goes his or her own way. Grown children are as anxious to leave home as their parents are to be rid of them. Those retired elderly who can afford to, prefer to live away from their adult children so as not to be the subject of ridicule or suffere the stigma stemming from social or economic dependence.[3]

The increased mobility of our population, the growth of metropolitan areas, the change in the character of families, the separation of residential areas from places of work have all served to render the old concept of community meaningless. Certainly the notion of community based on the long-term geographical juxtaposition of families with similar ethnic origins and economic ties is gone. Patterns of friendship are no longer concentrated within the areas immediately adjacent to our homes but extend throughout the city and to many distant areas within the country and beyond.

One of the untoward consequences of these changes is that urban residential neighborhoods have become fluid and transient. Any appearance of change or threat often sends everyone scurrying; it is not uncommon today for residential neighborhoods to experience a complete turnover in population in as little as five years as a result of the influx of a few low-income or racially different residents. The questions, then, are: Is our noninvolvement with our residential neighbors something we have obtained by choice or is it the consequence of unpremeditated circumstance? Are there really no benefits which can accrue in today's society from sharing in community with our neighbors? If there are benefits in contemporary communities, what are they —and how, given our realities, are contemporary communities best achieved?

The Interest Community

In an article entitled "Order in Diversity: Community Without Propinquity," Melvin Webber, of the University of California at Berkeley, developed and explored the concept of the "interest community." Webber suggested that the old concept of community based on a grouping of people united by common background, similarity of pursuits, and physical proximity had given way to communities of people sharing similar interests but separated by physical distance. In the case of professionals like himself, the members of his interest community are often separated by hundreds, if not thousands, of miles. They communicate via journals, letters, and telephone calls and come together for face-to-face contact as infrequently as once a year at national or even international symposia.

Most other interest communities are neither as impressive as those shared by professionals nor do their members live that distant from one another, but they function in very much the same way. Interest communities can consist of bowling clubs in a particular town, a concert society, or even a group of skilled workers making up a union local in an assembly plant. Many of us commonly belong to a few such interest communities and our corresponding interest in and ties to the community of physically adjacent neighbors has waned accordingly.

While no one can fail to recognize and appreciate the compelling qualities of Webber's insights and arguments, there are a few important things which go unexplained: If the concept of community based on the shared values of proximate neighbors is of such little import, why do entire neighborhoods bolt and run when a few strangers of a different race, ethnicity, income, or life-style move in? There is the possibility that in addition to our professional interest communities, many of us also belong to an interest community whose existence and purpose depends on the physical proximity of like-minded people. It is perfectly reasonable for social scientists to take the traditional concept of the physically contiguous community, to redefine it in terms of a community based on the shared interest of its members, and then to make it independent of distance. But in so doing, we may have belittled the importance of that interest community centered around our homes and directed at either the raising of children or the pursuit of daily companionship and of leisure-time activity. These physically dependent types of interest communities do not grow casually as a consequence of propinquity but rather are chosen by their occupants for the activities they provide—and propinquity is an essential component in allowing them to fulfill their purpose.

With other planners and social scientists, I share the view that it is no longer possible (and perhaps not even desirable) to attempt to replicate the old neighborhood communities based either on extended families or on a similarity of backgrounds and/or ethnicity. I share the belief that most communities today are formed for the purpose of pursuing narrow interests and limited associations. However, physically based "communities of interest" are no less purposeful or single-minded than the interest communities of professionals; their only difference is that they require the physical proximity of their members to function. Successful *physical* communities of interest are created by people who select themselves into defined three-dimensional environments to be able to live in close proximity with others who share similar needs which depend on physical proximity to be satisfied. The distinctive quality of contemporary physical communities, as compared to the older communities, is that they are, in fact, set up to satisfy particular and limited goals.

A physical community of interest may include groupings of family units whose *raison d'être* is little more than the provision of a safe environment outside the home where children can interact with other children and society at large. It also involves the provision of schools and other institutional facilities. The physical proximity of its members is obviously a necessity to the creation and survival of this sort of community of interest. Since one of the adults in the family will commonly be at home on a continuing basis in a community of interest centered on child rearing, the nature of the physical community will be of importance to that adult as well as to the child. To other adults and members of the family who are away from the community for a long period of time or on a daily basis, the physical community of interest their home is in may be of little consequence. However, as membership in the propinquant community may involve a substantial investment (i.e., the purchase of a home), all members of the family will be interested in the stability of their physical community of interest. Should it collapse, even the nonparticipating members may find themselves moving, and this move may affect their ability to retain their involvement in other, professionally oriented, interest communities.

The retired elderly, who, like young children, spend much of their daily lives in and around the zones of their homes, have similar needs for propinquant communities. For low- and moderate-income adults or families who cannot afford a car and do not have access to dependable mass transit, the communities of interest they are able to create for themselves within walking distance from home will be much of the world that is available to them for socializing, recreation, and entertainment.

Community of Interest

Rather than lament the dissolution of the old communities in urban America, we must recognize and accept the nature of change that has taken place and look for new definitions and patterns for physical communities. We must examine what the concept of a physical community means in contemporary American society: what purpose it serves, how it is held together, and what makes it come apart. Finally, we must examine what the concept of a physical community of interest promises as a mechanism for achieving economic and racial integration without the attending disruption of neighborhoods and of urban communities that past integration efforts have wrought.

In a postindustrial society such as ours, in which most proximate dwellers are strangers to one another, it may be that the only way to ensure that neighbors share some common needs is by grouping dwellings together for residents of similar age and life-style characteristics. This rarely occurs in practice. Most developments and multifamily buildings were intentionally conceived to be occupied by a mix of different age groups and family types. That is, they were designed with apartments ranging from one-room efficiencies to four-bedroom units. This is considered to make good real estate sense as it gives the building manager a range of units to rent. The policy of mixing different apartment sizes in the same building has also been defended by planning philosophers as a mechanism to provide each building with a cross section of society — to create a mixture of young people, families with children, and elderly in every microenvironment so as to give each group the experience of living with people of all ages. It is also said that this form of integration, in contrast to segregation by age group, prevents any age group, such as the elderly, from feeling that its members are living in isolation or that society has ostracized them.

The idealism behind this sort of planning is the desire to create, in the modern world and among total strangers, the same cross section of age groups living together as exists in societies composed of large extended families. The image is one of the elderly living among young families, playing with and caring for their grandchildren; of respected elders who are a source of wisdom and are recipients of reverence. It is an ideal that unfortunately depends for its existence on a stable, static society, one in which neighbors are related by birth, live in extended families, and follow life cycles in which economic interests are pursued in common and the ritual of interaction largely predetermined. However, in the world in which we live, where neighbors are not normally related to each other either by birth or common professional pursuit and do not share a common past, culture, or ethnic root, the mixing of different age groups is often a highly *undesirable* proposition to each age group. The respect for the elderly by children and young adults in these circumstances is minimal. The relationship actually may become openly hostile if there is also a racial difference between the very young and the very old.[4] Reciprocally, the tolerance among the elderly for noise and activity generated by children and young adults who are unrelated to them is next to nonexistent. In a mix of different family types, the needs of each age group for areas outside the dwelling is decidedly different. Children want areas in which they can run around, yell, throw a ball — activities that frighten and antagonize the elderly who are sensitive to sound, see and move about with increased difficulty, and are afraid of physical contact and falls because their limbs break easily. Under these circumstances, the housing of different age and life-style groups together does not produce the utopia predicted. It is certainly not the mechanism for facilitating the interaction of neighboring residents and will not lead them to the adoption of areas outside the dwelling units for communal use.

In contemporary society, two American families of different ages may be as disparate in their need for and use of areas outside their individual dwelling units as the populations of two widely divergent cultures. Such differences do not result in the development of collective, semiprivate realms outside the individual dwelling to replace the amorphous public space that are increasingly making no man's lands of our cities.

In building the urban megalopolises of the latter half of the twentieth century we did not appreciate that the areas left open outside our homes would not automatically become centers of activity or take care of themselves. Nor did we realize that there would be a limit to our ability to hire others to police and maintain these public areas. The environmental forms we have been building to accommodate the new concentrations of disparate populations has made much of our evolving urban milieu impossible to maintain, control, or use.

With the ubiquitous construction of new high-rise residential buildings, we have witnessed the creation of urban environments in which our ability to influence the nature of activities taking place immediately beyond the confines of our apartments has all but disappeared. The nonprivate areas of our cities have become vast warehouses of depersonalized space, public no man's lands with which no one can identify, feel comfortable, or be concerned. This vast continuum of public space begins in the corridors of multifamily buildings and runs down through the lobby and out the door to the grounds and streets that border our developments. Our neighborhood parks, once alive with people, are now barely usable.

It may be that the shifting of populations into dense, urban concentrations and the parallel dissolution of extended families, while providing opportunities in one area of our lives, have also deprived us in other areas. But it is unlikely that the present pattern will be reversed either by universal accord or by government incentives (whether federal, state, or local in origin). The older urban neighborhoods we occasionally look back to, nostalgically, as models for contemporary communities contain too much of what was also restrictive: they were either composed of ethnically similar people with a common set of values and life-styles, to the exclusion of all others, or they were hierarchically structured societies composed of different classes interacting within the context of clearly codified relationships. Some of these older forms of society still exist in areas of our country, but they are characterized today by a commonly shared problem: their young people are fleeing to distant cities to find both the freedom and the opportunity that their parent societies cannot give them. A community form which is both utilitarian and realizable for contemporary society cannot be one which harks back to the old days. We must find models which are contemporary with current, metropolitan aspirations. Our task is complicated because we desire to create community while also maintaining heterogeniety and the opportunities which come with an open society.

By clustering similar age and life-style groups together in small communities of from fifty to five hundred dwellings, we will be able to achieve both the sense of community desired by Americans and the integration of different ethnic and economic groups. These individual communities of interest can then be placed next to other communities, housing different life-style groups to, together, make up a total urban fabric. By creating communities of interest for occupants identified by a similarity in age and family structure, it may be possible for us to re-create cities made up of recognizable and active communities, with outdoor areas which are intensively used by residents and safe enough for everyone's passage.

If, instead of a random grouping of dissimilar people, we can create groupings of people who share a common need for areas outside their dwellings in which to interact with others, then areas which were previously public and undefined for any use can now be designed to facilitate specific uses and be removed from the nebulous classification as "public space." For example, families with young children need space outside their dwellings units where children can run around and play together. These families may be of different incomes, background, and ethnicity, but their one common need provides an important rationale for bringing them together and allows designers to define collective areas outside their dwelling for them to interact in together. If their need for children's place space is genuine and continuing, the residents will identify with the common outdoor area, adopt it as their own, and work to ensure that it remains safe, secure, and usable. This collective play area will then become an extension of the individual dwellings into the outside world. It will also provide a buffer between the private world of the dwellings and the public world of the city beyond. If properly conceived, it can become the first of a growing hierarchy of collectively held areas which spread throughout the city to take over the unutilized public space we have inherited. If one could create communal outdoor areas, each serving a grouping of people with shared needs, by extension we might find needs which would be common to two or more such groupings, and a good portion of our present network of underutilized urban public areas could be reassigned to particular groups for their use, supervision, and control.

Community of interest is a concept for creating contemporary physical communities structured around the satisfaction of the shared needs of similar types of residents — needs which can only be met as a consequence of the common geographical location of community members. Community of interest has as its premise the assumption that for most people, at different stages in their lives, there is a need for areas immediately outside their homes which can be used for activities that involve others like themselves — places to play, to gather and gossip, to meet members of the opposite sex. The pattern in contemporary cities has been to house people together of different backgrounds, ages, and life-styles and to place them in buildings which have areas outside them which are amorphous and highly public. Under such circumstances it is difficult for neighbors to consider adopting areas outside their home for communal use. Community of interest is a mechanism for the creation of intermediary zones between the private home and the public street — zones which are the shared terrain of a small group of neighboring residents, which address their common interests and provide them with a form of collective identity. The creation of these zones also serves an additional purpose: it takes unused and unsafe public space which is costly to maintain and police and turns it into intensively used semiprivate space which is identified with the particular group of families who use, maintain, and control it. The process of changing this space from public to semiprivate status does not mean that it will no longer be available to nonresidents; it only means that use of the newly defined terrain by nonresidents will be with the approval of the contiguous resident population and must meet their criteria of acceptable usage.

The creation of community of interest cannot, however, be accomplished simply by setting up zones outside the dwelling for the collective use of proximate dwellers. It requires the grouping together of people of similar life-style and the establishment of covenants in housing management or among groups of residents to maintain the nature of the occupant group vital to the maintenance of that particular form of community of interest.

Different from the utopian planner's ideal, the creation of a surrogate form of extended family in contemporary society requires the provision of physical environments designed for the specific needs of a group of families pursuing similar life-styles: for example, residential environments exclusively for families with children, as different and separate from environments exclusively for young adults or for the elderly. It is this form of *segregation* which is the key to the *integration* and *interaction* of neighbors of different racial, ethnic, and economic backgrounds. The grouping of people by similar age and life-style allows for the provision of facilities, beyond the individual home or apartment, which are directed at the communal needs of residents. Community of interest is an effort to create a contemporary equivalent of the extended family. Elderly persons living together in their microenvironment, families with children in theirs, working couples and singles in theirs—this may sound like a planning program that is simplistic, if not regimented. But this segregation by life-style need not be maintained beyond the individual grouping: a microenvironment serving one life-style group can be juxtaposed with other types serving other groups to produce a complex, integrated society at the macroscale.

The limit on the number of families that can be combined into a collective habitat for any one group is governed by the extent of the uniformity among the families in that type: that is, uniformity in shared needs, ages, and life-styles. The greater the disparity among members sharing a similar life-style, the smaller the grouping that can be brought together to share a collective area. In families with children there are both adults and children sharing the one environment; a single maverick in such a group may be all that is needed to destroy the viability of a collective area and cause all other participants to withdraw from its use. By contrast, in an all-elderly environment, uniformity is very pervasive and embraces many things: age, life-styles, and codes of behavior. In this setting, a grouping of from one hundred and fifty to five hundred elderly families may be both workable and desirable. Among children-oriented families, a grouping of from sixteen to sixty families may be the upward limit.

Communities of interest are being advocated as a planning tool because they facilitate the interaction of neighbors who are new to each other, and they serve to make areas of the urban environment more usable and less costly to maintain. But what of the public areas beyond the boundaries of specific communities of interest—the areas that form the interstices between adjacent communities? In creating particular communities, are we just pushing our problems elsewhere? There are three reasons why creation of communities need not result in the displacement of these problems into the more public of public arenas. First, by relieving municipalities and housing agencies of the burden of maintaining and controlling *all* nonprivate areas, we enable the limited resources available to be concentrated in particular public areas: the public interstices between communities of interest. Second, the act of creating a community of interest is one of defining a group of people who share a common need for communal areas outside their dwellings. Having brought such a group into being in a particular geographical area, we are now in a position to think about what other type of group might share a need for additional communal areas common to two or more communities of interest. For example, a grouping of elderly families and a grouping of working singles and couples may each have their collective needs more readily satisfied in their own microenvironments, but both might share a common need for a collective area which contains commercial facilities they both use frequently: restaurants, dry cleaning establishments, movie houses, etc. The third reason the creation of communities of interest are likely to minimize the extent of unused, poorly maintained public areas is that each community of interest is also intended to house a predominantly middle-class community, with low-income residents of similar age and life-style forming only about one third of the population of the community. Thus, there should be sufficient funds generated by the adjacent communities both for the direct support of commercial facilities located within the interstices between communities and for taxes to provide for the maintenance and supervision of these public areas.

The Mixing of Income and Racial Groups

The pervasive problem facing American cities is one which neither allows itself to be addressed easily nor which appears to be receding with time: it is the problem of the low-income blacks. Their concentration in particular urban areas has in the past inevitably prompted white flight. Low-income blacks are accused of being responsible for the large increase in urban crime, the deterioration of schools and neighborhoods, the decline in property values, and, finally, the eradication of that subtle and complex phenonenon, the urban milieu. For all our government subsidies, we have not been able to do much about breaking the pattern of black poverty in successive generations. But it is also by no means certain that we want to do so. As Americans we hold the achievement of personal success and the accumulation of wealth of great importance. But as a society we also have something of a rule system which frames acceptable means for achieving this success. We are jealous of our individual attainments and tend to measure our successes by the comparative accomplishments of others. There is little room in such a competitive system for providing assistance to others, for allowing them to easily rival our success.

For better or worse, our society's means of distributing wealth to successive generations is inequitable. Those who inherit wealth from their parents are the most likely to be wealthy and successful; those who have the connections which lead them to opportunities also have the best chance for succeeding. It is in the nature of men and society that those who are born into a wealthy family also have the best connections and the greatest opportunities to develop their native capacities. Only a person's perseverance to succeed is somewhat independent of inherited wealth—but it, too, is a trait that must be acquired and nourished in youth. As children learn by following the example of others, the acquisition of the trait of perseverance is best nourished by bringing the young into continual association with those whose perseverance has led to success. Unfortunately, such example givers are most often the rich and they, like most of us, tend to lavish what attention they have on their own young.

But our society has come a long way since feudal times and the days of early capitalism. We have learned that we must be altruistic in order to insure our, and society's, perpetuation. We are cognizant of our need to provide training and opportunity to *all* of our young people — even if not quite equally. How then does all of this enable us to deal with our pervasive problem? Poor blacks have neither the inherited wealth, the know-how, nor the social or business connections to ease the way for their children. Except for what little our society provides in the way of free public schooling, their children receive little in the way of opportunities to develop their native skills and intelligence. Finally, the trait of perseverance to succeed is rare in those who have had their hopes and efforts thwarted too many times and too often for the reason of the color of their skin. Just as success breeds success, and wealth, more wealth, so poverty breeds further poverty, and failure, hopelessness. From experience, we have learned that the task of pulling the poor out of the cycle of poverty is not easily achieved, but, unforgivably, it would appear that we have become reconciled to accepting the poor black as a permanent fixture in our society. The change in attitude that comes with each new presidential Administration is not a change in substance but one of programs: more welfare rather than less; more housing; more conscientious busing. There is some doubt as to whether the majority of middle-class Americans — from the skilled working class to the wealthy upper class — really wants to see the poor and the black assimilated into middle-class society. Aside from government-financed programs which keep the poor concentrated together and in a state of dependence on welfare that runs for generations, there is little evidence of any attempt to bring them into the fold of middle-class society. The message has not yet been brought home to us that the cost of ever-increasing generations dependent on welfare, of spreading crime and neighborhood abandonment, is too high a price to pay, even for affluent Americans. We must find a way of bringing the poor and black into the fold, if for no other reason than to keep from going broke ourselves.

In my advocacy of residential environments which are designed to entice neighbors to interact with one another, I have rejected a planning goal that has dominated community planning for thirty years: the mixing of different ages and life-style groups in the same, immediate environment. There are two reasons for my doing so. The first grows from my desire to provide areas outside the dwelling for the interaction of neighbors, which I believe is best achieved by grouping similar age and life-style groups together — at least in their immediate environment. The second reason is that it will facilitate racial and economic integration. I am convinced that the future of American cities lies in the creation of housing environments which consist of a fine-grained mixture of different income and racial groups — dominated in numbers by the higher income group. To accomplish this, while maintaining stable neighborhoods, requires the minimization of conflict. Antagonisms between residents growing from differences in age and life-style are, in my view, well worth minimizing by keeping these groups separated from each other in order to be able to integrate residents of different race and income — but of similar age and life-style. My plan for integrating different economic and racial groups is to build on their unity of purpose resulting from the needs and goals common to them at a particular age or period in their life cycle. I am suggesting that this can be accomplished through the creation of small, distinct subhabitations within the larger urban milieu which are clearly defined for specific groups and designed to answer their specific needs. By serving each group's needs within these subworlds and by strongly defining these worlds with real and symbolic elements, we can integrate residents of different race and income within each subworld and still be able to place subworlds housing different age and life-style groups in close juxtaposition to each other. Thus, where we have segregation by life-style in the microcosm we also have integration by race and income. In the macrocosm composed of a grouping of such segregated environments, we have a mixture of life-style groups and a predominant middle-income milieu — with purchasing power large enough to support a varied urban life-style.

To date, we have solved our problems by putting increasing distance between middle-class whites and low-income blacks and we have paid a very high price for it in the form of abandoned residential neighborhoods, business areas, and social and cultural institutions and in the high cost of commuter travel. We have paid an even higher price in the disappearance of our urban life-style. The middle-class response was a rational and effective, if shortsighted, reaction to a serious and threatening problem. The mechanism chosen — one of total separation — was selected because as a society we could not face up to adopting a program of dispersing the ghettos into the middle-income communities on a tightly controlled quota basis. We thought such a program smacked of totalitarianism and would be unacceptable both to the ghetto resident and to the host community. Now, some twenty years and billions of dollars later, we are no nearer to solving the problem. If we genuinely desire to reduce the concentration of crime and social malaise that eat at stable neighborhoods in an ever-spreading cancer, we have no option but to disperse our ghettos and provide real educational and social opportunities to allow ghetto youth to enter into the mainstream of American life. By dispersing concentrations of low-income families into middle-income communities, both new and old, in numbers these communities can absorb without trauma, we can both contain the criminal activity of the young and provide the education, contacts, and behavioral traits necessary to allow them to break out of their cycle of poverty. Busing programs do not provide these opportunities because the milieu of the school is too foreign and infrequent an experience. The combination of the instillation of the values of ambition with the high levels of teaching and supervision common to middle-income communities is what is needed by the children of the poor, and they can best get it by associating on a continuing basis, in school and around the home environment, with the children of the middle-class.

The liberal establishment is often the unwitting coconspirator of the most conservative and bigoted elements of society. The most radical housing authorities and the most conservative often share the same policies—each for their own, very different, reasons. Radicals feel that quotas are discriminating and that public housing should be made available on a priority basis for the poorest of the poor; conservatives push to concentrate low-income blacks in public housing ghettos so as not to "contaminate" the rest of their city. Both policies result in concentrations of low-income black residents in environments which are hell to live in and impossible for successive generations to get out of. The nature and extent of past housing failures also serves those opposed to our goals in another way: every failure raises doubts about the desirability of further government subsidy of housing.

Quotas

The success of past government assistance in providing housing for *upper-* and *middle-income* groups cannot be debated. Unfortunately, in the area of low- and moderate-income housing our past efforts leave much to be desired. The one area of housing policy that has shown the most resistance to implementation and long-term stability has been racial integration. Racially mixed developments, of both uniform and mixed incomes, have, over time, tended to become increasingly occupied by blacks. And yet racial integration in housing must be the primary goal which underlies all forms of housing assistance, as no policy which provides assistance to the creation of segregated housing can promise either community stability or the conservation of urban areas over time. For all their past problems, moderate- and middle-income housing programs which have had a percentage of their units allocated for the poor are still the best means for housing low-income families. If our long-term goal is the assimilation of the poor and black into the mainstream of American middle-class life, the establishment of quotas for economic and racial integration in *all* housing receiving *any* form of government subsidy is essential. This notion of quotas has been suggested and halfheartedly implemented over the past twenty years. It has also been the recipient of much abuse by liberal and conservative alike. It is now time for us to take another look at quotas because we have not acheived very much in the form of economic and racial integration in housing without them. The sum of my experience with urban communities leads me to conclude that quotas governing racial and economic integration are not only essential to the stability of government assisted housing developments and their surrounding communities, they are vital to the long-term stability of all residential communities, including the now-distant suburbs.

The notion of quotas in housing has been abhorrent to the liberal, the conservative, and the black community. Conservatives do not want integration at any level; liberals, on the other hand, find the establishment of percentage quotas for blacks or low-income residents a restriction of housing opportunity. Blacks find the notion of quotas insulting, and some black community leaders see the initiation of quotas as their political death. The consequences of the conservative position can be seen in the exclusive, white, middle-class, suburban communities which now surround every American city; the consequences of the liberals' position can be seen in the all-black, all-poor, hard-pressed, public and moderate-income developments, and in decaying communities of subdivided single-family houses which surround them. Black leaders are also finally learning how little power there really is in representing an all-black, predominantly low-income community. Each antiquota group has had its day—and American housing and society are no better for it.

Another argument that has been raised against quotas is that most blacks prefer to live in all-black communities. But the contrary proves to be the case: a nationwide survey conducted by *Newsweek* in May 1967 revealed that 74 per cent of blacks interviewed preferred to live "in a neighborhood which had both whites and Negroes."

The legal scholar Bruce L. Ackerman has marshaled a volume of evidence for his position advocating racial integration by quotas. Not least of his contentions is that most blacks would prefer to live in an integrated community:

A 1968 national poll which asked blacks to identify their needs showed 93 percent of the respondents listing "more desegregation in schools, neighborhoods, and jobs." Another survey of 214 low- and moderate-income white and black households in Dayton, Ohio, found two-thirds of the low-income black families, 88 percent of the male-headed, moderate-income black households, and 100 percent of the female-headed, moderate-income black families preferring a "racially integrated environment."

An examination of reasons offered by blacks for favoring integration suggests that black families seeking housing in white areas do not wish these areas to become predominantly black. In an August 1963 national survey of black attitudes Harris pollsters found that 49 percent of the blacks supporting housing integration said they favored integration because they believed that the "races should mix." Another 26 percent of the interviewees said that they thought that living in an integrated area would mean a neighborhood that was "quieter, cleaner, etc." . . .

The racial harmony motive might be viewed as too idealistic or abstract to sustain a continuing interest in integration once black families enter previously all-white areas. However, the more practical concern — that predominantly black areas receive lower quality municipal services and are more vulnerable to urban problems — does support an expectation that the substantial number of blacks sharing these practical concerns do not want the predominantly white neighborhoods which they enter eventually to turn all black.[5]

As long as government intends to continue to subsidize housing — and this means continued subsidizing of housing for upper-income groups as well — it should be a requirement that *all* such assisted housing (or communities) provide 30 per cent of their units to comparatively lower-income groups and that 40 per cent of those in turn be provided to blacks. In light of America's commitment to the concept that success has its just rewards, our government's involvement in preventing the creation of exclusive economic communities may be seen as a deprivation of individual rights. But if public monies are being used to subsidize the creation of such communities, it would appear that government is also obligated to serve some greater public good. It seems reasonable that there should be no government assistance to moderate- and middle-income housing developments which does not provide some units for low-income and black families. There should be no tax breaks available on housing and schools in middle- and upper-income communities unless these communities make land available for housing for moderate- and low-income groups—a significant portion of whom should be black.

However, based on past experience, if we expect housing developments and communities to provide below-market-rate rental housing and to provide a percentage of it for blacks, we will have to be cautious if we also expect to maintain these communities as stable housing resources. The establishment of racial and economic quotas appears to be the only path open to the realistic achievement of these goals. A quota system is the other side of the coin of the federal government's intervention requiring racial and economic integration. But quotas should only be established if they are based on what past experience has demonstrated can be successful. These quotas must then be publicized and scrupulously adhered to if we expect the host community to remain both *stable* and *host* for some time to come. If the maintenance of quotas requires that we also subsidize the rich and middle-income families to live among the poor, then that is what we must do. We are already subsidizing middle- and upper-income families more heavily than anyone else—let us at least try to accomplish a greater social purpose with these subsidies.

There are two types of quotas under discussion: racial and economic. Because most blacks are of a lower-income group, an economic quota is often also a racial one. It is important, however, always to distinguish between the two. In varying instances, the one is easier to achieve than the other. The matter becomes particularly complex when a housing agency or manager is trying to fulfill two sets of quotas simultaneously.

II

Urban Growth and Housing Programs

Over the past fifty years our nation has experienced a growth and concentration of population that has significantly altered where most people live and work and the way they perceive their residential neighborhoods. Most Americans now live within large, metropolitan agglomerations, at comparatively high densities, in communities segregated by race, religion, and income.

As job, housing, and educational opportunities for blacks opened up in our northern cities in the 1950s, there was a dramatic shift of population from southern towns and cities to the large metropolitan areas of the Northeast, Great Lakes, and Northwest (see Table 2.1).

In 1940, 77 per cent of the nation's black population lived in the South; by 1970, only 53 per cent did. The immigrating populations from small towns and rural areas have tended to be of lower income and have moved in to occupy the older central areas of our cities. In response to the influx of low-income populations to the central cities and to the new housing opportunities being made available in the suburbs, the existing middle-income urban populations moved to the surrounding areas (see Tables 2.2 and 2.3).

Past Housing and Urban Policies

Since the Roosevelt years, various types of programs have been formulated to provide housing assistance to the low-income urban migrants. The federal government's first sally into housing assistance in the 1940s was the public housing program which took the form of providing federal funds to municipalities to construct housing for lower-income groups. Almost 1 million units of public housing were constructed between 1945 and 1970.

In the 1950s a second method was devised for providing housing to lower-income groups. It involved a two-step procedure: the federal government initiated the first step by providing housing assistance to middle-class families who, by building and occupying new housing, freed old housing for working-class families, who, in turn, freed their housing for the poor. The success of this program depended on there being no net increase in the demand for housing among middle-income and working-class families. If there was, little of the old housing would ever get handed down.

For the most part, the effect of this program was as predicted, particularly in those cities which were already losing their middle-income population: working-class and poor families found themselves the inheritors of an abundance of sound older houses at extremely good prices. The problem was that many of the new owners had neither the know-how nor the incomes to maintain the housing. When, after a few

Table 2.1: Movement of Blacks, 1960–70

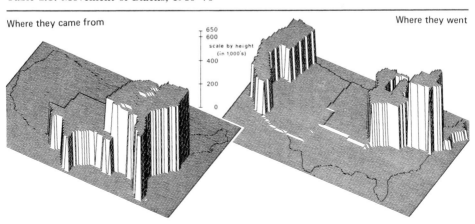

SOURCE: U.S. Bureau of the Census and Harvard University Mapping Service – Laboratory for Computer Graphics.

years, the housing needed major repair, they abandoned it—along with their federal government-guaranteed mortgages. The houses were then picked up, even more cheaply, by realtors who used still other government subsidies to patch up and subdivide the housing and rent it to an even lower-income group.

In the 1960s another set of federal programs were created which were intended to more directly provide housing to low- and moderate-income groups. Section 221–D3 of the 1964 Housing Act, and then its replacement, Section 236 of the 1968 Housing Act, provided low-interest, low-equity mortgages to nonprofit groups or limited-dividend developers to build housing which would rent at below market rates, with some 30 per cent of the units to be leased to even lower-income residents. For this latter group, the housing was seen as a desirable alternative to public housing in that it would house equivalently low-income families in a middle-income milieu. The housing could also be built more rapidly and cheaply than public housing and would not require a costly bureaucracy to administer it. The developments were intended to be run by nonprofit institutions such as churches or unions. In some cases, the developer received a direct government supplement to pay the difference in rent for the 30 to 40 per cent of his tenants who

**Table 2.2: Population in Metropolitan
Areas by Race, 1940–70**

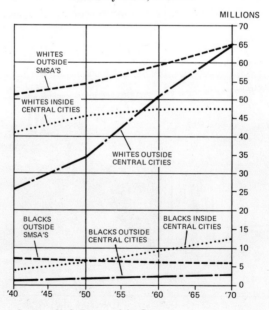

SOURCE: U. S. Bureau of the Census.[1]

were of very low income, in other cases the low-income residents received the rent supplements directly.

Some of these developments are proving viable even today — ten years after they were built. Most, however, have suffered three problems: (1) unanticipated increases in maintenance costs, (2) poor management, and (3) a too-rapid change in the characteristics of their tenants. Poor management can be endemic to nonprofit and co-operative groups, just as it can to public housing. What is worse, for small management groups, the resources of federal, state, and city governments are not available, as they are to public housing authorities, to bail them out in times of need. The other problem, the too-rapid increase in the ratio of low-income tenants, was compounded by the fact that the low-income residents were often also black. Limits on the percentage of low-income residents could be easily administered, whereas limits on racial characteristics could not. Since the percentage of apartments in any development that could be leased to low-income residents was determined by the amount of supplementary funds provided by government, the limit of low-income tenants was easily maintained. In some developments, the issue initially was one of requiring the developers to make as many as 30 per cent of their units available as subsidized apartments. However, when these developments proved costly to run — as was the case when the building type was inappropriate to the needs and life-style of the occupant group and the cost of heating oil doubled — the vacancy rate rose and management became desperate. The margin of profit in these developments was too small to enable management to wait out a crisis or be too careful about selecting new tenants. Thus, vacant apartments which were originally designated for rental to middle-income families were leased to low-income residents who came with their own rent supplements or re-

Table 2.3: Location of Income Groups in Suburbs
Versus Central Cities

SOURCE: U. S. Bureau of the Census.[2]

ceived welfare payments which covered the rent. Other vacant units were leased to the local public housing authority for its tenants. Once this process began, it was with very rare exception that management made any effort to limit the percentage of welfare or public housing units to a specific number. The project then entered into a spiral of rapid decline, and management tried to bail out with as little injury to itself as possible. This usually entailed embarking on a program of minimum maintenance and quick write-off.

The adoption and maintenance of racial quotas in subsidized housing proved even more difficult than the maintenance of income quotas. There were management firms who strove to achieve racial integration and openly stated what their ratios were (usually, two white families to one black family) and there were those management firms who set racial limits quietly and stuck to them without publicity. Families who applied to the latter type of development, whether white or black, were informed by management of the racial leasing strategy and, according to the managers, raised few objections.[3] The goal seemed reasonable to both white and black families. Management was able to attract either whites or blacks to fill its quotas by actively seeking those families it wanted through directed advertising or by sending out inquiries to particular organizations.

Those management firms who advertised their racial-mix quotas openly were occasionally taken to court by civil rights groups and inevitably lost their case on constitutional grounds.[4] For either of the above types of management quota practices, the history of racially mixed developments is that once the ratio exceeds 40 per cent black, a slow exodus of whites begins, followed by increased difficulty in attracting new white families, followed by a further exodus of white families with every incremental increase in black families until the project turns all black. Those developments which did not openly proclaim their racial quota system were not taken to court and have been able to achieve some degree of racial integration and stability. In fact, the publication of management policy on racial mix itself can act as a stabilizing force which even allows a slight excess of black families over the published quotas.[5] The corollary, therefore, is also likely true: a publicized management policy of being flexible on the percentage mix of black families can act to prompt a more rapid exodus of white families and black middle-income families.

By 1970, overwhelmed by the "hidden" costs of government-assisted housing (by which was meant the ever-expanding Department of Housing and Urban Development [HUD] bureaucracy at federal, state, and local levels), the federal government decided to embark on a multimillion-dollar experimental housing allowance program. The program provided direct cash assistance to lower-income households to enable them to rent better housing on their own. Two experiments were built into the program: one to determine how various households used these cash assistance payments in the purchase of better housing; and the second to see how the housing market in particular communities was affected by a full-scale housing allowance program – it was hypothesized that this form of government assistance to lower-income groups could act to drive up all housing rental and purchase prices in a community.

The results of the experimental housing allowance program proved surprising on many fronts. First, less than one half of the qualifying households agreed to be recipients of the housing allowance and to participate in the program. Second, the assistance monies did not appear to induce the low-income renter households to move any more frequently than they already move (25 per cent of these households move each year). Third, of those households in the experiment who received unconstrained assistance, less than 10 per cent of their assistance monies was used to improve the quality of their housing. Lower-income households paid so much of their income toward rent (40 per cent and more) that any additional assistance not constrained for use as rent was more frequently used in meeting other living expenses like food, clothing, transportation, and education.[6] A direct housing allowance to lower-income groups is clearly not the way to improve the quality of the housing they live in.

In 1974 a new program was introduced into the Housing Act that provides assistance to lower-income groups in the form of a subsidy specifically earmarked for use in housing. Entitled "Section 8," it provides private developers, nonprofit groups, and housing agencies with funds to build new housing (or to rehabilitate existing housing) by guaranteeing the rental income of a certain number of units leased to lower-income families. The federal government pays the difference between the rent the low-income occupant can afford and the rent the unit demands in the market place. There were two goals to this program: (1) to provide the mechanism by which lower-income families could obtain housing in moderate- and middle-income developments; and (2), to reduce the cost to government of subsidized housing by doing away with the cost of institutionalized housing bureaucracies (public housing, et al.).

After five years of operation it is questionable whether the program has achieved either goal. Most of the Section 8 monies have been allocated by HUD area offices, not to allow lower-income households to rent housing in middle-income developments but, rather, to bail out failing HUD subsidized moderate-income housing developments that

have lost their full-rent paying occupants. Through the priority allocation of Section 8 funds to these developments, HUD has been rehabilitating and converting them into occupancy by 100 per cent deep subsidy tenants.

The cost of Section 8 housing has also proven to be much higher
than expected. The latest Congressional Budget Office paper found
that the means originally used to determine the long-term subsidy commitment by government underestimated actual costs by as much as
three times. For example, the direct subsidy costs of a forty-year Section 8 commitment was found to actually run from $242,600 to
$710,300 (or $500,000 more than the $203,900 that was initially
reserved).[7] The paper concludes with the recommendation that greater
reliance be placed on the use and reuse of existing housing and that
lower-income tenants be asked to pay a higher percentage of their incomes toward rent. The current limit on the percentage of their incomes that Section 8 tenants can be charged toward their rent is from
15 to 20 per cent; the remainder of the rent cost is assumed by the federal government.

The Congressional Budget Office also re-examined the forty-year
public housing subsidy commitments and found that the actual direct
subsidy costs, including the operating subsidies that must be paid to
housing authorities following the Brooke Amendment, will run between $226,800 to $426,800 per unit. The budget authority initially
reserved $141,600 per unit.

Future Housing and Urban Policies

Our nation's public housing program was conceived, in the 1930s
and 1940s, as housing for low-income working-class families. During
the past fifteen years, in most American cities, it has come to be seen as
"housing of last resort," that is, housing for the poorest of poor. This
change in image is the result of many factors, but three seem to have
played a dominant role: (1) the urban renewal programs of the 1950s
and 1960s gave priority access to public housing to families displaced
by urban renewal; (2) tenant and civil rights groups successfully
challenged the tenant selection procedures employed by housing authorities; and (3) the moderate-income housing programs created in the
1960s made it possible for working-class families living in public housing to move up to better housing or even home ownership. As a result,
a large number of low-income, one parent families were moved into
public housing without the normal screening procedures. With time,
these families became the dominant occupants—they simply never
moved out. Two-parent working-class families came and went in public

housing, but the one-parent welfare families neither could afford moderate-income housing nor were knowledgeable enough to be able to apply for the rent supplements available for from 30 to 40 per cent of the occupants of federally assisted, moderate-income housing.

When it became obvious that public housing was becoming a haven for one-parent families receiving welfare under the AFDC (Aid for Families with Dependent Children) program, even the few remaining lower-income working families began moving out. With their departure, things became even more bleak. Under occupancy solely by one-parent welfare families, the crime and vandalism problems became so intolerable that even *they* began to move out, producing high vacancy and turnover rates. Some cities, like New York and Wilmington, Delaware, prevented this erosion process by holding to their screening procedures and income ratios, even under pressure from government and various interest groups. They insisted on keeping the majority of the families in their family projects either working-class or two-parent. As a consequence, these housing authorities have been able to weather the crisis of public housing long enough to see government change its position on both tenant selection and income criteria. These authorities are among the few who still have full occupancy and actually succeed in providing housing for as many of the poorest of the poor as the other authorities with high vacancy and abandonment rates. The housing authorities of other cities who surrendered too easily to the pressures of interest groups and government now have unoccupied projects.

In recent years it seems to have become accepted that the poorest of the poor—the chronically unemployed and unemployable, the welfare mother with a large number of children, the ex-offender, the drug addict, and the alcoholic—are to have priority in public housing. If our national goal is to lead the next generation of the poor up from poverty, then the sum total of our nation's housing and welfare programs does not seem to be directed at this end. In fact, what we appear to be perpetuating is immobility of the poor by making dependence inviting to those at the borderline who might otherwise strive to stand on their own. Allowing public housing to become "housing of last resort" is an erroneous policy for many reasons. The "last resort" projects are almost universally occupied by black welfare residents. When these projects are located in white communities, their "all-black" character makes them peculiarly vulnerable to community action to have the projects torn down. A project's high vacancy and crime rates are normally the reasons given. But no such community action would have been undertaken if 50 per cent of the project residents were white.

Some housing authority boards and city councils are quietly pleased with the action of pressure groups that have served to make their public housing concentrations of welfare blacks. These cities are now able to use their housing projects as internment camps for the poor and black, leaving the rest of the city free of them. With time, the all-black housing projects are allowed to deteriorate and become increasingly abandoned. With no other place to go, it is reasoned, the welfare blacks will move away and become some other city's burden.

Finally, the very recognition that public housing is being provided on a priority basis to one-parent welfare families effectively creates a further government-financed incentive for families to break up in order to qualify for admission. This is not to say that the *majority* of one-parent welfare families now living in public housing broke up their marriages, first, in order to be eligible for welfare aid intended for families with dependent children and, second, in order to get into public housing. But with equal certainty there are many families in borderline situations for whom the incentive of priority admission to public housing provides sufficient impetus to end a marriage and adopt the welfare syndrome. In a similar vein there are pregnant girls in their teens whose partners might be willing to marry them but whose immediate chances for income and housing are greater without a husband than with one. The corollary of this proposition might hold as well: if housing authorities adopted a policy of giving priority admission to two-parent working families, they might affect the same borderline families in the opposite way. It might provide them with the incentive necessary to keep the family intact and working.

Although we can debate how many families are so affected, there is little doubt that by defining one form of government-subsidized housing as being primarily for the poorest of the poor, we help to create a market for it, just as in the past, by creating new interstate highways to solve congestion, we stimulated new automobile ownership and new suburban development which in turn created more highway congestion and a whole new set of unanticipated problems. People who may not see themselves as being among the poorest of the poor may, under a continuing policy which gives priority to the poor, see the tangible benefits of being so classified even if it means breaking up their families and adopting welfare as a way of life. The benefits of priority housing and welfare may be too much of an economic incentive to make holding on to a marriage, job, or social status worthwhile.

It is the "American dream" that the equality of opportunity provided by a democratic and capitalistic society, coupled with the benefits of technology, laissez-faire, and an ever-expanding economy, will bring the poor into the middle class. This is probably why our nation's public housing was initially envisioned as a program for providing way stations for poor immigrants from rural areas and abroad. It was seen as temporary housing for the working-class poor until they acquired the skills and know-how to move out and acquire homes of their own in the competitive market place of the expanding metropolis. And for the first twenty years public housing was just that.

The postwar program of providing low-interest, federally guaranteed mortgages to the mass of skilled working-class and middle-income Americans was a further step within this same philosophical framework. Government intervention removed the sting of risk from banks' investment in housing mortgages. The program succeeded beyond expectation in that it demonstrated even to those banks who did not make use of federal guarantees that housing mortgage loans were not as risky a business as they had previously supposed. Interest rates on all mortgage notes were, as a consequence, lowered.

It was only with the large influx of low-income populations to metropolitan areas in the 1950s and 1960s that the notion took root among social scientists and housing experts that there were ranks of Americans who were not upwardly mobile and who could not now nor in any subsequent period of their lives ever afford anything but substandard housing, let alone the initial and carrying costs of subsidized mortgages. At that juncture the values of the American dream gave way to those of the welfare state. The concept of public housing changed from temporary housing for the young and working poor to permanent housing for the poorest of the poor.

Along with our need to provide the immobile poor with the shelter and funds to sustain life, we have had to absorb the significance of the headlong flight of middle-income Americans to the exclusive and homogeneous enclaves of suburbia. We are only slowly beginning to recognize that we now have an urban poor who do not appear to be very taken with the vision or responsive to the incentives of fulfilling the American dream. We have not given much thought to what will be the sociophysical nature of an American society composed of a divided and calcified structure of rich white versus dark-skinned poor, nor have we any notion of what government programs should be created to either continue to perpetuate this polarization or strive to dissolve it.

Over the past twenty-five years the series of makeshift programs we have been employing, like school busing and subsidized housing projects, have not been able to keep pace with white, middle-class America's negative reaction to them. If one were to seek, in the response of average middle-American, an indicator of the emerging new philosophy, it would be one which appeared to be advocating permanent segregation of rich and poor, white and black. Its consequence is formal recognition of the dissolution of the American dream — a notion our society has neither the cynicism nor the strength to endorse. It would require us to give the stamp of legitimacy and permanence to our current programs of welfare maintenance and segregation, and we are unwilling to do either—some of us for moral reasons and others for financial ones. The question then is, is there an alternative open to us other than our current mode of sliding slowly into what appears to be the inevitable?

Employing Our Largest Area of Subsidized Housing for Social Purpose

The pros and cons of various forms of government housing subsidies to low- and moderate-income groups receive much public discussion. But what is not commonly known is that the largest government subsidy for housing is provided to middle- and upper-income groups. Upper-income Americans who purchase homes without any direct government subsidy, even in the form of a guaranteed low-interest loan, receive two hidden government subsidies which residents of most other Western countries, including Canada and Great Britain, do not receive. American homeowners do not have to pay federal income taxes on those portions of their income spent on mortgage-interest payments and local school and property taxes. These savings in federal taxes by middle- and upper-income Americans are together the largest form of government housing subsidy for any income group in the nation.

> Overwhelmingly the largest housing subsidy is favorable tax treatment of homeowners which, in 1966, left them with at least $7 billion more in disposable income than they would have retained if they were taxed as are other investors. The estimate would be larger if it included tax savings arising from accelerated depreciation on rented housing and other items. Only 8 percent of this subsidy accrues to taxpayers with incomes of less than $5,000. Taxpayers with incomes of more than $50,000 per year saved $487 million, slightly less than the total value of low rent public housing subsidies.[8]

The saving on school taxes produces a further social inequity in that it is an incentive to the creation of exclusive suburban enclaves and segregation by income and, therefore, race. In typical upper-middle-income communities, the annual school taxes on a $100,000 home range from $2,000 to $4,000. This is a tax-free subsidy for the creation of private and segregated educational opportunities. For those in very high tax brackets, as much as 50 to 70 cents of every dollar spent in local school taxes is assumed by the federal government. By contrast, no tax breaks on schooling are available to middle- and upper-income families who choose to live in the city and feel obligated to send their children to private schools.

Such inequitable subsidies may be justifiable if they are being used to achieve a greater social purpose, but if they are not, they are unforgivable. There is, of course, the opportunity to use tax incentives to homeowners as a mechanism to achieve racial and economic integration and, with the current mood of the country, this may be the only remaining option available for achieving it.

Government Intervention and Constitutional Deprivation

Having witnessed the failure of many government efforts in providing new housing for the poor and the black in urban areas, some planning and housing groups desire now to embark on a program of integrating the poor into communities of the suburban middle-class. Few Western nations have attempted this and fewer still have succeeded: some British, Swedish, and Dutch housing programs claim to be directed at this goal, but in reality most of their housing developments suggest that integration by income and race is as uncommon there as it is here. Most countries have been content to slip back into doing what we have been doing since the late 1940s: providing low-income groups with new housing developments which, by their size and location, continue to produce ghettos for the poor.

Our nation's commitment to improve the social mobility and housing of low-income groups may be' commendable, but it comes into conflict with two basic tenets of American society: that hard work and achievement is rewarded with improved status and tangible goods, not the least of which is good housing in a good neighborhood; and that we have the right to live among neighbors of our own choosing, that is, in quality communities made up of people like ourselves. If *what* we live in and *where* we live is better than it is for others, we are the obvious recipients of a conspicuous, tangible reward and a clear expression of status. To assume, as some planning and housing groups have, that, as a result of court rulings, exclusive communities of the middle-class and the wealthy will be opened to the poor, the black, and the working class is naïve because it flies in the face of these two fundamental precepts which structure our society.

If we recognize the futility of constructing large, low-income housing developments in existing urban ghettos, then let us also recognize that large, low-income housing projects built even in the most desirable of suburban neighborhoods transport the ghettos with them. If we perceive suburban, middle-class neighborhoods as the soil for transplanting ghetto residents, then let us also recognize that such relocation cannot be accomplished by threat, government sanction, or legal fiat and be expected to last out the decade. If it is to be done, it must be done with persuasion and by demonstration that similar efforts of a small scale have not destroyed the stability of the host community.

The recent push to open the suburbs to low-income housing is the result of recognition by the liberal establishment of the failure of the other two major federal programs directed at improving the lot of low-income minority groups while bringing them into the mainstream of American life. The first program—that of providing over a million units of low-income public housing—has, some twenty years later, proven to have accomplished little more than the creation of large new ghettos which replaced the old. Much public housing is now in a bad state of repair. It suffers a high vacancy rate and is even being abandoned in some cities. Their problems were generated by the large concentration of low-income families in a single development, the inadequacy of the housing designs in meeting the needs of the occupant families, and the high crime rates generated by both these problems. Moderate-income housing programs which were created to address some of the weaknesses of public housing programs by providing vehicles for integrating low- and moderate-income families are faring little better. The problem is that many moderate-income housing developments, just like the public housing, were built in low-income urban areas and were rarely able to attract a permanent majority of middle-income residents in which to integrate low-income groups.

Court rulings which have prevented the Department of Housing and Urban Development from continuing to build low- and moderate-income housing in low-income ghetto areas, and rulings requiring suburban municipalities to provide zoning for multifamily housing, are both being perceived as victories of equal impact to the Supreme Court decision on school integration. However, these court rulings, just like the busing decision, are likely to have unanticipated and deleterious side effects. These decisions will not only prove difficult to implement (and, in the process, cause much trauma and disruption of communities) but are also likely to achieve the opposite effect from the one intended: no housing will be built anywhere for low- and moderate-income groups.

The school desegregation decision gave impetus to hundreds of thousands of white middle-class people to leave the cities where school integration was to take place. The influx of poor and minority groups to our large cities, in combination with the school busing decision and the availability of new, federally subsidized single-family housing in the suburbs led the white middle-class urban dwellers to abandon their neighborhoods and move to new suburban municipalities where school busing to achieve integration at a local level was inconsequential. The net effect of this large shift of the white middle-income population to the suburbs was that the black children who were now being bused to schools in previously white urban neighborhoods found themselves attending schools which were becoming increasingly black.

The urban middle-class who saw their chosen life-styles and moralities threatened, who found their integrated schools unacceptable as educational and social milieus, who abandoned their old neighborhoods and housing for new communities with little history and few roots are not now likely to stand by and have their lives uprooted again, court decisions notwithstanding. There may be a court requirement to locate low- and moderate-income housing in the suburbs, but in the current atmosphere there is not likely to be an allocation of government money with which to accomplish it. The flight to the suburbs of middle-class America may in retrospect appear abhorrent, but the universality of the movement begs the question as to whether the liberal establishment is properly attuned to the problems and is correct in classifying all people who are concerned with the quality of their children's educational environment, and with preserving the stability of their neighborhoods, as bigoted. We cannot have it both ways — we cannot recognize the desirability of the stable social milieu of a middle-income community and at the same time embark upon federally assisted policies that destroy it — for the poor and black will, in the course of a few years, again be living only among the poor and black.

It does no good to tell the residents of the Irish, Jewish, German, Italian ethnic middle- and working-class communities that federally assisted public and moderate-income housing projects will not destroy their neighborhoods if their inhabitants perceive that they do. We must become attuned to and learn to cherish each community's own sense of the ingredients necessary to the maintenance of its milieu and stability rather than wildly rushing about projecting our own values and commitments upon others.

Our goal has to be the creation of stable neighborhoods and housing developments which are occupied by a mixture of income groups but are primarily occupied by the higher-income population so as to maintain quality communal services in the form of schools, shops, parks, police and fire protection, and job and business opportunities. The questions are these: Under what conditions is it realistically possible for government to encourage the mix of different economic and racial groups? To what degree can the creation of a community of interest among residents by grouping people of similar age and life-style together minimize the effects of racial and economic integration sufficiently to allay fears among neighbors? What policies and percentages of racial and economic mix have, in the past, proven to have the longest life expectancy?

Racially Integrated Housing

The problems attending efforts to create stable interracial housing have been examined in neighborhoods of privately owned homes, in private developments of co-operatives, condominiums, and rental units, and in public housing. The term *tipping point* has been commonly used to describe the racial transition and succession phenomenon that has occurred in neighborhoods of privately owned homes. The pattern it describes is one of nonwhites entering a neighborhood in sufficient numbers to start an increasing exodus of white residents. Eleanor Wolf reviewed the literature on the tipping point and found that definitions included the following ideas: a *preference point*—the verbal indication by individuals of their willingness to participate in some social situation with varying proportions of members of another group; a *leaving point*—the point at which residents attempt to sell their homes, affected by housing market conditions; and an *entering point*—the point at which new white residents are no longer willing to enter an integrated neighborhood.[9]

E. P. Wolf and J. S. Millen have pointed out that there is no consistent evidence of a specific proportion of nonwhites that will cause whites to move out or refuse to enter. Millen stresses the importance of local circumstances. Wolf demonstrated in her research in Detroit that there was no marked acceleration in rate of racial transition, as would have been expected if the tipping point were a fixed racial proportion. She argues that decisions to enter or leave are actually based on people's own estimates of the *future* composition of the neighborhood rather than on current proportions. J. T. Little et al. have documented the importance of residents' expectations regarding the possibility that their properties will decrease in value with in-migration of low-income nonwhite families. Bradburn et al. and Rapkin and Grigsby also stress the importance of the current residents' expectations.

Income Mixes and Stability

In some neighborhoods, racial transition and socioeconomic change are followed by property speculation and exploitation, weakened market conditions, disinvestment, and, finally, abandonment. In its case study survey on abandonment in various cities, the Center for Community Change of the National Urban League describes the abandonment process as the operation of an *economic* tipping point, the point following racial and economic transition when owners and financial institutions decide to milk the property and walk away. Anthony Downs also emphasizes the importance of an economic rather than a racial tipping point.

George Sternlieb has studied the factors leading to housing abandonment by landlords. Some of the statistically significant factors he found which predicted abandonment were neighborhood housing vacancy rate, deterioration of neighborhood housing, racial composition of tenants, tenants considered a "problem" by their landlord, various financial characteristics, and the size and qualities of the landlord's other properties.

Whereas Sternlieb's studies relate specifically to factors affecting privately owned housing and not to public housing or publicly assisted housing, his findings are important in that they show that a high vacancy rate is a precursor of further abandonment, just as is evident vandalism and deterioration of property. He also found that "deterioration of neighborhood housing is highly correlated with poverty, crime and vandalism. . . ." A further finding of Sternlieb's is that a landlord's decision to abandon his property often hinges on his perception of his tenants as troublemakers, and this perception is often the result of racial difference and the income status of his tenants. Landlords frequently decide to let their property run down once they have agreed to accept one or more minority-group tenants with rent supplements. And this is so even when a landlord is actually receiving more rent than he was from previous tenants.

However, the fact that many neighborhoods have changed from white to black and that some have been abandoned should not lead one to assume that no stable, racially integrated neighborhoods exist. They do, as Bradburn, Sudman, and Gockel have documented comprehensively. According to their *process* definition of integrated neighborhoods—that is, when both black and white families are moving into the neighborhood and into houses of comparable quality—they estimate that 36 million Americans in 11 million households live in *stably integrated* neighborhoods.

According to Bradburn, Sudman, and Gockel, white and black buyers in integrated neighborhoods and white buyers in segregated neighborhoods described similar criteria in selecting their new homes. The most frequently cited advantages were convenience to work, the size of the dwelling, specific features other than size, and financial considerations. Wolf and Lebeaux indicate that buyers are also concerned with the quality and cost of public services, especially education, and, in some areas, the level of crime. These same concerns have been reported by residents in private interracial developments by the Potomac Institute and by Grier and Grier in their 1960 study. From the point of view of blacks, high-quality services and low crime rates are more likely to be found in integrated neighborhoods. In an opinion poll taken in 1968 by the Survey Research Center, blacks who preferred integrated neighborhoods gave the following reasons: learn to get along better, less crime, quieter, and better services. It seems that if the quality of the dwelling units, the public services, and the over-all condition of neighborhood are reasonably high and are maintained at that level, the chances of a community remaining stable and integrated are greatly improved. Grier and Grier, Little et al., Millen and the Potomac Institute make similar recommendations. These recommendations apply to privately developed housing just as they do to subsidized housing.

Several writers have suggested that successful, stable racial integration can best be realized in rental housing and owner-occupied housing that is managed by a central agency, that is, a co-operative or condominium. In rental housing, because of the size of the operation, the mangers are not as vulnerable to real estate pressures and community changes as are individual homeowners. Managers are also in a position to implement policy that can contribute significantly to neighborhood stability and integration. Both the Potomac Institute and Grier and Grier both document cases in which racial mixing has been restored and community attractiveness has been improved through management policy. The Potomac Institute also recommends that sales and management staff be trained to show respect to members of all groups and that resident involvement and responsiblity in community affairs and maintenance are essential. Housing management can facilitate entry by different racial and ethnic groups in desired proportions by screening applicants or by directing advertising or promotion to recruit different groups. This does not vary whether the housing is owner-occupied or rented. The manager or developer is thus able to assure prospective residents that the minority population will not exceed a certain figure.

The spatial distribution of nonwhite residents is thought to be a factor in stability, affecting the white residents' decisions to move out and prospective white residents' decisions to move in. Freeman and Sunshine have attempted to organize previous findings on residential integration into a computer simulation; they have simulated various housing market models under various conditions of ethnic constraint. In their models, each house in the neighborhood has a stimulus value dependent on the distance from the seller's or prospective buyer's house and on the proportion of blacks in the neighborhood. Their conclusion is that density and spatial distribution should be considered in any integration policy because the spreading of nonwhites through-out the neighborhood can slow the transition process. In fact, Grier and Grier report that developers of interracial housing do attempt to do this as a conscious practice.

Interracial occupancy patterns and biracial building occupancy pat-terns in public housing have been investigated by social psychologists Deutsch and Collins; Wilner, Walkley, and Cook; and Johoda and West. These studies indicate that physical proximity to blacks encour-ages interracial neighborly contacts which, in turn, encourage the de-velopment of favorable ethnic attitudes.

The Jahoda and West study is particularly interesting because the authors investigated the attitudes that seem to account for sudden neighborhood transition. Jahoda and West interviewed the residents of integrated public housing about their expectations of the proportion of blacks who would live there in the future. Among those who believed in segregation and found current race relations unfavorable, 67 per cent predicted that the project would become entirely black. Even among those who were in favor of integration and found race relations favorable, 47 per cent believed the black proportion would increase substantially. Furthermore, of those who expected the project to become entirely black, 75 per cent reported they were going to move. Jahoda and West assert that the beliefs of the white tenants were ripe for the self-fulfilling prophecy of invasion to occur; it did not occur because management maintained equal proportions of the groups. In a similar project without a quota, the equal proportions changed to 80 per cent black.

Economically Integrated Housing

Many of the writers who have addressed the question of interracial housing argue that it will work best when the members of both races are of equal socioeconomic status. It has been a consistent argument of social psychologists that for optimal contact and the consequent reduc-tion of prejudice to occur, neighbors must be of equal status. Many of the critics of economically integrated housing have used these argu-ments to conclude that such housing will not be successful because social interaction will not occur between members of different status groups. However, it is questionable whether social intermingling along the lines of personal friendship is *required* for a community to be stable and crime-free. Marrett, in reviewing these writers, indicates that they believed the objectives of economic integration were to "improve per-sonal relations in society" and "to upgrade low-income people educationally, socially and culturally." These need not be the only or even the most important objectives of socioeconomic integration, as she points out. If the objective is the achievement of stable, low-crime communities, perhaps the design of a community to facilitate intense socializing between neighbors can be viewed as a secondary goal.

In an ongoing research project at our Institute, we have found that in two economically and racially integrated developments in New York neighboring contacts such as casual conversations with one's neighbors and helping a neighbor keep up the yard were reported to occur frequently, whereas going to the movies and lending money occurred very infrequently. Furthermore, both these projects were judged to be very friendly places by the residents.

In one of the very few studies specifically about economically integrated housing, Ryan et al. address the widely held view that mixed-income housing will not work because residents will not interact socially. In both mixed-income developments and in developments that were not mixed, the median number of neighbors with whom a visiting relationship was maintained was only two. The authors' conclusion is similar to my own contention: for a community to be safe and stable, one's neighbors need not be one's close friends — they need only be good neighbors. Ryan et al. also found that the two factors which most related to people's satisfaction with their neighbors were the belief that neighbors were friendly and that they were well behaved. They conclude that "this is probably all that's required."

A major finding of this same study was that residents' satisfaction was highly related to housing design, construction, and management variables and was not directly related to income or racial mix:

> ... we can say that income mix "works" or does not "work" according to whether or not the mix occurs in a well-designed, well-constructed, well-managed development. These latter factors are the crucial determinants of satisfaction. Income mix and racial mix are, in themselves, of no particular relevance.[10]

This conclusion is similar to the findings reviewed earlier on interracial neighborhoods and developments: the quality of the dwelling and of the neighborhood are important determinants in the selection of a home and increases the possibility of stability and a low crime rate; and the quality of the development and the management is essential in maintaining the stability of interracial developments. Similarly, Franklin Becker, in studying tenant satisfaction in multifamily housing built by the New York State Urban Development Corporation which is economically integrated, found that the most frequent sources of tenant dissatisfaction were related to physical design, the location of the development, management, *maintenance,* and *security.*

The evidence in favor of or against economically mixed housing is limited; the ideology both for and against is strong. Grier and Grier, Frieden, Kain and Persky, and Downs call for the integration of low-income minority groups with moderate- or middle-income groups as the most significant and realistic solution to the finaicial and social problems of the city and of the low-income population living in the city. Downs cites the evidence that high crime, vandalism, and delinquency rates are found in predominantly black low-income areas as a major problem both for the city and for the residents who are being victimized.

Grier and Grier write:

> If Negroes were more evenly dispersed throughout the metropolitan areas, not only would the concentration of urban problems be reduced, but the resources available to deal with them would be immensely increased. And the tendency of those problems that center on race to extend themselves geographically and to perpetuate themselves in time would be sharply curtailed if not entirely eliminated.[11]

The authors also describe the severe effects of population change: it destroys the social fabric of a neighborhood; increases in crime and delinquency occur because normal vigilance no longer exists.

Both Grier and Grier and Kain and Persky believe that programs intended to solve ghetto problems within the existing structure of the ghetto will not be successful for the very reason that their focus is entirely within the ghetto. Kain and Persky argue for the integration of low-income persons into moderate-income neighborhoods on a pragmatic basis and on the basis that such a strategy is consistent with the goals of American society.

Downs presents the most detailed, comprehensive argument for such a strategy. His position is that both the upgrading desired by low- and moderate-income households and the protection of neighborhood quality desired by middle-income households can be achieved in the same neighborhoods if a significant number of low- and moderate-income families live there and if middle-class dominance is maintained. Downs is interested in creating such integration on the scale of a neighborhood or even larger area; he suggests three geographical scales of economic integration: (1) by *commuting zones,* to provide convenient access to suburban jobs for low- and moderate-income residents (size approximately 117,000 people in 10.6 square miles); (2) by spatial separation of groups but integration in *school attendance areas,* to create economically integrated schools; and (3) by *block,* to create daily personal interaction between households. He concedes that this last scale would be the most problematic. It is my contention that the creation of socially and economically integrated communities that are stable and relatively safe even in multifamily dwellings will require integration both within buildings and within the development as a whole.

In describing what he calls "neighborhood linkages," Anthony Downs in his book *Opening Up the Suburbs* asserts that the quality of life in households is created in part by associations with other people in the vicinity of the dwelling unit. He then outlines five of the most important linkages: (1) movement into, around, and out of the dwelling unit, which requires personal safety; (2) children's play interactions; (3) school interactions; (4) aesthetic impact of neighborhood, including property maintenance; and (5) use of shared public facilities such as parks and public transportation. Downs asserts:

> These interactions establish "external" or "spillover" effects that link the quality of life in each household to the behavior of other people living or working nearby. All urban households are affected by such linkages, so all are concerned about the behavior of their neighbors (and others who frequent the area).[12]

Furthermore, the establishment of a peaceful and safe local environment requires that residents can effectively prevent certain types of behavior in their neighborhood.

These ideas are essentially similar to those being advocated here. It is through the residents' use and perception of areas exterior to the dwelling unit that a community is truly made or broken in the most concrete sense. It is in such spaces — in the corridor, stairs, lobby, common entry, and grounds of the development — that neighborly contacts are made, that children play and that many crimes and acts of vandalism occur.

Throughout the literature on interracial and economically integrated housing runs the underlying issue of occupancy controls or quota systems. As we have seen, there is no evidence for a consistent tipping point that holds true for most situations, but there is evidence of neighborhoods and developments that have experienced complete racial transition. Writers in the field agree that people's expectations of the future racial and economic composition of a community do determine whether they move in, stay, or move out and consequently determine the future composition of that community. It appears that if current and prospective residents believe that the proportions will not change drastically and if the proportions are maintained through management policy, the community will remain stable. This has been documented for public housing (Jahoda and West), for private, federally assisted housing (Ackerman), and for privately financed developments (Grier and Grier). As the Griers point out, if it is the stated intention of the developer or public agency to create and maintain an integrated community, they are obliged to meet the expectations of prospective residents, current residents, and the larger community.

The use of selective advertising and promotion to different groups has been cited as an alternative to occupancy controls. However, this does not always result in long-term integrated housing nor does it provide prospective residents with the assurance they seem to need. Although quotas do meet these requirements, they are a highly controversial tool. On the other hand, the use of quotas can provide low-income minority persons with the opportunity to live in integrated communities because it would provide more opportunity for the construction of integrated communities. The Griers describe the case of a development in Ohio in which the developer's sales staff presented the quota policy honestly and respectfully to black applicants who could not be accepted because the quota had been filled. The developer reported that almost all the hundreds of prospects turned away were willing to accept the policy and that some appreciated its purpose, which was openly stated to be the maintenance of a fully integrated community.

The legal questions regarding occupancy controls in housing have not yet been resolved. Recent court decisions are confusing, such as in the Otero case, involving a suit brought against the New York City Housing Authority for establishing ethnic quotas. Ackerman describes the conclusion in this case as upholding integration ceilings in certain situations. In his comprehensive review of empirical findings and legal decisions regarding racial occupancy controls, Ackerman concludes that "policy arguments and empirical analysis support the case for using benign quotas in Federally subsidized housing."[13]

In addressing the argument that integration quotas will disadvantage black homeseekers, Ackerman states:

> What pro-civil rights quota opponents must recognize, however, is that a governmental decision not to implement racial occupancy controls will result in a denial for some blacks of the housing integration opportunities they seek.[14]

III

Housing Design and
the Control of Behavior

In the Introduction and the first two chapters I have tried to demonstrate that the dissatisfaction most Americans feel with their home environments is the consequence of our being a highly mobile people who have concentrated ourselves into large urban megalopolises and into housing developments and communities which often consist of a dense amalgam of incompatible age and life-style groups, all strangers to one another. To compound the problem further, there has been a large shifting of low-income black population from southern towns and rural areas into the larger cities of the North. I have then suggested that the sum total of our nation's housing assistance programs (for low-, middle-, *and* upper-income populations) that were created to address these problems has had much the opposite effects of those intended: they have facilitated middle-class flight to the suburbs, polarized our new megalopolises into black and white, poor and rich, and have been a catalyst for the abandonment of urban neighborhoods and communities. Although the importance of economic and racial integration as a mechanism for assimilating the poor and black into the mainstream of

American society is recognized, the means for achieving it remain elusive. To this end I have presented research findings which demonstrate that the establishment of racial and economic quota systems in housing developments serves a critical function in the stabilization of integrated communities. Research into tipping points has shown that residents' decisions to move are not in fact based on certain magic numbers but rather on their perceptions of what the racial makeup of the community will likely become; established quotas therefore act to remove uncertainty about the future.

Finally, I have presented findings from research on community instability and dissatisfaction that have shown that the quality of housing design and maintenance is as important in determining the desirability of a community to higher income residents as is its racial and economic mix. The form and maintenance of housing strongly affect residents' images of themselves and of their neighbors and, as a consequence, their satisfaction with their community and their desire to stay. In this chapter I discuss the different housing types in use today and their evolution in response to the pressures of increasing density. I also try to demonstrate how different housing forms affect residents' abilities to determine and control activity within their buildings and their willingness to accept responsibility for the maintenance and security of the areas outside their homes.

The housing environments we have been building to accommodate our new urban concentrations have taken a variety of forms, many dating literally from the time of their construction no more than twenty years ago. High-density environments can bring people into contact with each other in new ways—some of which prove to be unsettling, particularly for those who have had no past social tradition for this form of living. By building at high densities, we have created new options in our living environments just as we have removed old ones. While it is not certain that we have gained more than we have lost, it is now clear that high-density housing is more than the simple accretion and concentration of single-family houses.

High-density housing is normally the consequence of two factors: the universally perceived desirability of certain locations and the comparative income of the resident population. Competition for a particular parcel of land in a choice location drives up its cost. The high cost, in turn, restricts the purchase of the land either to those who are rich or to those who are prepared to share that parcel with many others. Obviously, the lower the income group, the higher the number of residents who must be brought together to share the cost of expensive land. The operation of these mechanisms has created many of our most serious housing problems, because inevitably a large percentage of the lowest-

Fig. 3.1: Farmhouses in northern Holland.

income groups in any metropolitan area will have to live in the highest density housing.

A superficial glance at the variety of housing being built today suggests that there are infinite types available. More careful examination reveals that there are only a small number of prototypes in common use, although there are many variations within each type. Examined from our area of interest — the effect of the design of environment on the residents' capacity to control and determine the use of the areas outside the confines of their dwelling units — the number of residential prototypes of significant difference can be generally limited to three: (1) single-family houses; (2) walk-ups; and (3) elevator buildings. Single-family houses include detached, semidetached, and row houses. Walk-ups include garden apartments and open gallery buildings. Elevator buildings commonly range from six to thirty stories in height and house anywhere from fifty to five hundred families per entry.

We shall examine these three prototypes, their evolution, the basic subclasses within each, and the comparative differences in the living environment and urban fabrics each produces.

The Single-Family House

Figure 3.1 shows a few farmhouses along a road in northern Holland. It illustrates the origins of the traditional concept of the single-family house. Each of the farmhouses is located on its own piece of property or, to put it another way, on the farm owned by a particular family. Within the three-dimensional envelope of each farmhouse is the private word, or domain, of that family. The land on which the farmhouse sits is equally private. The land may be defined by fences or simply by the edge of the public road or ditch that passes along it, but each family determines the nature of the activity that can take place on their own property, just as they do the activity in the interior of their home.

Figure 3.2 illustrates a row of nineteenth-century Dutch houses located in the town serving the farm community shown in Figure 3.1. This is a residential setting of an entirely different scale and density: where each farmhouse occupied from ten to fifty acres of land, the urban houses here are built at over thirty units to the acre. However, in spite of the fact that the density is several hundred times that of the farm community, there is in the urban setting, as in the rural one, a very clear notion of defined property. Each of these row-house units serves a single family. Every item located within the exterior walls that define the house is unmistakably understood as belonging to a particular family. Nor is there any question as to who has the right to determine the use and users of the interior areas: it is the members of the family themselves.

On the front façade the windows of each dwelling unit face the street directly, minimally encumbered by curtains or blinds. At the rear of each unit is a yard that belongs to the occupant family and serves as its exterior private space. This yard abuts the yards of other houses on

Fig. 3.2: Nineteenth-century Dutch single-family houses in an urban setting.

both sides and opposite in what has come to be known as the "row-house pattern."

At the front of each house there is a small extension of the private realm of the dwelling out into the street: this is defined by a brick line in the cobblestone running parallel to the façade. Note that the bottom of the stoop in front of the building entry also ends at this line.

The street that runs between the parallel rows of dwellings is public, in that it is for the collective use of all the residents on the street and the village and outsiders. The public street is a means of getting from one residence to another or to any part of the town and the outside world. Theoretically, everyone is free to walk along this street without being interfered with and without having his presence questioned. Should a passer-by decide to move from the public portion of the walk onto the rough cobbled area defined by the brick line — even though he is still in a public street — he will be perceived by residents as having moved from a zone that is essentially public and trespassed into the private domain of an individual family unit. A passer-by who is not recognized as a resident of the street would be required, with such movement, to make his intentions more clearly known.

Because the houses on each side of the street are so close together it is unlikely that a stranger would be able to stand still in the center of the street for very long without being questioned by someone, whether by a resident of the dwelling or a neighbor. The fact that the windows of the dwelling unit are so large and face so closely and directly onto the street allows residents from within the unit to make their presence felt on the public portions of the central walk some ten feet away. Of course, this also serves to make the private domains of the dwelling unit visually accessible from the street.

Because of its narrow dimensions, this street is much less public than one might at first suspect. The twenty feet separating the buildings brings the public street into the sphere of influence of the adjacent homes. The juxtaposition of the dwellings units and street is too close to allow residents to tolerate activity in the street that they perceive as a departure from the communally defined norm of acceptable behavior or that they consider is an invasion of the privacy of the individual dwelling unit.

Where the central portion of the street allows for a broader range of activities to occur within it, the rough-cobbled portion of the street has a more limited use: it is an outside space perceived as belonging to particular families and so can serve only a limited range of activities.

The stoops and the change in paving texture are devices of demarcation that create buffers between the public street and the private household; these marking mechanisms are also symbols defining the

Fig. 3.3: Semidetached housing in urban America, circa 1920, built at twelve dwellings to the acre.

zone of influence of the private dwellings within the public street. These symbols reinforce the residents' view that they have the right to question activity taking place on the brick portion of the street as well as on the immediately adjacent cobbles and stoops.

In any conflict which might arise because of public activity engaged in by passers-by on the street, the residents' view will prevail as their sphere of influence within the privacy of their adjacent dwellings is unquestioned and their permanent presence within their homes does not allow them to withdraw too far from such a conflict. By contrast, the nature of the rights permitted the passers-by on the public street is undefined. They have no claim to stationary presence. Even in a prolonged conflict over spheres of influence, the passers-by must, with time, withdraw, because in addition to permanence, residents up and down the street share a community of interest with each other. The nature of residents' influence is so clearly understood by all parties (residents and passers-by) that such open confrontations rarely occur; the victor is predetermined and few people enjoy the humiliation of public defeat.

Figure 3.3 is a view of semidetached American houses built in the 1920s at a density of twelve dwelling units per acre. This is a solution that falls between the detached house and the row house in comparative density and luxury. Like the row houses in Holland, the grounds

Fig. 3.4: A block of row houses built in America at the turn of the century for moderate-income populations.

are defined in front and back — the front doors have been provided with the equivalent of stoops. The street is wider here, and the sidewalk more distant from the houses. The change in level also contributes to the disassociation of the dwellings from the street. There is no question that the sidewalk still is within the sphere of influence of the abutting houses, but because a forty-foot road separates the two sidewalks, it is only one row of houses, rather than two, that abuts each sidewalk. Here the planted lawn rather than the cobbled paving defines the private terrain of each dwelling. The stairs and landing function equivalently to the stoop in the Dutch example — they provide an extension of the dwelling into the street.

Figure 3.4 shows a street of turn-of-the-century American row houses. The dwellings were built for moderate-income and skilled working-class families and achieve a density of thirty-two units to the acre. Less generous and expensive than the semidetached houses shown in Figure 3.3, they nevertheless contain all the mechanisms identified in the Dutch nineteenth-century urban houses: the stoop and fenced-off grass areas, however meager, succeed in creating a semiprivate buffer zone between the private dwelling and the public street. The close juxtaposition of the buildings with the street brings the sidewalk into the sphere of influence of the dwellings more strongly than was the case with the sedidetached dwellings. Here, too, the rear yards are the private outdoor area of the dwellings' inhabitants and are accessible only from the interior private zone of the house.

Looking at the entire city block and from it to the fabric of the city that is composed of these blocks, one finds that almost all of the ground area has been designated as the private space of particular families. Very little is left over as public street and sidewalk. In fact, because of the close juxtaposition between dwellings and sidewalk and the unbroken run of individual dwellings along the sidewalk, much of the public street falls under the penumbra of private dwelling units.

The Walk-Up

Figure 3.5 shows a few blocks of old three- and four-story brownstones, a New York idiom of the row house. These old brownstones, built originally as individual family homes, have since been subdivided and turned into flats. They are now occupied by four to eight families rather than one. Access to the flat of each family is from an interior vestibule, staircase, and corridor. The subdivision of these houses for multifamily occupancy has produced a new phenomenon that has no precedent in any of the single-family houses previously discussed. The

Fig. 3.5: Aerial view of a few blocks of New York City brownstones, now converted to flats.

entry to the private domain of individual dwelling units no longer occurs on the public street but off a nonprivate area which is located within the building. These buildings, therefore, have areas within their interiors that are public in that they do not belong to any one family but are shared by all the families living in the building. Actually, these common circulation areas are more *semiprivate* than they are *public* because they are shared by only a small group of families.

The creation of a living environment that has areas *within* buildings that are not part of the private realm of particular families is a radical departure from the tradition of the single-family house. This departure involves not only the nature of the building interior, but also the grounds around the building. Because the grounds are shared by many families, they now have a public and ambiguous quality. It is not clear to whom the grounds belong or how they can be used. Not surprisingly, therefore, one finds that when the rear yards are not assigned to individual families they are used as long-term storage areas—collectors of junk might be a more accurate designation. No resident maintains these grounds or feels comfortable in using them for prolonged periods of time.

However, should the building owner happen to live in the building —say, at the ground level, which was the custom for a while—or should the building owner acquire an agent such as a superintendent or a concierge to maintain the building and act on his behalf, then the owner or agent will undertake control of the interior public areas of the

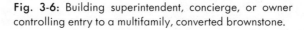

Fig. 3-6: Building superintendent, concierge, or owner controlling entry to a multifamily, converted brownstone.

Fig. 3.7: A three-story, multifamily apartment building of the 1920s. The provision of very large apartments (eight to ten rooms) and generous interior lobbies and circulation areas were part of an endeavor to make this housing form a substitute for the single-family house.

building and the grounds surrounding it. The people who come through the entry vestibule will undergo a screening process (Figure 3.6). The nature of the activity permitted in the interior public circulation areas, under these circumstances, will be determined by the owner or agent. Although the individual flats or apartments in this building are the private domains of individual families, their realms do not extend beyond the doors to their apartments. If the owner or concierge is not in residence, the interior public areas will be readily accessible to outsiders. The maintenance of these interior nonprivate areas will likely be subject to residents' whim. The grounds, if not assigned to a particular resident, will suffer a similar fate.

These converted brownstones are able to provide housing for as many as two hundred families on one acre of land. They function best when occupied by single people or families with few children.

Newly constructed three- and four-story multifamily residential structures, known as walk-ups became a common phenomenon of higher-density, middle-income housing constructed in the 1920s. They were built as an attempt to reproduce the environment of the single-family house, but at a density of thirty-five to sixty families per acre of land (Figure 3.7). This housing type is normally both very wide and deep (one hundred by sixty feet) and provides families with children a large, comfortable apartment as an alternative to the single-family house.

Fig. 3.8: The entry lobby to a three-story, middle-class, urban apartment building of the 1920s.

Fig. 3.9: Foyer serving two apartments in the three-story, middle-class building.

Fig. 3.10: Three-and-a-half story walk-up apartment buildings located opposite a park. The housing on the internal street are single-family detached units. The luxury of the park frontage required a higher-density development.

A variety of devices were used both in the design of the interior circulation areas of the multifamily building and in the provision of large exterior balconies to capture some of the flavor of the single-family dwelling unit. The entry lobbies were made spacious and were occasionally treated as small courtyards (Figure. 3.8). Many of these lobbies were glazed at the rear of the building, allowing in light and providing access to an exterior courtyard that could be used in pleasant weather. At each floor level, entries to individual apartments were defined by separate alcoves and occasionally by a transitional step or two. In general, the treatment of the common corridors and lobbies was sumptuous, involving carpeting, the placement of chairs and side tables, ornamental lighting, and textured wall surfacing (Figure 3.9). A very conscious attempt was made, through interior design and decorating techniques, to replicate, in the public circulation areas of the building, the mood of the inside of a home.

Each of these buildings serves from six to twelve families. The superintendent and his family occupy the basement apartment. Seen from the street, the three-and-a-half story walk-up apartment blends in unobtrusively with neighboring single-family housing. Few of these buildings, however, are able to provide adequate outdoor play facilities for children. They work best when located opposite city parks, as many of them in fact were (Figure 3.10).

Fig. 3.11: A three-story walk-up building placed on a street of single-family detached houses has required the owner of the adjacent house to define his grounds as private with a small fence. The single-family houses further down the street are not fenced because everyone understands them to be private. The grounds around the three-story walk-up, though, are public and hence the need to differentiate them from the private grounds of the adjacent single family house.

Fig. 3.12: Parking and entrance to a contemporary suburban, three-story apartment building, built at thirty-five apartment units to the acre.

The walk-up most commonly built today is the garden apartment building illustrated in Figure 3.12. This prototype has a density limit of about thirty-five units to the acre. In the garden apartment illustrated, each entry, expressed by a recessed alcove on the façade, serves only six families, two per floor. The lobby contains the intercom, mailboxes, and stroller storage room. A common stair in the entry hall serves all six apartments. In some walk-up buildings a second exit from the entry hall is provided to give access to the outside area at the rear of the building.

Possibly the most important feature of this design is that only two families are required to share a corridor at each floor level. It is therefore not unusual for families in these buildings to extend their proprietary feelings out of their apartments and into the corridor; many residents see the corridor landings as extensions of their private homes. They include the corridors outside their apartments in their weekly cleaning and place such items as welcome mats, dried plants, or wall hangings in the area to give it a personalized touch and help mark the space as their own. With only six families sharing an entry, it is comparatively easy for residents to come to recognize and know one another, and equally simple for an implicit understanding to grow among them as to what constitutes acceptable usage of these common interior areas.

The grounds outside the garden apartment building, as shown in this photograph of a typical suburban prototype, normally have parking areas opposite the front entries and common green areas at the rear. The grounds are public in that no attempt has been made to assign any of the areas to particular families or even to the six families sharing an entry.

An interesting variation of the three-story walk-up, which manages to avoid interior public circulation areas completely, evolved in Montreal, Canada. Figure 3.13 shows a view down a typical urban street composed of these flats. The ground-floor unit is entered from its own fenced-off patio. The second- and third-floor units share a common exterior stair that springs from the public sidewalk to a balcony serving two entry doors. One of these doors enters the second-floor unit; the other leads to an interior staircase, which leads up to the third-floor flat. This interior stair is within the private realm of the family occupying the third floor and is therefore not a public stair. This building type is also unique in that it achieves a very high density (up to sixty-five dwellings units per acre) while completely avoiding the creation of any interior public circulation areas.

All the units are floor-throughs — that is, the apartments extend from the front to the rear of the building. The windows of the units thus face both the street and the grounds at the back. The balconies and entries in front of the building are within the zone of influence of the units because of their placement next to the windows. The families occupying the ground floor unit have the use of the front and back grounds. The families living on the second and third floors are compensated by having their own private balconies, front and back.

This building type has one advantage over most other three-story walk-ups in that the front door to every unit is visible from the street.

Fig. 3.13: Three-story, walk-up flats in Montreal, Canada, built at fifty apartments to the acre. All apartments have front doors which face onto the street. There are no interior circulation areas serving more than one family.

Young children can play outside on the balconies, in the sun, in view of street activity, while still being next to the door to their apartments.

The construction technique used in the Montreal walk-up is very economical in that it makes use of a continuous slab of building to which individual wooden balconies and stairs are affixed. More costly and elaborate variations were built on slightly larger sites, as seen in Figure 3.14. Here the entry to the upper two floors is beyond a small transitional buffer area rather than immediately off the street.

The European variation of the walk-up flat is the open-gallery block, which takes two forms: those built with one-story apartments and those with two-story apartments (or maisonettes). Figure 3.15 illustrates a small four-story gallery walk-up building composed of single-level apartments. All units are accessible from a staircase at the far end of the building and the common gallery at each level. Aside from the half-hidden stair, there are no other interior public areas. The windows and entries of the units face the public access galleries. This prototype can house as many as sixty families on an acre of land. The grounds at the front and rear are for the common use of all the residents in the building and are symbolically fenced off.

Figure 3.16 shows the two-story apartment, or maisonette, variation of the four-story, open-gallery block. The four-story building consists of one two-story dwelling unit (maisonette) sitting above another two-story unit. Access to the upper maisonette is by staircase. The lower maisonette unit has the private use of some of the front and rear grounds.

Fig. 3.14: A more luxurious version of the Montreal three-story flats. The building's facing material consists of ornamental stone and the site is larger, permitting a buffer area between the sidewalk and the outside stairs leading to the second- and third-floor units.

Fig. 3.15: Example of a typical European four-story walk-up, this one located in London. All apartments consist of one-story flats and the entries to the units are from the single-loaded corridors which face onto the street.

Fig. 3.16: European four-story walk-up with each apartment consisting of a two-story maisonette.

Fig. 3.17: Five- and six-story tenements located on Manhattan's Lower East Side.

The Medium-Rise Building

Figure 3.17 is an aerial view of a grouping of tenements located on the Lower East Side of Manhattan in New York City. These tenements were constructed at the turn of this century for working-class families. They were designed for multiple occupancy and accommodate from ten to as many as twenty-four families per building entry. Twenty-four families per building entry was typical of old-law tenement buildings built in New York before 1890. As a building type responding to the demands of density, the tenement environment represented a quantum jump in the number of families required to share the interior public areas of a building and the grounds around it. Because of the large number of people involved in this sharing, the interior circulation areas were made very public.

It is unlikely that the owner of a tenement will be found in residence here, although there usually is a tenant family assigned the duty of acting as resident superintendent. A resident superintendent, or concierge, was commonly provided in multifamily buildings both in

Europe and America in the nineteenth and early twentieth centuries. It was a tradition that came into being with the evolution of high-density housing and unfortunately has been abandoned in contemporary fed-erally-assisted housing. The concierge's (or superintendent's) respon-sibilities used to involve not only taking care of the building and keep-ing it clean, but, more importantly, screening all the people who entered and left the building. With as many as twenty-four families (one hundred and more persons) sharing an entry, the tenement produced a collective living environment in which it was difficult for residents to recognize other residents and even more difficult to distinguish intruders from friends of other residents; hence the importance of the concierge's screening function. In order to reduce their work load, resi-dent superintendents got to know the troublemakers among the chil-dren and watched them with special care: this proved a very effective form of preventive maintenance.

The typical five- or six-story old-law tenement is twenty-five feet wide and ninety feet deep. It houses four families per floor, for a total of twenty to twenty-four families per building and as many as four hundred families per acre. The so-called new-law tenements were an improvement on the tenements built before 1890 in that they let in more light and air. Nevertheless, they were built to house more than one hundred families per acre of land (Figures 3.18a and b). The six-story air shafts and the space at the rear of the buildings were paved at

Fig. 3.18a: Old-law tenements built in New York prior to 1890. Each floor, shown in the section, serves four families.

Fig. 3.18b: New-law tenements, built after 1890, with better light and air provisions. Each floor, shown in the section, serves four families.

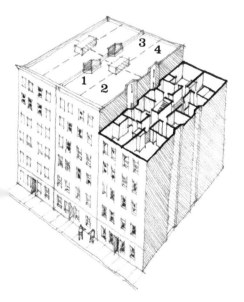

the ground level. Over the years, these areas became covered with glass and litter. The sidewalk and city street were the only places for occupants of these buildings to sit or children to play; the stoop and the sidewalks in front of the building thus became the converging area for residents of every age group. The frequency with which one sees photographs of tenement residents clustered on the front steps on a summer's night attests to the fondness with which this image of a tenement community is held by sociologists and architects. But this gathering of people on the steps of the building is probably less born of social inclination than of a search for cooler air. Given an alternative private space of a more secluded nature, these apparent social proclivities would likely have vanished. As long as there was little automobile traffic, the streets in front of the tenements served as useful play areas. However, the frequency of today's automobile traffic and parked cars renders the streets virtually useless for children's play.

The obvious inadequacies of tenement housing for families with children led to the public housing movement, and with that, the advent of the high-rise building. If a housing authority was required to use the same urban sites to rehouse the families living in the dilapidated tenements, it meant finding a building form that could reproduce equal densities.

The low cost of hydraulic (direct-plunger) elevators, compared with electric (wire-rope-suspended) elevators led in the late 1940s to the adoption of the six- and seven-story building; seventy feet is the effective height limit of the hydraulic elevator. The medium-rise elevator building normally has double-loaded corridors and takes the form of a cross.

These buildings house eight families per floor, a total of fifty-six families sharing a building entry. One elevator serves all the families in the building. The double-loaded corridors (apartments on both sides of a central corridor) are dark and narrow, but not as long in this building type as they are in slab buildings. The corridors at each level and in the common lobby serve too many families to allow any of them to feel comfortable about extending their realm of concern outside their individual apartments.[1] As a result, these public areas—the lobby, elevator, and stairs—have to be cleaned and maintained by the building management. Such areas are also very prone to vandalism. The elevators in particular are attractive playthings for children. They break down continually and their repair is very costly. Finally, because these common circulation areas are both public and hidden from the view of residents, they have proven to be, in public and moderate income housing, where most crimes, particularly robberies, assaults, and rapes, take place.

Fig. 3.19a: Seven-story cruciform-plan buildings with mechanical elevators and double-loaded corridors, serving fifty-six families per building entry.

The medium-rise elevator project shown in Figure 3.19 achieves a density of a little under fifty units per acre. The buildings differ from the three-story walk-up schemes in that they free a high percentage of the land for parking and recreation (14 per cent land coverage, compared with 33 per cent land coverage for three-story walk-ups built at

Fig. 3.19b: Typical floor plan for cruciform building.

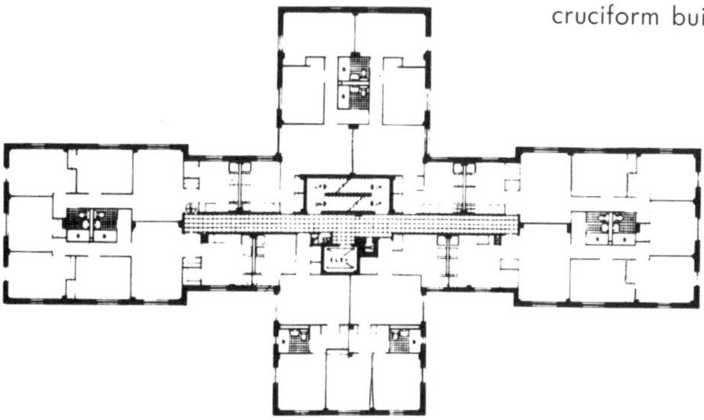

the same density). In the scheme illustrated, the architects have left all the grounds areas open and unassigned to any building. As a result, parents are apprehensive about allowing their younger children to play unattended on the grounds below.[2] Even though more ground area is left open for children's play in a seven-story development than in a walk-up, the same population living in a walk-up at the same density would result in many more children playing on the grounds below.

But the medium-rise elevator building at fifty units to the acre still does not replicate the density of the six-story tenements. Not surprisingly, electric elevators, which have no limit on height, were adopted by developers as the logical next step in the evolution of urban housing.

The Elevator High-Rise

Figure 3.20 shows a public housing project on the Lower East Side of Manhattan. The buildings are fourteen stories in height and house nine families per floor, for a total of one hundred seventeen families per building entry. The project is built at one hundred units to the acre — the same density as the tenement slums it replaced. This solution provides green areas and open space for sitting, play, and parking, but it is accomplished at the price of raising families into the air and away from the grounds below. The high-rise environment proves little better than the tenements it replaced in providing outdoor play areas for children which are close to home and easily supervisable. The economics of operating high-rise elevator buildings require that in excess of one hundred families share a common entry and interior circulation system. The exterior grounds and interior circulation areas therefore tend to be anonymous and easily acessible to outsiders. There is no easy way for residents to influence or control activity in the public areas immediately outside their apartments because there are just too many people sharing access to each building and its grounds.

As in the tenements, the large number of residents in a high-rise complicates the recognition process among neighbors and discourages the development of a commonality of goals and interests among them. For agreement on any matter of common concern to take place, too many people are required to concur — it cannot grow from the casual ad hoc concurrence among a half-dozen neighbors. The very public nature of the interior circulation areas has also succeeded in producing places within the buildings where residents are vulnerable to criminal attack. The additional height of the high-rise block makes it a less useful environment for families with children than the six-story tenements. The increased distance to the ground makes access to play areas difficult for young children and complicates their supervision by their parents. The

Fig. 3.20: Jacob Riis Houses, one of the first fourteen-story, high-rise public housing projects. It was built at a density of one hundred units to the acre, the same density as the six-story tenements it replaced.

high-rise blocks do, however, provide more room per family in each apartment. They also provide more light and air and better utilities.

The retrogressive aspects in the evolution of housing we have witnessed were the consequence of two forces working at cross purposes: the desire to improve the standard of individual dwelling units and the need to house families at increasing densities. The impossible density of tenement housing built one hundred years ago is now being reached again with the advent of twenty- and thirty-story high-rises. Where the individual apartments in tenements were woefully inadequate in terms of plumbing, sunlight, and size (three hundred square feet for a family of five), contemporary high-rise apartments provide eight hundred to twelve hundred square feet per family, receive abundant light, are supplied with modern plumbing facilities, and are serviced by high-speed elevators. However, when occupied by families with children, they provide poor access to play facilities, high maintenance costs, and a high vulnerability to crime.

Fig. 3.21: View of the new thirteen-story Aylesbury Estate in Southwark, London, being built to replace the nineteenth-century working-class row houses in the foreground. Both the old and the new housing are built at the same density: thirty-six units to the acre.

Fig. 3.22: Construction of the first of three phases of the Aylesbury Estate. The housing being replaced appears at the right. Residents believe that the new housing is being built at a much higher density than the old.

Options Available for Meeting High Densities

Given the problems of designing a development at thirty-five units to the acre, many architects chose the six-story scheme shown in Figure 3.19a when they could have achieved a similar density with the three-story garden apartment scheme shown in Figure 3.12. The options available to architects and the contrast of environments which can result from their decision to adopt one or another is most startlingly demonstrated by Figures 3.21 through 3.26. Figure 3.21 is a view down an eighteenth-century row-house street in London toward a housing project that is being built to replace it.

An aerial view of this new high-rise project is shown in Figure 3.22. The interesting, if frightening, point is that both the row houses and the high-rise are built at the same density: thirty-six units to the acre. The high-rise scheme was built at a much greater cost than row houses could be built today, because of the need for elevators, heavier foundations, multilevel car parking, and elevated sidewalks. The row-house scheme gives every family a piece of ground in front and back that they themselves maintain and that can be used for a variety of purposes. This ground area is useful play space for very young children but is inadequate for older children who need larger, collectively accessible play areas.

Fig. 3.23: Children and cars in the unpermitted areas of the Aylesbury Estate. Children find the elevated walkways unsuitable for play and adults find the enclosed parking areas too dangerous to leave their cars in.

Fig. 3.24: The Interior grounds of the St. Francis Square housing development in San Francisco, also constructed at a density of thirty-six units to the acre.

The high-rise frees more communal ground area, but the children still do most of their playing in neighboring streets, and residents will not park their cars in the provided elevated garages because of vandalism and theft (Figure 3.23). As much parking and collective play space is actually provided in the row-house scheme as in the high-rise, but it is in the form of street paving, parking, and asphalt play surfaces — unacceptable solutions to housing officials. In fact, strictly residential streets can be designed to produce minimal through-traffic and so facilitate their double use as play areas.)

Figures 3.24, 3.25, and 3.26 show a garden apartment scheme in

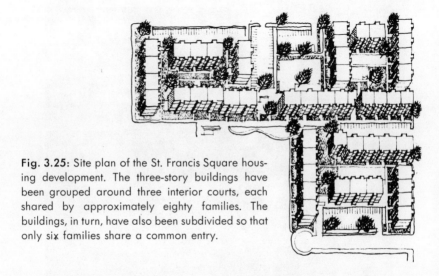

Fig. 3.25: Site plan of the St. Francis Square housing development. The three-story buildings have been grouped around three interior courts, each shared by approximately eighty families. The buildings, in turn, have also been subdivided so that only six families share a common entry.

San Francisco built at the same density as the Aylesbury Estate — thirty-six units to the acre. It provides both outdoor private areas for each family and collective areas for grouping of eighty families. All parking areas are at the ground level and the collective play areas are separated from vehicular traffic. Individualized private outdoor areas are provided in the form of patios at the ground level for ground-floor residents and balconies for families on the second and third floors. The collective courts at the rear of the dwelling are large enough to bicycle in or throw a ball around in and contain play equipment for six- to twelve-year-olds. Note too that front access to each building entry is from the street or parking area and egress to the play courts is from an opposing rear entry.

Housing Form and Residents' Control over Neighboring Streets

The layout of a row-house building is simple compared with a walk-up or high-rise. The individual row-house dwelling units do not have a communal interior circulation system, there are no elevators, the grounds abutting the units can be assigned to individual families, garbage disposal involves no complex machinery, and so on. The simplicity of row houses extends as well to their political nature: each unit is the domain of a single family. What happens within a row-house unit or its assigned grounds is clearly the responsibility of the family which inhabits it and controls access to it.

Row-house developments, when contrasted with high-rises, also set up decidedly different relationships between the dwelling unit and the city street. The family within the row house has complete control of the

Fig. 3.26: Street entrances to the buildings of the St. Francis Square development. Each entry serves only six families.

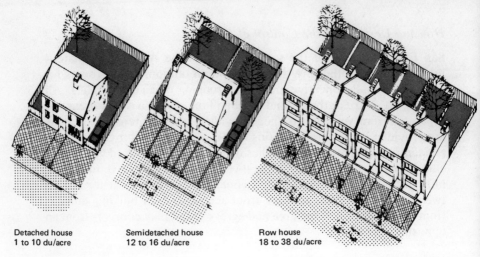

Detached house
1 to 10 du/acre

Semidetached house
12 to 16 du/acre

Row house
18 to 38 du/acre

Fig. 3.27: Single-family houses.
—All interior spaces are within the private domain of the family.
—All grounds around the private unit are for the private use of the family.
—There is a direct abutment between private grounds and the sidewalk.
—The domain of the house encompasses the street.

Private   Semiprivate   Semipublic   Public

Fig. 3.28: Walk-up buildings.
—Private space is within the apartment unit only.
—The interior lobby, stairs, and corridor are semiprivate.
—Grounds can be designated for one family but are usually shared by all the families in the building.
—Only a small number of families (three to six) share the interior circulation areas and grounds.
—The street is within the sphere of influence of the dwellings.

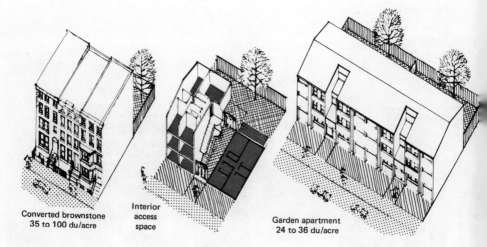

Converted brownstone
35 to 100 du/acre

Interior
access
space

Garden apartment
24 to 36 du/acre

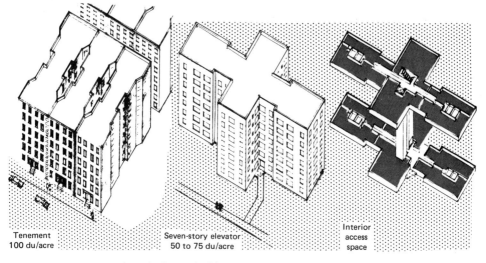

Tenement
100 du/acre

Seven-story elevator
50 to 75 du/acre

Interior
access
space

Fig. 3.29: Intermediate high-rise buildings.
— Private space exists only within the apartment units.
— The anterior circulation spaces (stairs, lobby, elevators, and corridors) are shared by many families and so are semipublic in nature.
— The grounds vary in nature from semipublic to public.
— The street is only marginally associated with the domain of the building or dwellings.

Private   Semiprivate   Semipublic   Public

Fig. 3.30: Tall high-rise buildings, from one hundred to two hundred fifty dwelling units per acre.
— Private space exists only within the apartment units.
— The interior circulation areas and the grounds are public in nature.
— There is no association between buildings and street.

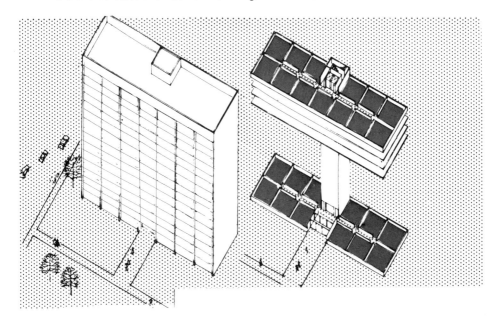

interior of the unit and its grounds, and because the grounds are in close juxtaposition with the public street, there is an extension of family influence to the street. Because of the family's unambiguous control of the unit and the close physical juxtaposition of unit and street, what transpires on the city street is affected by and affects adjacent homes. The individual row-house resident does not require the approval or acquiescence of his neighbor to either formulat expectations or to control activities on the public sidewalk immediately in front of his home. He can make that determination as independently and as directly as going out on his lawn and telling someone parked in front of his house to stop honking his horn or ask children playing in the street to stop knocking over the garbage cans. By contrast, families living in a high-rise development have apartment doors which only face onto corridors in the interior of the buildings. In many cases, even the entrances to the buildings will not face onto the streets, but onto the grounds of the project. Residents of high-rise.buildings perceive the neighboring public streets as something which, somewhere, borders their development and which is beyond their control. If the corridor on their floor is long and serves much more than ten families, it is likely that residents will also view the activities at the other end with similar detachment, suspicion, and impotence.

Summary

A family's claim to a territory diminishes proportionally as the number of families who share that claim increases. The larger the number of people who share a territory, the less is each individual's felt rights to it. Therefore, with only a few families sharing an area, whether it be the interior public circulation areas of a building or the grounds around it, it is relatively easy for an informal understanding to be reached among the families as to what constitutes acceptable usage. When the numbers increase, the opportunity for reaching such an implicit understanding diminishes to the point at which no usage other than walking through the area is really possible, while every use is permissible. The larger the number of people who share a communal space, the more difficult it is for people to identify it as being in any way theirs or to feel they have a right to control or determine the activity taking place within it. It is easier for outsiders to gain access to and linger in the interior public areas of a building shared by from twenty-four to one hundred twenty families than it is in a building shared by from six to twelve families.

If we examine the various building types we have been looking at from the viewpoint of residents' ability to exert control over areas in and around their dwellings, then the primary difference between a single-family building and a multifamily building is that in the single-family building all the interior spaces are the private domain of the occupant family, whereas in the multifamily building the interior circulation areas within the buildings are shared by many families and are public in nature (Figures 3.27 through 3.30 present the distribution of public and private areas in different building types measured according to dwelling units per acre [du/acre]). Similarly, the grounds surrounding a single-family unit are understood as being for the private use of the occupants of that dwelling unit, while the grounds surrounding a multifamily building are seen as space for the collective use of all the building's inhabitants. Control over the use of grounds surrounding a multifamily building must be maintained continually by the building's management. Because of the number of users and the access to and use of the interior, the common circulation areas of a multifamily building are open to all the members of the families occupying the building, their friends, and, of course, strangers. Control of access can be limited, but this requires the continual presence at the main entry door of an agent of management.

In a current study at our Institute, *Factors Affecting Crime and Instability in Federally-Assisted Housing,* we are learning that the size of buildings has a statistically significant, direct causal effect on: residents' use of public areas in their development (−.50); their social interaction with their neighbors (−.31); and their sense of control over the interior and exterior public areas of their development (−.29).[3] These results are from a study of forty-four moderate-income housing sites and twenty-nine public housing sites in three cities: Newark, St. Louis, and San Francisco. The results are from a path analysis, in which the influence of other factors, including socioeconomic characteristics, management effectiveness, quality of city police and security services, and form of ownership are taken into account. In the case of residents' use of public areas, the numbers in brackets mean that an increase of one unit in building size will cause a reduction of .50 of a unit in residents' use of public areas. This demonstrates that building form has a very strong predictive capacity on public area use, independent of the other factors which are most likely to predict it.

IV

Crime and Abandonment in Urban Residential Areas

Parallel with the growth and concentration of its population, our nation has been experiencing a rapid rise in its crime rate. The number of serious crimes rose from 4.5 million to 10 million between 1964 and 1974; even allowing for the nation's growth in population, the rate of serious crimes is 91 per cent higher today than a decade ago.[1]

Just as our nation's population has been concentrating in larger urban areas so has its crime. In 1960 cities of over 250,000 population experienced crime rates 50 per cent higher than cities with smaller populations. Even though crime rates increased in both small and large cities, by 1972 cities of over 250,000 population had crime rates 100 per cent higher than smaller cities (see Table 4.1).

Within cities, the distribution of the crime rate closely follows the distribution of income groups. In the maps of Minneapolis illustrated in Figures 4.1 and 4.2, the crime rate suffered by different precincts increases with the decrease in the income of the population. This pattern holds for all areas of the city except the central business district. The crime rate in the central business district is as high as it is in

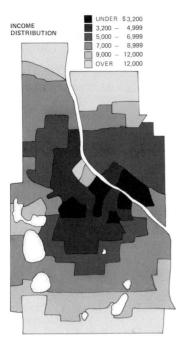

INCOME
DISTRIBUTION

UNDER $3,200
3,200 — 4,999
5,000 — 6,999
7,000 — 8,999
9,000 — 12,000
OVER 12,000

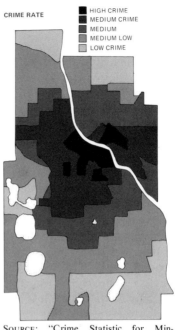

CRIME RATE

HIGH CRIME
MEDIUM CRIME
MEDIUM
MEDIUM LOW
LOW CRIME

SOURCE: "City of Minneapolis, 1972 Income Profiles," Minneapolis Planning and Development, Minneapolis, 1974.

SOURCE: "Crime Statistic for Minneapolis," Memorandum prepared by the Planning and Research Division of the Minneapolis Police Department, Minneapolis, 1974.

Fig. 4.1: Distribution of income groups in Minneapolis, 1972.

Fig. 4.2: Distribution of crime rates in Minneapolis, 1972.

Table 4.1: Comparative Rise in Reported Violent Crime Rates by Size of Community, 1960–72

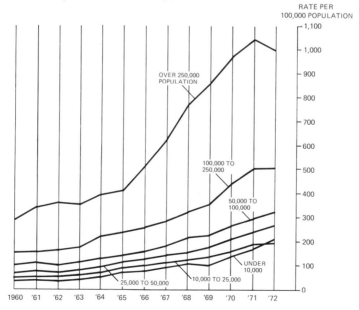

SOURCE: *Social Indicators, 1973: Selected Statistics on Social Conditions and Trends in the United States.* Office of Management and Budget, U. S. Government Printing Office, Washington, D.C. 1973, Chart 2/3, Ch. 2.

lowest-income areas elsewhere in the city, but most of the crime in this area is committed against commercial property and entertainment establishments.

Increasingly over the last ten years, crime throughout the nation has been shifting from commercial to residential areas. The *FBI Uniform Crime Reports, 1973*, showed that 61.9 per cent of all burglaries took place in residential areas.[2] The reports also showed that robberies committed in residential areas accounted for 29 per cent of all robberies taking place in buildings; this included banks, chain stores, commercial houses, and service stations (Table 4.2).

More disconcerting is the rate of increase of crimes taking place in residential areas as compared with crimes in nonresidential areas. FBI statistics show that residential robbery increased by 105 per cent between 1967 and 1972, while the over-all robbery rate increased by 85 per cent.[4] Similarly, during the same period, residential burglary increased by 73 per cent while over-all nonresidential burglary increased by only 46 per cent.

In the six years between 1967 and 1972 there was an increase of over 25 per cent of the population who said they were afraid to walk alone at night (Table 4.3). Not suprisingly, the most rapid increase occurred not in the largest or smallest communities, but in average-sized cities between 2,500 and 500,000 in population.

Initially, the fear of crime kept many people from the use of unsafe commercial and entertainment areas, but recently it has also kept them from the use of the public streets outside their homes and, in high-rise

Table 4.2: Residential Crime as a Percentage of Total Crime

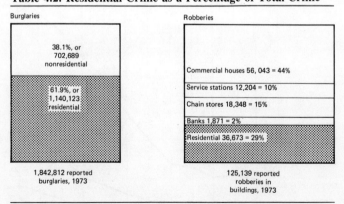

Burglaries

38.1%, or
702,689
nonresidential

61.9%, or
1,140,123
residential

1,842,812 reported
burglaries, 1973

Robberies

Commercial houses 56, 043 = 44%

Service stations 12,204 = 10%

Chain stores 18,348 = 15%

Banks 1,871 = 2%

Residential 36,673 = 29%

125,139 reported
robberies in
buildings, 1973

SOURCE: *FBI Uniform Crime Reports, 1973*. Totals represent reported crime from 4,343 agencies representling a population of 128,611,000.[3]

buildings, from the use of the interior circulation areas of their own building. There is no doubt that self-imposed restrictions can lower crime rates, but it is at the cost of our withdrawal from social and communal life, from the use of commercial and recreational areas, and from the attendance of cultural activities that require community-wide support for their continued survival.

In an effort to deal with the nation's crime problems, municipal police forces have been increased in size from 340,000 men in 1967 to 445,000 men in 1974, at an increase in cost from $3 billion to $8.6 billion.[5] But police manpower deployment and effectiveness studies conducted in Kansas City, revealed that the doubling of manpower for patrolling in residential areas had no measurable effect on the reduction of crime.[6]

In a recently completed study of residential crime in the Boston area, Thomas R. Repetto concluded the following:

> Although police are commonly thought of as the first line of defense against crime, their actual effectiveness against residential crimes seems extremely doubtful. Of approximately 2,000 police reports on burglaries analyzed for this study, less than one percent of the crimes were discovered in progress by patrolling police. An additional six percent were discovered while still in progress by citizens who summoned the police, and the remaining 93 percent of the crimes were not discovered until

Table 4.3: Increase in Persons Afraid to Walk Alone at Night, by Size of Community, 1965–72

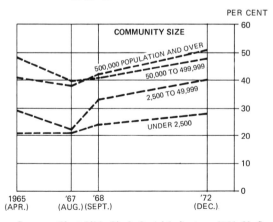

SOURCE: *Chart 2/21, Ch. 2, Social Indicators, 1973,* U. S. Government Printing Office, Washington, D.C. 1973.

sometime after they were committed. Only four percent of the cases surveyed resulted in arrests, of which approximately half took place at the scene of the crime, and the other half through detective follow-up investigation.[7]

An examination of the most recent crime reports indicate a decline in the crime rate after some ten years of rising crime. Before becoming too exultant, we must consider the possibility that the reduction in crime is not necessarily the consequence of improved law enforcement, but may be the result of the restrictions we ourselves have placed upon our own activities. Humans are immensely adaptable creatures; if people are afraid of being victimized, they will stop engaging in activities and in the use of areas they know to be dangerous.

The Crime Resistive Capacities of Middle-Income Communities

By the nature of their taxing powers, most municipalities rely heavily on their own revenue sources for the public services they provide — from schools to police protection. Federal and state grants-in-aid, although often distributed on a per capita basis, are not always provided where they are most needed. The lower the average income of a city's residents, the more needy that community is for funds to provide its residents with welfare services and police protection — but the less able it is to generate these funds from its own resources. As a consequence, municipalities composed only of middle- and upper-income residents have clear advantages in providing their residents with secure living environments: they have a strong tax base from which to finance municipal services and to hire police and are less likely to generate criminal activity from within their own boundaries. Middle-class youth have many more options open to them for recreation activity and for legally acceptable peer-group initiation. They also have their monetary needs satisfied by allowances from their parents or by acceptable forms of income-earning activity. Middle- and upper-income families also tend to have fewer children and normally have both a male and female head in each family. Residents of middle-income communities also have strongly expressed desires for the maintenance of safe, crime-free neighborhoods. They have a more universally shared set of expectations about what constitutes acceptable behavior in public streets and parks and are adamant about seeing to it that these rules are kept and, in their breach, demand, receive, and support police intervention.

By contrast, communities composed of a high percentage of low-income residents experience a compounding of problems and deficiencies which produce the opposite effect. Although a majority of residents in low-income communities may hold an attitude toward crime and criminals which is similar to that held by residents in middle-income communities, it is not one shared by all residents, particularly when their children come into conflict with city police. Among low-income populations, particularly those of racial minorities, there is some condoning of criminal activity: police are not commonly viewed by low-income residents as agents who are acting in their interests. There is not always support for police presence even when police have been called there by one of the local residents.

In the early 1960s municipalities which were unconcerned with what they read as a small decline in their middle-income populations were surprised to see how quickly the combination of increasing crime and a declining tax base mushroomed into a crisis which sent wave after wave of middle-income residents scurrying to the suburbs. Some municipalities experienced a turnover in their populations within five years that no urban renewal program could redress in twenty. The circumstances in St. Louis, Detroit, Newark, Cleveland, and Washington bear witness to the uniformity of the malaise and the inevitability of the results. Municipalities which were not able to maintain a majority of middle-income residents entered into a declining spiral in which their initial descent only served to accelerate their further fall. In such circumstances it was not uncommon for middle-income residents to become critical actors in a self-fulfilling prophecy: their fears as to what would happen to their property values if they did not leave their neighborhoods quickly were realized—partly as a result of their own attitudes and hurried departures.

In the 1960s and early 1970s one could actually see the change in population taking place on a month-by-month, block-by-block basis. Once the pattern of change was perceived, further increases in crime only served to confirm community suspicion, and the subsequent momentum of middle-class flight could no longer be stemmed. The replacement of a middle-income population with low-income residents living in subdivided houses further increased crime rates and the final pattern of community deterioration took effect. Middle-class flight serves to increase crime rate in urban areas in five ways: (1) it replaces a middle-income population with a lower-income population which is both more vulnerable to crime and has a youth with a greater proclivity toward engaging in criminal activities; (2) it leaves a lower-income population to live in subdivided houses with many families sharing a common entry to a building—a design which makes occupants more vulnerable; (3) it results in a higher density occupancy; (4) it lowers the urban tax base and the funds available for police services; and (5) it removes a population with a low tolerance for crime, a strong demand for police presence, and a support of police activities which deter crime.

Case Study: The Decline of the City of St. Louis

Although there are local conditions and pressures which have given
the pattern of abandonment in St. Louis its particular form, it is not too
different there from what is being experienced by many other cities,
like Newark, Detroit, Cleveland, and Washington and in boroughs of
larger cities like Chicago and New York. From the early 1950s, when
St. Louis attained a maximum population of 880,000, the region began
to experience population shifts and changes which drastically altered
the character of the central city.

Between 1960 and 1970 the metropolitan region of St. Louis
showed a net increase in population of 12 per cent, but this increase
was solely due to a 29 per cent increase in the population of the suburban areas. During this same period, the population of the city itself
declined by 17 per cent. These population shifts were the result of a
massive migration of whites from the city to the suburbs, while the city
itself began to become occupied by a high percentage of low-income
black families. Between 1960 and 1970 the black percentage of the
city's population rose from 29 per cent to 41 per cent; it increased only
from 6 per cent to 7 per cent in the rest of the metropolitan area. In
1959 the median income of city residents was 79 per cent of the median
income of the entire metropolitan area; by 1969 it had decreased to 68
per cent. The proportion of relatively high-income families declined
sharply: In 1959, 11 per cent of families in the city had incomes double
the city's median family income, but by 1969 only 4 per cent had such
incomes. The proportion of relatively low-income families rose in a
parallel fashion. In 1959, 16 per cent of families in the city had incomes
below half the city's median family income, but by 1969, 21 per cent
had such incomes.[8]

Demographic change did not occur uniformly over the entire city
but was concentrated in particular areas (Figures 4.3 and 4.4). The
northern half of the city, and in particular the northern half of the central east-west corridor, became populated almost exclusively by black
families, while the southern half remained predominantly white. The
black-populated half of the city was characterized by lower-income
families, greater levels of multifamily, unsound, and dilapidated housing, lower levels of owner-occupied housing, higher vacancy rates, and
higher numbers of tax-delinquent properties.[9]

The poor black families who came to St. Louis during the migra-
tions from the South following World War II inherited the dilapidated
housing of areas in and around the central business district. The massive urban renewal clearance of the downtown areas in the mid-1950s
displaced the black population and forced them to relocate to other

parts of the city. The large, high-rise public housing projects, like Pruitt-Igoe, which were built to house these families became crime-ridden and difficult to manage, and the population from the projects began to move into adjacent residential areas composed of single-family housing which had been subdivided. Real estate speculators took advantage of the situation by preying on the fears of white homeowners and the ignorance of black home buyers and renters. They used "blockbusting," panic-sales techniques, and the general deflation of property values to change neighborhoods to their advantage.

As the process continued, a growing number of black families who had purchased homes under contract with the speculators found them-

Figs. 4.3 and 4.4: These detail the racial component of the demographic change that has occurred in St. Louis between 1960 and 1970. Those census tracts that exhibit the greatest decline of white population during this period closely correlate to the census tracts having the highest vacancy rates.

PER CENT CHANGE IN WHITE POPULATION,
1960 - 70
(St. Louis Census Tracts)

Increase or no change
0 - 9.99% decrease
10 - 49.99% decrease
50 - 100.00% decrease

PER CENT BLACK POPULATION, 1970.
(St. Louis Census Tracts)

0 - 9.99%
10 - 39.99%
40 - 69.99%
70 - 100.00%

ꞮURCE: U. S. Bureau of the Census, *Census of Population*
d Housing: 1960 & 1970, Census Tracts, St. Louis, Mo. -
. Standard metropolitan statistical area.

SOURCE: U. S. Bureau of the Census, *Census of Population and Housing: 1970,* Census Tracts, St. Louis, Mo. -Ill. Standard metropolitan statistical area.

Fig. 4.5: A single remaining abandoned house, standing on what was recently a stable residential street in St. Louis.

selves unable to meet the taxes, the inflated debt structure, and the maintenance costs of homeownership. By the nature of their contract, the houses then fell back into the receivership of unscrupulous realtors. In time, the houses were broken up into multifamily apartment buildings. Although the rent per apartment was comparatively low, the total rent received for an entire house was large. With a minimum of maintenance, the realtor was able to recoup the investment of his original purchase several times over within a ten year period.

As this speculative process continued into the late 1960s and early 1970s, large numbers of white families left the city completely for the new suburban housing created by other federal housing programs. The result was a large increase in vacancies in the central city. Between 1960 and 1970 the vacancy rate in the city rose from 5.4 per cent to 12.3 per cent. The consumer price index in St. Louis rose 31 per cent between 1960 and 1970, while the rent index increased by only 10 per cent. With supply exceeding demand, the landlords of moderate-income housing were unable to match rents with rising taxes and maintenance costs. Those landlords who had initially made large profits from the conversion of single-family houses to multifamily units now found themselves caught in a financial bind. Increased maintenance costs, higher real estate taxes, and less rental income threatened their investments, and so they began to neglect their properties. As conditions became intolerable, tenant turnovers increased and apartments were subdivided into rooms for transients, to be rented by the day and week. After a year or two, the owners abandoned their properties completely, and the structures, left to vandals and arsonists, quickly became hazards to the safety, health, and stability of the surrounding area.

In response, the city of St. Louis developed a policy of demolishing vacated buildings. A drive through some neighborhoods of the city today reveals block after block of cleared property, with only one or two houses left standing like remnants of rotten teeth in a decayed mouth (Figure 4.5). No more than five years ago, houses on these streets were occupied by single families and sold for over $25,000.

During the period when the nation's crime was increasing by 144 per cent, crime in St. Louis was increasing by 240 per cent.[10] In an analysis by the St. Louis City Plan Commission, the 1970 index crime rate of St. Louis was compared to an average rate for twenty other cities. The total crime index for St. Louis exceeded the average for the twenty cities by nearly 35 per cent. In every category of comparison but one, the St. Louis crime rate exceeded that of other cities (Table 4.4).

Even when compared to its own metropolitan area, the city fared poorly. While the city was experiencing a crime rate of 74 per 1,000 population, its surrounding metropolitan area was experiencing a rate 71 per cent lower: 27 per 1,000 population.[11]

Table 4.4: Index Crime Rate per 1,000 Population, (1970)
Average for Twenty Cities[a] Compared to St. Louis

	Average 20 cities	*St. Louis*	*Per cent difference*
Total index crime rate	55.30	74.05	+34
Crimes against persons	9.50	15.07	+59
Murder	.25	.43	+72
Rape	.49	.88	+80
Robbery	5.34	8.54	+60
Aggravated assault	3.48	5.20	+49
Crime against property	45.82	58.82	+28
Burglary	19.81	30.66	+55
Larceny over $50	13.63	7.31	−46
Auto theft	12.37	21.01	+70

SOURCE: St. Louis City Plan Commission, *St. Louis Redevelopment Program,* (St. Louis, Mo., June, 1973), p. 52.
[a]500,000 to 1,000,000 population

Fig. 4.6: The 2,740-unit Pruitt-Igoe public housing project in St. Louis in the process of being torn down.

One effect of these changes was that young middle-income families in the region no longer considered the option of purchasing a house within the city limits of St. Louis; they preferred the safer investment in the suburbs. The decline in newly formed households was further reinforced by the "redlining" practices of many of the banks, according to a RAND survey. "Redlining" is the term used to describe the decision of the mortgage division of a bank to declare a particular neighborhood as no longer safe for investment and to refuse to make mortgage money available for the purchase of homes within it. By adopting a collective redlining policy, banks further served the self-fulfilling prophecy of neighborhood decline. Where a bank's evaluation of the soundness of a community may be cautious, once a collective decision is made by a group of banks to redline a community, that decision itself can become the critical factor in determining the community's future. When residents of redlined communities endeavor to sell their homes, they find that prospective buyers cannot get mortgage money. The market value of their homes thus declines rapidly and residents become very vulnerable to the wheelings and dealings of blockbusters.

The change in the characteristics of the city's population, the decision by banks located within the city to invest in property and opportunities outside the city limits, and the inability of the city of St. Louis to attract new, young, middle-income families combined to reduce the attractiveness of the city for businesses, new and old. In the past twenty years St. Louis has seen the dramatic exodus of its existing commercial establishments. The loss of businesses and retail sales as well as personal incomes produced a significant shrinkage in the city's tax base. With diminished taxes the city found itself increasingly unable to keep up those services and amenities — schools, parks, police, fire protection, street cleaning — that would continue to make it attractive to the remaining residents and businesses. Once the city had entered into a spiral of decline, the pace quickened. Erosion in one area contributed to erosion in another. Where, at the beginning of the spiral of decline, it might have been possible for the city government and its financial institutions to embark upon a course of action that would have stabilized certain areas and arrested the blight, once the pace and extent of the decline increased, the amount of investment required to stem the change was too great for the resources available. All that anyone could do was sit back and watch.

Crime and Abandonment in
Public and Moderate-Income Housing

The pattern of crime and abandonment in the nation's public and moderate-income housing follows a somewhat similar pattern to that experienced by residential communities composed of single-family houses. While the original occupants of public housing included only a small percentage of one-parent welfare families, over the years the percentage of these families increased so that they now form the majority. The deleterious effect of the high percentage of one-parent welfare families is aggravated by the large size of many public housing developments and aggravated still further by the fact that many of these developments are constructed of buildings with a large number of families sharing a common entry. Many of these large public housing projects have vacancy rates of 25 per cent and more: Cabrini Green in Chicago, Columbus Homes and Stella Wright in Newark, the Plaza in San Francisco, Raymond Rosen and Schuylkill Falls in Philadelphia, Columbus Point in Boston, and Kerr Village in Oklahoma City are just a few of the projects which have experienced high vacancy rates in recent years. The 2,740-unit Pruitt-Igoe project, built in St. Louis in 1957, became a symbol of the malaise. By 1974 it was completely abandoned and was torn down in 1976 (Figure 4.6).

Although nothing equivalent to the failure of our nation's large public housing projects can be found in moderate-income housing developments, the problems they face are equally serious. In a 1975 survey of developments by the office of the Assistant Secretary of HUD for Housing Management, it was found that two hundred fifty developments throughout the country faced foreclosure in the next two years. Although many of their problems stem from underfinancing and mismanagement, much of their high vacancy rates can be initially attributed to high crime and vandalism rates. Foreclosure of these projects will mean that the federal government will come into receivership of over $500 million in abandoned housing.

Once the process of deterioration and abandonment has gotten underway, it is almost impossible to reverse. New moderate-income families cannot be enticed to move into these developments to fill the vacancies and the higher-income families already in residence wait only for an opportunity to move out. Vacant units are vandalized to a point where they cannot be rehabilitated easily, and criminals, vagrants, and drug addicts use these vacant units as bases of operation.

In cities like Seattle, Newark, and San Francisco, where moderate-income developments suffering high crime and vacancy rates are located adjacent to public housing, the managements of the moderate-income housing blame many of their problems and failures on this proximity. Adjacent residential communities composed of privately owned, single-family houses suffer similar problems.

An understanding of the factors which contribute to the creation of high crime rates in low- and moderate-income housing developments is helpful not only for devising remedies to solve their problems, but also for developing strategies for stabilizing neighboring communities composed of single-family housing.

Table 4.5 represents the results of an analysis of the influence of different social and physical factors on the crime rates in low- and moderate-income projects operated by the New York City Housing Authority. This analytical technique, called "stepwise regression analysis," is employed when many different factors interact to produce a particular effect (e.g., a rise in crime rates). The technique isolates those factors which contribute to the effect most strongly and independently of other factors. In Table 4.5 the percentage of population receiving welfare is shown to be the most important factor, followed by building height (or the number of families sharing the entry to a building).

Those social variables which correlated most highly with different types of crime are also very highly correlated with each other. They include the percentage of resident population receiving welfare (excluding the elderly), the percentage of one-parent families receiving welfare through AFDC (AFDC families are normally one parent households), and the per capita disposable income of the project's residents.

Interviews with residents, management, and police suggested the following explanation for the correlations of these social factors and crime rates: that a one-parent household headed by a female is more vulnerable to criminal attack; that families with only one adult present are less able to control their teen-age children; that young teen-age AFDC mothers are often victimized by their boy friends; that the criminal activity of the poor is tolerated, if not condoned, among the poor; that the poor, and particularly the poor of racial minorities, are unable to demand much in the way of police protection; and that the commission of crime against residents in ghetto areas requires minimal skill and risk.

The physical factors which correlate most strongly with crime rates are, in order of importance: the height of the buildings which, in turn,

Table 4.5: Crime Rates as Explained by Social and Physical Variables

	Correlations with dependent variables			
Social and physical variables	*Indoor felony rate*	*Indoor robbery rate*	*Robbery rate*	*Felony rate*
Percentage of population receiving welfare	(1)[a].51	(1) .46	(1) .47	(1) .54
Building height (number of units per entry)	(2) .36	(2) .36	(2) .36	(5) .22
Project size (number of apartments)	(3) .27	(3) .26	(3) .25	(3) .22
Percentage of families with female head on AFDC	(4) .44	(4) .41	(5) .36	
Number of publicly assisted projects in area	(5) .25	(5) .26	(4) .33	
Felony rate of surrounding community				(2) .41
Per capita disposable income				(4) .49
Multiplier	.68	.66	.66	.67

SOURCE: N.Y.C. Housing Authority police data for 1967: 87 housing projects. .01 level of significance at ± .27, .05 level of significance at ± .21.[12]
[a] Numbers of brackets indicate rank order of correlation in creating stepwise multiple regressions.

correlates highly with the number of apartments sharing the entry to a building; the size of the housing project "or the total number of dwelling units in the project"; and the number of other publicly assisted housing projects in the area.

The above analysis suggests that there are two classes of *physical* factors that contribute to crime rates: those such as "project size" and the "number of publicly assisted projects in the area" which reinforce social weakness and pathology; and those such as "building height" and "number of units per entry" which facilitate the control of the environment by its inhabitants. The first class of physical factors may also be considered as another class of social variable: for instance, if certain social characteristics such as the percentage of AFDC families correlate highly with crime rate, then we can anticipate that a large number of such families gathered together in one area may aggravate the crime problems still further and increase the crime rate per capita. The significance of this is not simply that the presence of more potential criminals creates proportionally more crime, but also that a concentration of potential criminals actually increases the rate of crime. Thus large low-income projects or low-income projects surrounded by other low-income projects suffer a higher crime rate than small or isolated projects even when the percentage of AFDC families remains the same in all projects.

A frequent complaint of residents of communities surrounding large public housing projects is that the teen-age criminals living in the projects make use of the large, anonymous environment of the housing project as a place to run back to and hide in. For example, there is a particularly notorious project in Jersey City which is located adjacent to U. S. Highway 1 entering New York City. A traffic light at an intersection which borders the project forces truckers to stop there on their way into New York. Teen-age project residents have developed a pattern of hijacking trucks at the stoplight, throwing the driver out, and then driving the truck into the project. The truck is then emptied in a matter of minutes and the loot hidden in vacant apartments.

The relationship between the socioeconomic characteristics of residents and a project's crime rate had long been suspected. The most fascinating new information to come out of our analysis, therefore, was that of the influence of building height and number of units per entry in predicting crime rate. Regardless of the social characteristics of inhabitants, the physical form of housing was shown to play an important role in reducing crime and in assisting residents in controlling behavior in their housing environments. The smaller the number of families sharing a residential environment (whether a portion of a project's grounds or the access and circulation areas within a multifamily building), the stronger will be each family's feelings of possession and, ultimately, of responsibility and control. This explains why in a three-story walk-up building occupied by only six families, the two families sharing a landing will maintain the hallway outside their apartment doors. It also explains why play equipment located in a defined area designated for the use of a small number of families is both more frequently used and better maintained.

In addition to the fact that buildings with a larger number of families sharing an entry experience higher crime rates than those with few families per entry, they are also vulnerable to additional types of criminal activity. Most of the crime experienced by residents of single-family buildings is burglary, committed when members of the family are either away from home or asleep. By contrast, the residents of large, multifamily dwellings experience both burglaries and robberies (muggings). The higher crime rate experienced by residents in large multifamily dwellings is mostly attributable to the occurrence of robberies (Table 4.6) in the interior common-circulation areas of multifamily buildings: lobbies, hallways, stairs, and elevators. These are also the areas where criminals wait to approach their victims and force them into apartments for the purpose of robbing them.

Of a total of 8,611 felonies reported in all New York City Housing Authority projects in 1969 (excluding intrahousehold incidents), 3,786, or 44 per cent, were committed in the interior public areas of buildings.

Table 4.6: The Location of Housing Crime
in Relation to Building Height
(Reported Felonies per 1,000 Families)

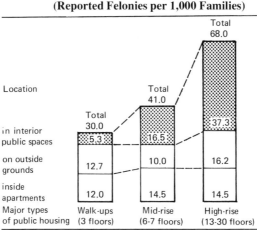

SOURCE: N.Y.C. Housing Authority data 1967; N = 87.[13]

Of the crimes committed in interior public areas, 3,165, or 84 per cent, were robberies. The breakdown by location of the felonies taking place in interior public areas was: elevators, 41 per cent; hallways, 22 per cent; lobbies, 18 per cent; stairways, 9 per cent; roof landings, 2 per cent; and other, 8 per cent.

Interaction of Social and Physical Factors

Although the socioeconomic characteristics of the resident population exert stronger influences on crime rate, the physical characteristics of the buildings and project can counteract the social. The physical form of residential environments can ameliorate the effect of many of the problems created by the concentration of low-income one-parent families with teen-age children.

The more complex and anonymous the housing environment, the more difficult it is for a code of behavior following societal norms to become established among residents. It is even difficult for moderate-income families with two adult heads of households to cope with crime and vandalism problems in poorly designed environments, but when poor and broken families are grouped together in such a setting, the results are nothing short of disastrous. The public housing projects now experiencing the highest vacancy rates are those which consist of the worst mixture of social and physical attributes.

Table 4.7 compares the vulnerability to crime of low-income one-parent families in different building types with the experience of moderate-income two-parent families living in the same building types. It shows that low-income one-parent families are more vulnerable to

Table 4.7: Variations in Crime Rate as Affected
by Different Combinations of Socio-
econmic Groups and Building Types

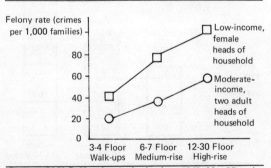

SOURCE: N.Y.C. Housing Authority data, 1969; N = 87 projects, significance at .01 level.

poor building design than moderate-income two-parent families. Although two-parent moderate-income families suffer higher crime rates in high-rise buildings than they do in walk-ups, the crime rate does not increase as dramatically with building height as it does for low-income families. Moderate-income two-parent families living in twelve- to thirty-story buildings experience a lower crime rate than low-income one-parent families living in six- and seven-story buildings.

Further results of our Institute's path analysis in *Factors Affecting Crime and Instability* in moderate-income communities (referred to earlier at the conclusion of Chapter III) show that building size has important causal effects on fear of crime (.38) and on community instability (.39), independent of socioeconomic, managerial, ownership, police, and guard service factors. Community instability is measured by apartment turnover and vacancy rates and by residents' desire to move. However, as in the New York City Public Housing study mentioned earlier in this chapter, the findings from our current study of moderate-income developments show that the socioeconomic characteristics of residents also have strong causal effects on fear, instability, and crime. Independent of other factors, the socioeconomic characteristics of residents have a total causal effect on fear of crime of .59; on community instability of .51; and on crimes against persons of .32. These findings can be interpreted as follows: a unit increase in the per cent of AFDC families living in a development will produce .59 of a unit increase in fear of crime and so on.

The data from the above analysis can be summarized in still another way by looking at the results of the regression analysis. The R^2 is a sign used to represent the percent of variance in one factor that is predicted by all other factors acting together. The effects of building size, socioeconomic characteristics of residents, management performance, form of ownership, and police and guard service together produce: an $R^2 = .69$ for fear (p < .001); an $R^2 = .67$ for community instability (p < .001); and an $R^2 = .39$ for crimes against persons (p < .05). Another way of stating these findings is that the combination of these factors predict 69 per cent of the variation in fear, for instance. But more important still, of all the factors in the predictive model, it is the socioeconomic characteristics of residents and building size which together predict *most* of the variation in fear, instability, and crime.

The Effects of Building Type on the Mix of Low- and Middle-Income Families

If a housing agency desires to mix low-income one-parent families in a stable mix with middle-income two-parent families, the percentage of one-parent families that can be included will be influenced by the building type employed. From the findings referred to above one would postulate that the lower the building height the larger the percentage of low-income families one could integrate into a middle-income milieu without causing crime problems and middle-income flight. One low-income one-parent family is normally easily accommodated in a middle-income walk-up building designed with only six families sharing an entry. With this degree of mix, it is comparatively easy for the five middle-income two-parent families to set the standards of acceptable behavior in the public areas of the building and the grounds around it and to exert social pressures to see that these standards are kept. By comparison, in a high-rise building designed with seventy-two families sharing an entry, the presence of twelve low-income one-parent families — the same percentage as that in the walk-up discussed above — is more than enough to produce high crime and vandalism rates and prompt the exodus of the middle-income two-parent families. The immediate effect of the departure of the middle-income families will be a high vacancy rate, which most building owners will resolve by filling the vacant apartments with additional welfare residents. With such policies, a previously stable, middle-income building or development can become fully occupied by welfare residents in as little as two to three years. With the building's life expectancy reduced, the owner will then become resigned to a quick write-off of his building and will provide it with minimal maintenance.

**Table 4.8: Percentage of AFDC Families in Stable Mix,
as Affected by the Number of Units Sharing
a Common Entry and the Size of the Project.**[a]

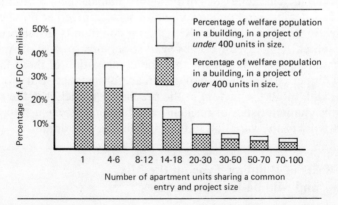

[a] Hypothetical representation based on the experience of housing managers of moderate-income housing containing a percentage of AFDC families.

Table 4.8 is a hypothetical representation of the contravening effect of two physical factors on the percentage of low-income one-parent families that can be housed in a stable mix with two-parent moderate-income residents. It shows that the percentage of AFDC families that can be housed in a stable mix with two-parent working families increases as the number of units sharing an entry decreases. The positive, ameliorating effect of units per entry is in turn diminished by the effects of the size of the development housing AFDC families. For example, in a housing development of fewer than four hundred units, 25 per cent of the families in buildings with ten families sharing an entry can be AFDC families. If the same buildings were used in a housing development greater than four hundred units in size, the percentage of AFDC families that could be housed in these buildings decreases to 20 per cent.

Other Factors Affecting Crime and Stability in Housing Developments

There are other factors which also influence both the stability of a housing development and the crime rates suffered by residents: the degree of shared values and life-styles among contiguous residents; the suitability of the environment type to resident type; the policies of management; and the quality of municipal services.

The upper limit on the number of families who can be grouped into a shared environment while maintaining stability is determined in part by the degree to which these families share a common life-style and values directed at maintaining property and controlling crime. If residents feel that they live among neighbors who do not share their concern for the maintenance of the interior communal areas of a building and its grounds or do not share a common desire to protect the housing development from criminal intrusion or vandalism, then the defensibility of the collective environment will be undermined.

The emergence of proprietary attitudes and control measures among residents requires that an environment be perceived by its residents as a desirable place to live. If residents feel that the reputation of their home environment has declined or that there is a new stigma associated with living there, they will withdraw their commitments and search for opportunities to leave. They will also stop exhibiting territorial involvement either in the control or maintenance of the environments outside their homes.

Such stigma and corresponding withdrawal may arise from either a social or physical change in their environment. Examples of physical change include a reduction in the quality of maintenance; deterioration of communal amenities; or boarded-up apartment units indicating vacancies and vandalism. Examples of social change include the influx of new residents pursuing a different life-style or from a different age group (for example, the influx of families with children into a pre-viously all-elderly building); the influx of a large number of low-income residents into a middle-income development which will reduce social interaction between neighbors and reduce the desire to control and maintain the nonprivate areas of the communal environment; an influx of a large number of new residents of a different racial origin or ethnic background (for example, an influx of black families, even of a similar income group, life-style, and sharing the same values, may still result in alienation and withdrawal).

Management Policies and Municipal Services

Just as conflict in values and life-styles among residents can influ-ence the desirability and stability of a community, so can the attitudes and performance of the housing agencies whose function it is to preserve the stability of the residential development. It is important that residents feel that management has a long-term commitment to their community, and that the maintenance staff and police are respon-sive to their calls for assistance. This is particularly important in the case of buildings that are shared by a large number of families. If the adult residents of a building do not occupy their homes more than fifty per cent of the time (in the case of working adults) or there is a conflict in values among residents, then control of the common areas within or outside the building will have to be maintained by a management agent acting in the interest of the residents. Such an agent will control access to common areas and type of activities permitted.

If management has a clearly stated set of rules regarding tenant in-volvement in maintenance and security and if management enforces these rules and penalizes residents for infractions, then residents are more likely to feel their environment is stable.[14] Similarly, manage-ment's policy and effectiveness in evicting residents who have been identified as vandals and criminals will improve the remaining resi-dents' sense of security and stability. A management policy of screen-ing new residents can also affect the stability of a development in three ways: first, by the influx of serious problem families; second, by main-taining an agreed to mix of economic and racial groups; and finally, by giving residents a sense of management's long-term commitment to its investment and their home environments.

The quality of building maintenance also contributes to stability and to a reduction of vandalism by giving residents a sense that their development is being cared for. The better the quality of maintenance, the more residents are themselves likely to engage in cleaning and maintenance activities. Quality of maintenance in this case refers to frequent garbage collection, sweeping, removal of graffiti, quick re-placement of broken windows and lights, lawn care, and respon-siveness to the requests and complaints of residents. Similarly, where security personnel and police are responsive to and share residents' concern for crime prevention and protection, residents will feel more confident about involving themselves in security problems and in as-serting their rights and control of public areas.

V

Housing Form and Housing Politics

In previous chapters I discussed how the sociophysical forms of housing environments affect people's life-style options and behavior. In this chapter I will explore how housing form influences the managerial and political climate of housing developments: the requirements of management; the comparative success of different forms of tenure; political interaction and dependency among neighbors; residents' perception of and influence over activities in the nonprivate areas of their developments, and, finally, how housing developments are viewed politically by the public and by various governmental bodies.

The forms of subsidized housing, their urban location, and the residents they serve are not accidental occurrences. Housing serves many political as well as social purposes, and the interest groups being served are not always the people who will be moving in or those whose housing needs are being talked about. In addition to providing some people with a place to live, housing provides jobs for construction workers, housing administrators, maintenance men, and social workers. It also provides business opportunities for city planners, architects, engineers, developers, realtors, and mortgage bankers. But new housing may also be used as a mechanism for changing the racial and economic character of an existing neighborhood or, conversely, as a means of preventing it from changing. Thus, much public housing was constructed to keep low-income and black populations from moving into neighborhoods whose rents they were beginning to be able to afford.

The Political Structure Inherent in High-Rise Buildings

The management problems inherent in high-rises, as contrasted with row houses and walk-ups, stem from the fact that high-rises are structurally and operationally complex. For their survival, they depend on the continued maintenance of a series of interconnected public service systems. The public grounds, stairs, lobbies, elevators, garbage chutes, and laundry rooms must all be maintained by management and policed by a security force. High-rise developments thus require a continuing investment by the owners in an organization which will see to their management: this can be either an owner-hired administrative unit or an association of residents. This management group must be continually present to address the problems of the development, many of which are in fact a by-product of the building form and the ensuing social environment created. As long as the funds for staff and maintenance continue to be provided, all will go well. But if wages skyrocket and residents resist rent hikes or if government subsidies become niggardly, then the continued maintenance and security on which these developments depend will diminish sufficiently to make the project unlivable or even dangerous. Broken elevators will not be repaired, rotting garbage will pile up in garbage rooms and chutes, washer-driers will remain broken, grass will turn into compacted earth, broken play equipment will not be replaced, and residents will be afraid to go out at night.

By contrast, row-house environments can, for the most part, be maintained by the residents themselves when maintenance money runs low. Walk-up buildings, which in our hierarchy are closer in nature to row houses than they are to high rises, are most often designed with interior, communal access stairs which can be maintained by residents.

High-rise buildings, while inadequate and unworkable for some groups of people, are highly desirable for others. There are people who pursue life-styles in which the use and control of the public areas adjacent to their apartments is not desired and is gladly relegated to someone else: working couples and singles, for example, pursue a life

style which keeps them away from their home environments much of
the time. They do not desire to be burdened with maintaining anything
beyond their own apartment—if that. Management's burden in a
high-rise occupied by working adults is amazingly light because the
maintenance and control of buildings and grounds for a largely absen-
tee clientele is minimal. In addition to producing a desirable living environment for working singles and couples, high-rise buildings work well
when occupied by an *exclusively* elderly population because residents
are careful to keep the interior public areas clean and orderly and to
control access to their building.

Luxury high-rise developments have been known to be able to accommodate some families with children and work reasonably well, but
only when there are superintendents and porters in residence in the
building and a platoon of doormen and elevator operators who together
control and maintain the interior public areas and grounds of the building. Management rules and regulations in such buildings are strict and
sometimes even govern the type of dress required of residents when
going down to the lobby to pick up their mail. As a rule, no loitering,
gathering of residents, or children's play is permitted anywhere in the
building or on its grounds. As long as there is no need among residents
for communal or outdoor recreation areas, this form of housing will be
satisfactory. But this is not a design solution which is easily transfer-
able to housing exclusively for families with children, particularly for
moderate- and low-income populations. Children's daily activities usually involve some very active play. For low- and moderate-income
populations these activities center heavily around their homes. The
wear and tear on the building and the control of access to the interior
public areas become heavy burdens on management. A high-rise building occupied by a mix of families with children, elderly, and working
couples can produce even more severe problems than one occupied
exclusively by families with children. During the day, children will be
running around inside and out and the elderly will suffer accordingly; at
night, with the children and the elderly asleep, the younger couples will
be staying up later and "carrying on" to all hours. In such mixes,
agreement on the nature of use of the interior public areas, the outside
grounds, and the interior of apartments will be difficult to achieve. Bit-
ter antagonisms will develop between neighbors even on how children
and young adults should be allowed to play within their own apartments. By contrast, a group of row houses along a street may house
families with children, working couples, and elderly, each pursuing
their own separate life-style without ensuing antagonisms. While each
family in a row house can go from its dwelling and individual grounds
to the street without interfering with its neighbor's ability to do the

same, in a high-rise development, people are closely grouped together and share a common access system to the outside world, and the pursuit of one's own individuality can seriously affect one's neighbors.

There are high-rise developments in the larger cities of the Soviet Union that are occupied by low- and moderate-income families with children that are said to work well. But they have their own equivalent of the superintendents and porters of luxury high-rises in America — the ubiquitous, old kerchiefed women who guard every square foot of public space — within the building and on the grounds outside. All one is permitted to do under their critical gaze is to move quickly through the building and its grounds to get to and from one's apartment. Let a casual visitor or resident drop a candy wrapper on the floor and our kerchiefed "baba" will pounce upon him and demand that it be immediately retrieved. In the Soviet Union, the state owns the housing and controls and maintains the public areas around the individual apartments; the individual resident has the tenure of a temporary occupant. Any infraction of the rules can mean the loss of an apartment which most residents have waited for a long time.

In Japan one finds another institutional form of high-rise, or mul-

Fig. 5.1: The Togo-cho Apartments, in Tokyo, built for the families of postmen by the Ministry of Postal Services. The grounds and interior public circulation areas are meticulously maintained by residents and management. It is common for Japanese to remain with a firm of life — housing and job often go together.

tifamily development for low- and moderate-income families with children (Figure 5.1) which also appears to be working well and that is without any of the problems which nomally attend high-rise housing in America. Large corporations in Japan commonly build developments to house their own workers. It is an institutional form that was prevalent in Western Europe and this country up to the time of World War II, before the state itself became a heavy investor in subsidized housing. In Japanese corporation-owned housing, one's neighbors are one's fellow workers. The hierarchy of dwelling types and floors parallels the hierarchy within the company, in carefully articulated levles. Of course, the loss of a job means the loss of a home. In such high-rise environments, there are few problems in maintaining and controlling residents' behavior; the nonprivate areas outside the apartment unit are company property — any transgression against it is equivalent to an act of vandalism within the company's factories or offices.

There is still another example of a type of social structure which will allow a high-rise developments to work well when occupied by moderate-income families with children. In 1973 an American black political group called "the Temple of Kawaida/Revolutionary Politics," led by LeRoi Jones (now Imamu Amiri Baraka), purchased a piece of property in Newark, New Jersey, in a moderate-income Italian community with the intention of building a high-rise tower to be occupied by members of the organization and their families. The decision to build a high-rise was dictated primarily by the group's desire to provide as many apartments as possible on the piece of land they had acquired — a motive common to most housing developers and nonprofit groups. When the building proposal was submitted for approval to the city of Newark, it was attacked by opponents of the project from the Italian community, led by State Senator Anthony J. Imperiale. Their basic argument was that, when occupied by families with children, high-rise buildings produce severe security and maintenance problems. Because of our Institute's (the Institute for Community Design Analysis) past studies, we received a request from the Italian community to provide expert witness that this would be the case at Kawaida Towers as well. We refused because we thought it highly unlikely that the future residents would experience much in the way of residential crime either generated from within the building or from outside it. The Kawaida Towers occupants would not be typical of the occupants of most market-building housing; they would not be a cross section of the local population. All the tenants of *this* building would be members of the Temple of Kawaida and the membership is a disciplined group. Once they had occupied the building, the residents would likely formulate a specific set of rules of accepted behavior in the interior public areas and the surrounding grounds. This could be done easily because they are already organized, accustomed to meeting regularly together, and have an established organizational hierarchy. A resident or individual who disobeyed the house rules would likely be severely reprimanded and, if the breach in behavior continued, would likely be ejected from both building and organization. Like the workers living in company housing in Japan, a change in group allegiance would require a change of residence.

The Kawaida project was approved by the city of Newark and the New Jersey Housing Finance Agency and construction of the foundation began. But the Italian community was adamant and construction was stopped under court order. After years of litigation, the court ruled that the project could be built if the composition of the residents was altered: it ruled out occupancy by families with children and approved occupancy by elderly, singles, and couples without children. This ruling was clearly unacceptable to the Kawaida group and so construction ceased. The empty lot and foundations remain as a testament to the political nature of housing.

In each of the high-rise developments discussed above, it is necessary for a strong institutional or political structure to be created which will allow the buildings to continue to function as housing. This then begs the question: Are there bureaucracies, associations, or political groups who stand to benefit from the creation of home environments which make residents dependent on the need of a pervasive authority for their continued operation? It may be of benefit to the Soviet government, to the boards of directors of Japanese corporations, to the leadership of the Kawaida group that the occupants of their buildings be dependent upon the leaders of these institutions for the control and maintenance of their buildings. The question must be asked whether it is also of any benefit to the chairmen, maintenance staff, and security forces of public housing authorities in America, England, Holland, Sweden, and France to create housing environments that make residents dependent upon the continued presence of the administrative bureaucracy to function.

In determining the nature of a resident body, a developer, housing agency, or co-operative can choose to bring either similar or dissimilar people together to share a housing environment. These varied groupings can then be provided with housing whose forms make it either easy or difficult for residents to develop a community of interest with their neighbors.

Residents can be provided with housing types which require only minimal interaction or agreement among neighbors to remain viable, or, conversely, residents may find themselves in a housing environment which requires continuous involvement with their neighbors to keep the housing functioning. If, in the latter case, the resident body cannot reach accord or if the residents do not have the time or inclination to devote themselves to the affairs of the building, the environment will either change or go under.

For grouping purposes, people can be classified in many ways: by age, life-style, income, race, ethnicity, religious persuasion, political allegiance, or place of employment. The questions remain: Should planners strive to group similar or dissimilar people together and what aspects of their similarity should be used in grouping them? Those building types which depend on resident interaction and accord for their continued survival will fare better if the residents that are assigned to them share similar needs and points of view. It will also help if these residents are, by nature, gregarious. On the other hand, those environments which do not require resident interaction for their continued survival can take a more varied mix of resident types without producing discord or instability.

When people are grouped together by similarity of race, ethnicity, age, or income, they become an identifiable body. This may work either to their advantage or disadvantage. If they are poor and black, being grouped together may be a decided disadvantage. On the other hand, if the residents who are grouped together are politically ambitious and can organize themselves to vote as a bloc, the common identifying characteristics can be beneficial. Unfortunately, low-income populations do not have a history of political activism. If people of similar traits are grouped together, the common characteristic that is chosen for grouping them should be the one which not only provides the most convivial community but the one which will produce the most political clout—if that is what is desired by those who influence the nature of the grouping. Another question follows: Who is to decide on which people are grouped together and to what purpose? Even where it is agreed that it is beneficial to group similar people together, the process can involve a complex juggling of options. For instance, one may choose to group only elderly families together in one high-rise building so as to reduce intergenerational conflict and to more easily provide communal facilities to address their particular needs, but one still has the option of either grouping residents uniformly by income and/or race or to provide a mix of one or the other, or both. A mixture of one third low-income rent-supplement elderly with two thirds middle-income residents will prevent the low-income elderly from being stigmatized as residents of low-income housing—as they would be if they lived in an all low-income public housing project. The mix of racial groups, if not equally balanced, may serve to make the minority group members feel that they are politically handicapped. On the other hand a fifty-fifty mix of racial groups may prompt the exodus of that group of residents that can more readily find housing elsewhere.

Just as it is true that those who pursue a life-style which is centered in areas away from their homes do not need much more than a place to sleep — on occasion — so it might be argued that if someone desired to keep a group of residents away from their neighbors, one way to accomplish it would be to provide them with home environments which were no more than "pads" for sleeping. Thus a government or corporation who desired to keep people distant from their homes (and neighbors) and rooted in other interests could begin by providing them with apartments in buildings containing a mix of different age and life-style groups and designed with no public areas where they could pursue activities in common with their neighbors or, for that matter, other members of their family. Areas for communal interaction would then only be provided within government-, school- or factory-designated areas. The provision of these institutionalized communal areas, coupled with the scheduling of events or activities within them, would lead people into the habit of learning to meet others to pursue communal activities within institutionally managed areas. The nature of the activities they pursued and whom they pursued them with could thus be more readily predetermined and monitored.

This is not to say that people who desired to get together with their neighbors would be totally deprived of association through the design of the environment — people find ways to get together with others even under the most restrictive of circumstances. But that may also be because they have a predetermined inclination to do so, whatever the restrictions. We are creatures of habit and very much influenced by what opportunities our environment makes available to us. Patterns determined early in youth are often adopted for the course of our lives without rethinking. We can be led, from childhood, to believe that interaction with others always takes place in institutionally designated areas and under institutional guidance and supervision. From that, we may be led to conclude, without conscious reappraisal, that the only areas of our lives that are intended to be truly private are those spent in sleeping and procreating; everything else is to be done within institutionalized areas and in institutionalized ways. The respect for individuality and the mixture of different types of people characteristic of environments that we cherish in the Western world are apparently difficult to achieve within high-rise or large multifamily environments. Intuition would have suggested the opposite — that dense multifamily environments would provide the greatest possibility for creating diverse mixture of different types of individuals in a common setting, but in fact when such a mixture does occur, it either becomes unlivable or else a strong and specific code must be developed to prescribe a uniformity of behavior. Diverse individuals cannot be brought together in anonymous environments which require communal accord to ensure survival. The social countermeasure required to make anonymous physical environments workable is a uniformity either of individuals or of purpose. If we desire to bring diverse individuals together without restricting their individuality, then we are required to define and spell out in physical terms, with a specificity equal to the social contract required in the anonymous physical environment, which areas are under the control of each living unit, and we must allow each unit direct contact with the public street. Interaction in such settings can be stimulated through the provision of additional areas common to a small number of diverse individuals. Interaction, when it occurs, will not then be born of necessity but of desire.

The Decline in the Social Status
of Residents over Time

All housing, whether built for single- or multifamily occupancy, with private funds or government subsidy, undergoes an evolution in the nature of its occupants over time. Thus, housing that was originally built for occupancy by middle-income families with few children will, over time, become occupied by progressively lower-income families with larger numbers of children and higher ratios of children to adult occupants. The average income of the tenant body will also decrease over the years as the buildings get older and new housing options become available for the originial tenants elsewhere. As a consequence, the funds available for maintaining buildings and grounds and for securing the residential environment diminish proportionately as the need for them increases. In these changing circumstances, those housing types which are dependent on the continued availability of maintenance men and security staff—that is, dense multifamily buildings—are the ones which will deteriorate most quickly when the building staff is reduced.

Once the process has started, these developments will enter into a comparatively rapid spiral of decline. As the deterioration of the residential environment becomes visibly evident, the remaining higher-income families will depart more rapidly, leaving behind the lowest-income groups, the families with the most problems and the least choice, and families with the largest numbers of children who, because of their lower disposable incomes, are most dependent on their immediate housing environment to provide them with all their recreational, outdoor, and communal activity. Thus the environment outside the apartment will begin to experience the most intensive use at exactly the time when the least funds are available to maintain and secure it. This is particularly true for high-rise buildings where residents have the greatest difficulty in maintaining and controlling the common areas outside their individual apartments. In such environments, there is little that the newly arrived lower-income residents will be able to contribute with their own labor to compensate for what the previous higher-income residents paid for with higher rents.

It is also true that if the grounds of a housing development are poorly maintained, everything about the place will take on a look of neglect – even if it is not otherwise so. A well-maintained look affects management's ability to continue to attract higher-income tenants. If, on the other hand, a development is designed with its grounds subdivided so as to be maintained by individual residents, the appearance of the entire project will benefit by the efforts of individual ground-floor residents.

Many of the problems now being faced by housing co-ops built from five to ten years ago arise from the fact that even though the resident group has remained much the same, the costs of maintenance and security staff have increased dramatically. The contracted rent structures did not permit increases in rent to correspond with increased costs.

In most high-rise developments, it is actually the intent of management that residents be made to feel that they control nothing more than what takes place within the four walls which define their apartments. Outside those four walls the nature of the activities and users is to be determined by management. When, for one reason or another, management is no longer able or willing to continue its responsibilities, it takes an incredible effort on the part of residents to adopt some of management's previous roles. As we have begun to learn from recent failures of moderate-income high-rise developments, there is very little in the way of new duties that residents can themselves assume to compensate for management's lack of funds or other deficiencies. The skills required in maintaining a high-rise building are complex and even those that can be assumed by untrained residents, on a individual voluntary basis, require the approval of other residents because of the collective nature of the environment. If residents want to contribute to a building's management or operation, they must first agree to get together. They then must agree to form a new political entity, decide what it is their entity will undertake to do, and how to do or pay for it, then they must decide how to monitor the results, and so on, in what is often an endless, time-consuming and frustrating process.

Fig. 5.2: A small portion of Lefrak City.

The history of the forty-eight hundred-unit, Lefrak City development in Queens, New York, is a good case in point (Figure 5.2). In
1960 twenty eighteen-story high-rise buildings were constructed on the
thirty-two-acre Astor estate in the Corona section of the borough of
Queens, New York City. The development, one of the most recent and
grand accomplishments of the Lefrak Organization, New York City's
biggest nongovernment landlord, was called "Lefrak City" and housed
a total of twenty thousand residents, mostly white and middle-class. It
was filled quickly because rents were low as a result of government
subsidy. The development was convenient to transportation and located in a white, middle-income community. The buildings were
provided with round-the-clock doormen, and management carefully
screened all prospective residents. The proportion of black residents,
although low in the early sixties, gradually increased to 25 per cent of
the population by 1972. The black residents, like the white, were
middle-class two-parent families. The project was thought to have
achieved stable integration.

In 1972, following accusations of racial discrimination filed against two other Lefrak buildings in different areas of the city, Lefrak signed a consent decree to integrate its residential properties. Even though Lefrak City was already integrated and the decree involved other buildings, Lefrak management contends that the fair-housing organizations realized that they had Lefrak on the defensive. Minority residents and those receiving rent supplements and welfare were steered by these organizations toward Lefrak City. Management dropped its tenant-selection and screening criteria and backed away from its rule of thumb of keeping its projects integrated at a two-to-one white-to-black ratio of residents. By 1976 the project was 70 per cent black. With the change in ratios, the project began to experience an increasing vacancy rate. It proved more and more difficult to attract middle-income residents, white and black. To fill up the vacant apartments, management began leasing to larger families and, increasingly, to those with rent supplements. Tenants who had a history of vandalism, neglect of children, and nonpayment of rent moved in. No effort was made to check their backgrounds. The increased vacancies, rent delinquencies, and excessive number of children produced further apathy in management. Broken doors, windows, mailboxes, and elevators remained so for a long time. Graffiti became the new decor in the lobbies, hallways, and elevators. The twenty-four-hour doormen were replaced with a few roaming guards.

With this state of deterioration in the Lefrak City development, the surrounding Queens community became concerned over its own future and the increase in neighborhood crime. Community leaders met with management and tenant organizations to try to reverse the decline. Local councilmen, representatives of the city's police, fire, sanitation, and human resources departments were all brought in to testify at borough meetings. The City Planning Department was even asked to prepare a plan to reverse the decline.

Resident groups held endless meetings with management, neighborhood groups, and city agencies. The first demand of residents was that all entrances to the Lefrak City buildings be locked twenty-four hours a day—including the garage doors. They claimed that even the newly expanded security force was not adequate and so worked out a schedule to man the security desks in the lobby of each building themselves.

Residents then adopted a tenant-selection program. Their first step was to try to persuade management to evict the "troublemakers" and "undesirables" among the tenants—a policy more easily formulated than implemented. The tenants' association then developed a screening procedure to be used by management in evaluating new applicants which was far more critical than the one management had previously abandoned. Anyone applying for an apartment at Lefrak City must now consent to submit to two check-ups: the traditional one for credit and income and a field check at his current home. An investigator from Lefrak goes to the home of the applicant, examines the state of the apartment, and checks with the building superintendent and neighbors to make sure that the new applicants will not cause "social problems." Between the tenants' association and management's review, more than half the current applicants are now being rejected. The screening method is legal, says the city of New York's Human Rights Commission, if the same criteria are applied to all parties and there is no discrimination by race or ethnic group.[1]

Through these and other efforts, the residents of Lefrak City have been able to make their housing livable again. Their efforts were successful, but at what cost? It is questionable whether many people are prepared to spend much of their days and evenings in endless discussions and meetings with neighboring residents on how to ensure that the interior public areas outside their buildings remain clean and safe enough to allow them to get to the street. Most people do not care to purchase, with their lease, an involvement with the petty politics of electing building representatives and collecting membership fees and contributions from recalcitrant residents. Nor are they prepared to give up their evenings and weekends sitting as tenant patrols in the lobbies of their building. The residents of Lefrak City are proud of their achievement but they also find themselves the inheritors of an environment which drains their social and economic resources. Co-op City in New York's Bronx and Cedar-Riverside in Minneapolis, like Lefrak City, with their uncontrollable public areas and sky-rocketing maintenance costs, are monsters of our own creation. They have cost the developers more to build than walk-up environments which, for Co-op City at least, could have been built at the same density (fifty dwellings per acre). Had the developers been a little more thoughtful and a little less greedy, they could have produced environments which were not as dependent on complex machinery, highly skilled maintenance staff, and round-the-clock guard service for their survival.

Why High-Rises Are Built

It is difficult to assign to any one of the professional groups involved in the production of housing the singular responsibility for the construction of high-rise buildings for families with children. Like much of what happens in our society, these housing developments are the result of the interaction of many separate and independent forces, each operating for its own interests under contracts of a limited nature and, usually, for a short term.

Developers are able to purchase parcels of land cheaply when the housing density permitted on them is low. They then appeal to the municipal planning board to have the land "upzoned" so that they can increase the number of units they can build on it — and increase their profits. The amount of "unearned" money they stand to make as a result of the upzoning more than covers the funds necessary to "convince" any recalcitrant board members. The only losers in the deal are the community surrounding the proposed development and the development's future occupants. Once the development is built and fully occupied, it will be sold for capital gains and a new venture started. The developers do not want to be around when the pieces start to fall apart.

Municipal housing authorities and development agencies, who should know better, often act as unwisely but for slightly different motives: the biggest problem most housing agencies face in developing new housing is finding new sites in desirable and acquiescent communities. Once a housing agency has succeeded in acquiring land and community approval for housing on a low-density site, the task of getting the zoning upgraded and additional government funds allocated to build more housing is comparatively simple — if somewhat unethical. Most housing agencies, like most developers and nonprofit groups, are anxious to build as much housing as they can on any site they own and in their haste do not spend too much time thinking about the consequences. A further mistake they make is to build even more projects in the same community. They concentrate development in particular areas just because land and approval is easily obtained there. The effect of these two forms of concentration — high-density housing and many adjacent projects — can, over time, have such a deleterious effect on the surrounding community that it will change its total character.

The demands of other municipal agencies in response to high-density proposals further aggravate the problem. Traffic departments demand that housing developers increase the ratio of off-street parking provided per unit — pushing buildings up still higher to free land below. Fire departments and insurance underwriters, in their *untested* determinations, require more emergency egress stairs for higher buildings — further increasing their already severe security problems.

As most housing in this country is developed by one group and then sold for management to another, there is little call for the long-term responsibility or precautions normally taken with long-term investments. The tax incentives for housing developments in America are short-term, whereas the economics of real estate investment and management are long-term. If developers and management continue to be separate parties, little attention will be given in the development stage to the consequences of having to manage that development in the twenty to forty years to come.

When architects design housing developments in the medium density range, their primary reason for choosing a high-rise building instead of a walk-up at the same density is to free as much ground space as possible for recreation, greenery, and parking. It does appear an obvious solution, particularly when urged by building codes which mandate minimum requirements for parking and open space on a per-unit basis. What is not recognized, however, is that different building types have varying capacities for enabling their residents to develop association with adjoining grounds. Ground areas which are free of buildings are an unquestionable resource; but the quantity of available open space is in itself a marginal factor in determining residents' concern for and use of the grounds adjoining their buildings. Rather, it is the degree to which residents identify the grounds around their buildings as their own that most influences the nature and extent of their use of these facilities.

In developing the high-rise solution for family housing, architects hoped that they could answer the urban need for higher densities and at the same time produce a living environment even more desirable than the traditional row house. The Swiss-born French architect Le Corbusier's concept—in Unité d'Habitation—of the high-rise residential environment, sitting free of the grounds below, was a solution internally consistent with the goals he hoped to satisfy and with his philosophic vision of modern man no longer obsessed with his individual hearth and garden. It was a solution based as well on a utopian view of a new society: a vision of all men living communally, sharing identical wealth, values, and pursuits. In his plans Le Corbusier intentionally strove to disassociate residents from any individual involvement with the grounds below. He viewed the grounds as a continuum of publicly-owned open space, of trees and grass growing freely between and under buildings. It was a strange concept to come out of countries like France and Switzerland where every square foot of ground and building is specifically assigned for the private use of particular parties and jealously guarded by individual owners or building concierges. Figure 5.3 shows Le Corbusier's design of Unité d'Habitation in Marseilles, in contrast to a traditional five-story building commonly constructed in Paris before World Was II. The traditional buildings are tied to the grounds; Le Corbusier's Unité begins nearly where the tops of the older buildings end.

American public housing authorities, in St. Louis, Chicago, and Newark, to name only a few, who constructed housing following Le Corbusier's model, are now comtemplating abandoning them. Many are already from 30 per cent to 40 per cent vacant. In St. Louis, at Pruitt-Igoe, as elsewhere, reality proved different from Le Corbusier's vision. The bountiful grounds, trees, and recreation areas were quickly vandalized because residents could not identify with or care for any area. Management could not afford to either maintain the grounds or watch over them on a continuing basis. In Pruitt-Igoe most of the outdoor play areas went unused because parents would not allow their young children to play where they could not be supervised. The distance to the grounds was too great and the interior public areas of the buildings were too dangerous to allow children to go out alone. The grounds below were too open, anonymous, and unrelated to any of the buildings or to particular apartments to allow residents to develop any set rules governing play area use. Children did most of their playing inside the apartment units and in the public corridors, which led to the rapid deterioration of the buildings.

In Pruitt-Igoe the "river of trees," as the grounds were poetically identified by the architects, became a sewer of broken glass and garbage. In public housing the response of the management of superblock projects increasingly has been to remove the vandalized play equipment and pave all the grounds between the buildings with asphalt (Figure 5.4).

Middle-income developments built along similar models fare better than do public housing projects, but this is conditional on the availability of funds for the continued maintenance of the grounds and for housing guards. The grounds surrounding high-rise buildings occupied by moderate-income residents are at times undistinguishable from the grounds of public housing projects.

Fig. 5.3: Sketches of Le Corbusier's Unité d'Habitation (right) and the traditional Parisian five-story walk-up apartment house.

Fig. 5.4: As the grassed areas, trees, and play areas of American housing developments deteriorate, the management paves them over. After six years of occupancy, the grounds are wall-to-wall asphalt.

The Comparative Costs of Building and Maintaining Housing

For many years it was accepted as general wisdom in the building profession that high-rise buildings cost less to build and maintain than walk-up buildings. This view was often the result of an inappropriate comparison between the over-all development costs of a housing project and its construction costs, and between the maintenance costs of buildings occupied by families with children versus those occupied exclusively by elderly or working singles and couples.

In calculating development costs, one includes the cost of the land; construction costs are calculated exclusive of land costs. The cost of land in housing construction normally ranges from 20 to 30 per cent of development costs. However, the more units that can be put on the same piece of land, the less the development costs per unit. For example, the construction costs per unit may be higher in an elevator building than in a walk-up building, but the development costs per unit may still end up lower in the high-rise as a result of significantly lower land costs per unit. Thus, in a high-density scheme with high per-unit construction costs, the savings on land costs per unit may produce a lower development cost per unit than a low-density scheme with lower per-unit construction costs.

To achieve exact equivalence, comparison of the construction and development costs of different building types should only be made when the density of the different types are identical. In such instances, the land costs per unit would be the same and could be canceled out of the equation. Unfortunately, comparable densities in walk-ups and high-rises only occur at the upper limits of the walk-up prototypes and at the lower limits of the high-rise prototypes. Such a comparison, therefore, may serve little more than to satisfy academic curiosity.

Comparison of construction and development costs of different building types is still further complicated by the different mortgage financing arrangements available under different housing programs, each program producing its own set of financial benefits. Significant variations are also produced by differences in the quality of construction and the quality of materials used in different developments. These variations will, in two developments which are laid out identically, produce different construction costs, maintenance costs, and life expectancies. A high-rise building intended for occupancy by families with children should be built with sturdier doors, glass, hardware, wall and floor materials, elevators and garbage chutes than a building for the elderly. Finally, building codes throughout the country require that buildings above three stories in height be of fireproof construction and meet special fire codes. This entails the use of materials with a higher fire-rating, more stairs and emergency exits, heavier walls, and supporting structures. Higher buildings also require, as intrinsic to their construction, the use of heavier foundations, the provision of elevators, and the provision of garbage chutes.

From all the above, it is clear that within the scope of this book, it is impossible to undertake a detailed comparison of the construction and development costs of different building types. However, a few recent studies have appeared on the subject and their conclusions are quoted here for general information.

In the late 1960s the National Commission on Urban Problems undertook a comparison of the cost of different housing types across the nation built under various government assistance programs.[2] Two of concluding tables in its report are presented here (Tables 5.1 and 5.2).

Both tables show, first, that the range in costs within any building type, whether elevator buildings, walk-ups, or row houses, is sufficiently large as to make a low-priced elevator building less costly per unit than a high-priced row house or walk-up. Nevertheless, Table 5.1 shows that in a comparison of over-all development costs per unit, row houses cost slightly less than walk-ups, and walk-ups, in turn, cost significantly less than elevator buildings. Table 5.2, comparing construction costs per square foot, shows that walk-up units are less costly than

Table 5.1: Development Cost per Unit by Type of Building

FHA 207−231 Multi-Unit Programs	Development Cost per Unit		
	High	Median	Low
1966 HUD study, 196 projects	$36,001	$16,524	$ 7,702
1962-66 medians, 87 projects	41,269	15,110	8,102
Elevator	41,269	20,826	12,464
Walk-up	20,954	13,388	8,102
Row	19,767	13,227	8,111

SOURCE: E. Eaves, *How the Many Costs of Housing Fit Together*, p. 56

Table 5.2: Construction Cost per Square Foot by Type of Building

FHA 207−231 Multi-unit Programs	Dollars/Sq. Ft.		
	High	Median	Low
1966 HUD study, 196 projects	20.88	12.49	7.74
1962-66 medians, 87 projects	21.66	10.16	6.70
Elevator	21.66	14.35	10.16
Walk-up	12.90	9.61	6.70
Row	13.63	9.66	8.25

SOURCE: E. Eaves, *How the Many Costs of Housing Fit Together*, p. 64.

row-house units, and row-house units in turn are less costly than elevator-building units.

The Housing Development Administration (HDA) of the city of New York recently undertook a comparative study of both the development and maintenance costs of different housing types.[3] Its study, based on 1973 construction experience, is neither as comprehensive nor as rigorous as the study by the National Commission on Urban Problems. But its conclusions are worth noting for the insights they bring to the problem of comparing building and maintenance costs.

The HDA study compared three-story three-family homes against state-subsidized (Mitchell-Lama) high-rise buildings (Figure 5.5). It determined that the three-story buildings, selling at approximately $100,000, were "among the best housing buys available." They found that development costs for a conventionally built three-family home were approximately $6,900 per room as compared with $11,900 per room in the high-rise Mitchell-Lama buildings. The maintenance and operating costs of three-family homes were approximately $135 per room per year, compared with high-rise Mitchell-Lama which were substantially in excess of $200 per room per year. The savings in the

Fig. 5.5: The three-story walk-up on the left is built at the same density as the seven-story high-rises on the right: fifty units per acre. The owner of each three-story walk-up lives on the ground floor and rents the upper two floors.

maintenance costs of the three-family homes were attributed to several factors, among them the willingness and ability of homeowners to make small repairs, the absence of large common circulation areas that require cleaning and maintenance, and the absence of elevators and other complex systems such as garbage chutes which requrie that repair work be done by expensive experts.

Both of the above studies appear to have similar conclusions; three-story multifamily walk-ups are the least costly means of providing medium-density housing; and walk-ups are less expensive to build and to maintain than both row houses and high-rises. The three-story walk-up manages to achieve an excellent compromise between the two-story row house and the high-rise apartment building, in that it does not require the elevators or elaborate fireproofing of the high-rise nor the extensive foundations, roofing, and exterior walls of the row house.

In the New York comparison, the differences in maintenance costs between high-rises and walk-ups are also affected by the different forms of ownership and occupancy inherent in each type of development. The owner of the three-story walk-up lives on the ground floor and does much of the maintenance work himself. This would be impossible in most high-rise housing. The program through which this walk-

up housing was built allows a small businessman or skilled worker who
has accumulated a few thousand dollars of equity capital to get a
guaranteed loan from the state and federal government to cover from
80 to 90 per cent of the cost of the building. Thus, with $10,000 to
$20,000 in capital, he can, with a second mortgage if necessary, scrape
together sufficient funds to purchase a $100,000 building. The rent he
will receive from the two apartments above his own will assist him in
paying off both the long-term mortgage on the building and the second
mortgage, if necessary. By the time the second mortgage is paid off, he
will need some of his rent money for repairs and maintenance. Meanwhile, the value of his building will be increasing with inflation, and
when the mortgage is finally paid off, his building will be worth six to
eight times his original equity investment (in 1978 dollars). The labor
that he puts into the building in maintaining it on a weekly basis goes to
increasing the net worth and long-term viability of his building and is
tax free. The incentive for him is quite clear: the sweat of his brow is
being directly translated into a dollar value increase in the worth of his
investment.

There is one more interesting aspect to the story of the three-story
walk-up building with its resident owner. In addition to proving to be
an inexpensive housing construction, management, and maintenance
program, it is also proving to be an inexpensive form of social welfare.
The landlord is usually of similar class and ethnic background to his
tenants upstairs. His tenants will be earning smaller incomes primarily
because they are either younger or more recently migrated. When his
tenants experienced financial difficulty, the landlord often helps out. It
is not uncommon for the landlord to stake his tenants to a few months'
rent when they are unemployed or in financial difficulty. This is a form
of social assistance without any of the stigma or self-deprecation that
normally attends institutionalized assistance. It is also a program with
built-in inducements to get people who are temporarily out of work to
find a job quickly so as to repay the favor and the rent due.

There are still other positives factors in operation in the three-story
building that are worth noting. The skilled worker who purchased one
of these walk-ups to live in and rent has, in the process of becoming a
landlord, also learned to become a businessman—to deal with banks, to
keep records, to nurture his investment, and to appreciate the benefits
of tax write-offs. Meanwhile, his two tenant-neighbors, through their
close association with him, also learn of like opportunities available to
them and are encouraged to follow in his footsteps.

One final point: the presence of the landlord and his family in the
ground-floor apartment provides the building with a natural form of
continual supervision of the outside grounds, sidewalk, and interior

public circulation areas of the building. This is the best and least costly form of security that can be provided any residential environment.

Much of the success of the three-family walk-up hinges on the peculiar combination of building form and tenure. The building is designed for a small number of families sharing an entry and is financed with the intent of having the owner in residence on the ground-floor apartment. George Sternlieb, director of the Center for Urban Policy Research at Rutgers University, in a study of the factors determining housing abandonment, found that buildings which were owned by landlords who had few, rather than many, investments were less frequently abandoned. Similarly, buildings whose landlords lived on the premises maintained a high degree of stability, even when the tenant body changed.[4] This model suggests that a housing policy which encourages residents to become involved in ownership and management is one which will prove the least costly to implement and maintain and one which has the greatest promise of producing long-term stability in housing.

This policy is further supported by the findings of the Urban Institute, a Washington, D.C. based research group under contract with HUD, in their study of the factors affecting occupancy and successful management in federally assisted moderate-income housing.[5] Those developments which were built as co-operatives fared significantly better than those that were built as limited dividend housing and were managed by an outside realty firm. If housing agencies and government decide to embark on a program of creating more co-operatives and encouraging small landlords, they should keep in mind that ownership and management both, in turn, are affected by building type. Co-operative ownership of a high-rise building, divided among over one hundred families, is rendered meaningless. In such settings, residents have a difficult time developing a sense of personal ownership, pride, and involvement in management. The generally poor performance of moderate-income high-rise co-operatives supports this view. The primary purpose for advocating resident involvement in building ownership is to instill in residents a sense of personal and financial involvement in the development, but if the form of the building negates the evocation of these feelings, this purpose is negated.

The provision of federal subsidies to allow moderate-income residents to become building owners and even landlords may be seen as conflicting with the interests of other taxpayers. The policy in nationally assisted housing in Great Britain, The Netherlands, and Sweden is briefly this: what government subsidizes, government will own. Postwar housing-assistance programs in these countries were directed at reducing the evil of housing landlords. But in the process of ridding themselves of the large, uninterested private landlord, these governments also rid themselves of the small, effective landlord. The governments than adopted the load of becoming the largest landlords ever and, with that, incurred the incredible cost of maintaining huge, inefficient housing bureaucracies that drained their nation's resources.

In the fall of 1975, two ministers from Great Britain visited our Institute in New York. In discussing the role of the British Government in housing, they admitted that the Labour government, which first initiated these housing programs, did not appreciate the full consequences of its action and that its government was now saddled with more than it had bargained for. But the admission of error and the reversal of policy does not make for good politics. It will have to take an *interim* change to a more conservative government to enable Parliament to rescue the nation from the burden of these programs.

To point out the potential pitfalls in any program, one of the British ministers told a story which not only provides an example of how good intentions on the part of government can lead to opposite results, but also serves to warn us that homeownership is not a panacea for all our housing problems.

As an experiment devised to test the benefits of homeownership for low-income families, the Greater London Council, which administers government-owned housing in the London area, sold one of its developments to its residents. This was a row-house development typical of the older English white-collar and skilled working-class housing one sees throughout the country. Those residents who had been living in the development five years or more were given title to the house they lived in and their monthly rentals were applied as payments on their mortgages, which varied in length with the number of years that they had been living in the development.

As anticipated, the look of the development changed almost overnight with the new form of tenure. Residents now saw their house and its grounds as their own property and began fixing them up. New fences and gates were put up, gardens were planted, window trim and shutters were painted, bricks were pointed and gutters repaired. Where previously the development had a run-down, forlorn feeling to it, it now took on the look of a prosperous British suburb. Housing officials were impressed that most of the cleaning and routine work was being assumed by the residents themselves. The repair of larger-scale items that required expert skills (plumbing, electrical, heating, and roofing repairs) was provided for through an insurance premium built into the monthly mortgage payments.

However, in the second year of the experiment, the unexpected happened. Residents began to sell their homes to middle-income purchasers at a nice profit. And, as their low incomes still allowed them to qualify for publicly assisted housing, they reapplied and moved back into other government housing projects. Government had, effectively, given each resident of the project a gift equal to the worth of their housing and had further removed a few hundred units from its housing stock. The final irony, said our British visitor, was that the new residents of the development voted Conservative in sufficient number to result in the loss of the district.

Housing Projects and the Expanding Bureaucracy

In our obsession with expanding the role of government and bureaucratic institutions and our pride in creating large bureaucracies for handling the welfare, education, and housing of our citizens, we have assumed a burden that we now seem unwilling to support further. We have created institutions for the housing of low- and moderate-income groups which run counter to the spirit and intent of housing assistance in this country. At the same time, unlike virtually every other nation in the world, including other Western countries, we have adopted a policy of providing large-scale federal assistance to middle- and upper-income Americans to become homeowners. The phrase "a nation of homeowners" perhaps most closely exemplifies the promise of our Constitution. And yet for our moderate- and low-income groups we have adopted a policy of institutionalized housing and the use of building forms which effectively prevent residents from controlling their own environment and participating in the maintenance and management of the buildings in which they live. The effect of this policy is not only the ever-increasing government burden of management and maintenance, it is a further example of the unintentional *growth* of government – the adoption by the state of yet more functions: first the ownership and then the necessary high costs of maintaining and controlling residential environments which are public in nature. These environments cannot be easily controlled by the residents themselves and the residents do not feel capable of performing any maintenance. Residents have been led both by the form of the environment and the institutional structure of management to abrogate to large bureaucracies their responsibilities for the areas outside the four walls of their apartment. The consequence of these policies is: first, the shrinking of personal freedom, responsibility, and control; second, the pervasive growth of unmanageable institutions; and, finally, the failure and abandonment of housing environments and cities because the increasing costs of managing, maintaining, and securing these environments have become prohibitive.

VI

The Private Streets of St. Louis

For many students of the dilemma of American cities, the decline of St. Louis, Missouri, has come to epitomize the impotence of federal, state, and local resources in coping with the consequences of large-scale population change. Yet buried within those very areas of St. Louis which have been experiencing the most radical turnover of population are a series of streets where residents have adopted a program to stabilize their communities, to deter crime, and to guarantee the necessities of a middle-class life-style. These residents have been able to create and maintain for themselves what their city was no longer able to provide: low crime rates, stable property values, and a sense of community. Even though the areas surrounding them are experiencing significant socioeconomic change, high crime rates, physical deterioration, and abandonment, these streets are still characterized by middle-class owner-occupied, residency—both black and white. The distinguishing characteristic of these streets is that they have been deeded back from the city to the residents and are now legally owned and maintained by the residents themselves.

Fig. 6.1: View of one of the original private boulevarded streets in St. Louis, built at the turn of the century.

The concept of privately owned streets, closed to through traffic, is not a new one to St. Louis. It was introduced at the turn of the century with the development of very wealthy communities at the periphery of the then rapidly expanding city. What is new, however, is the application of this concept to the problems of a contemporary city being decimated by change. Most of the new private-street associations are no more than one block in length, although there are some which incorporate as many as twelve blocks. In some respects, the private-street associations function as small, independent cities in that their residents have taken both legal and physical action to protect their investment in their homes and community and to set up a mechanism that allows them to reduce the incidence and fear of crime and to control the pattern of land use.

The original private streets of St. Louis were built between 1870 and 1910 as housing estates for the wealthiest of St. Louis' families. They were developed in areas which were then the periphery of the city. Virtually every house was a replica of a European mansion or villa (Figures 6.1 and 6.2). The private-street concept was, itself, also borrowed from the Continent.

In London private streets were built as exclusive enclaves for the rich and, by keeping title to their street, residents were able further to ensure their privacy. In almost all new residential subdivisions everywhere the developer deeds the streets in his development to the municipality he is working in once he has sold his houses to individual buyers. The residents of private streets, by contrast, collectively own the public right-of-way: the sidewalks, pavement, lighting, and trees — as well as their homes and the property upon which they stand. More importantly, they are further united in a restrictive covenant which limits the nature of use of their homes and property.

The original private streets of St. Louis were created to provide their residents with insulation, protection, and stability, not an automatic achievement on public streets in a thriving and rapidly expanding city. To guarantee their insulation and security further, the original private streets had watchmen minding their gates around the clock (Figure 6.3).

In the seventy years since the last of the great private streets was built in St. Louis, the many social and economic changes undergone by the city prompted the original families to seek out the greener pastures of suburbia. With their departure, the streets were occupied by an upper middle-income population. This transformation did not much alter the fundamental character or purpose of the private streets.

In the 1950s, with the onset of further racial and economic change in St. Louis, a trend for converting existing public streets into private streets came into vogue. As there was already a precedent for private streets in the city by-laws, it was a comparatively simple task for middle-income residents living on streets which had originally been deeded to the city to get together and petition the city to return the street to private ownership.

While the desire for exclusivity was the primary motive for the creation of the original private streets at the turn of the century, the middle-class residents of the 1950s replaced the importance of exclusivity with their need for security and stability. Residents claim that the physical closure of streets and their legal association together act to create social cohesion, stability, and security. The private association provides a legal framework which structures this cohesion, and the physical closure provides an effective tool for allowing residents to control the activities on their street.

The private streets of St. Louis (Figure 6.4) have two distinguishing characteristics: (1) each street is blocked off at one end to prevent through traffic, and (2) ownership of each street right-of-way by the residents is guaranteed by a deed restriction attached to all property. Closure is accomplished by the erection of a barrier across one end of the street, creating a cul-de-sac. As the cost of the barriers is borne by the residents, they vary widely in character — from simple posts and chain to elaborate walls, gates, and iron fences (Figures 6.5 and 6.6). The open end of the street is usually also defined, either through a narrowing of the pavement or the erection of a symbolic portal.

Fig. 6.2: Mansions on the original private streets of St. Louis. Each was built as a replica of a European baronial estate.

The legal instrument for creating the private street is an "indenture"—a set of deed restrictions incorporated into the legal description of each property abutting the street. These restrictions require the formation of an incorporated street association which then becomes the title holder of the street right-of-way. All property owners on the street are required to join the association. The deed restrictions empower the association to levy assessments on the landowners to pay for the maintenance of the street and its amenities. The deed also defines the land

Fig. 6.3: Guardhouse tower at entry gate to a private street.

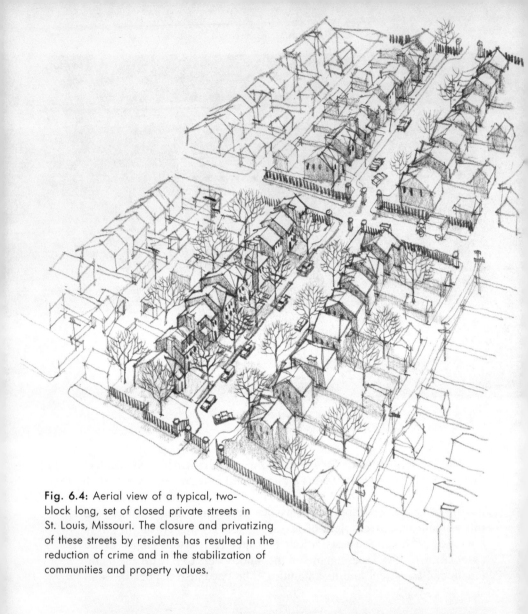

Fig. 6.4: Aerial view of a typical, two-block long, set of closed private streets in St. Louis, Missouri. The closure and privatizing of these streets by residents has resulted in the reduction of crime and in the stabilization of communities and property values.

use of the private homeowner's property. Of critical importance is the requirement mandating single-family residential occupancy. Private street associations continue to use the city's police, fire, water, gas, and sewage services paid for by the residents through regular property taxes, but residents do receive a small tax abatement from the city for maintaining the street right-of-way.

Variations in the configuration of private streets in St. Louis result from differences in existing urban fabrics, the location of the major arterial streets, and the number of streets that are grouped together in an

Fig. 6.5: A stone column, a sawhorse, and chain define the entry to a private street.

association. In most cases, the deed of ownership among residents involves no more than one or two city blocks, although it is common to find a number of private-street associations located next to each other.

University City, a suburb adjoining St. Louis, has a few private street associations which incorporate from six to twelve blocks. Economic and racial change in University City is a recent phenomenon compared with St. Louis, and as a result, the closed streets of University City are located adjacent to public streets which house a similar socioeconomic population. By contrast, the older closed streets of St. Louis are surrounded by public streets which, over the years, have come to house a lower-income population in homes which have been converted to multifamily occupancy.

The continued existence of the private streets in St. Louis and the

Fig. 6.6: Low stone walls and pillars define the entry to a recently converted private street.

increased petitioning by residents for the converism of public streets to private status suggest that there may be some validity to the claim of private-street residents that privatizing and closure provide increased security and stability. While surrounding public streets have lost their middle-income residents and have fallen victim to speculators, the private streets appear to continue to offer their middle-income residents some stability.

When questioned by our staff about the value of their homes, residents of private streets were almost unanimous in their feeling that their property had increased in value since they bought it—and that it would continue to do so. As the process of urban decay is critically dependent upon the loss of confidence by residents, any mechanism which serves to bolster that confidence can be of immense value to a city.

Our institutes' study of the private streets in St. Louis and University City shows that residents were influenced to purchase their homes because they liked the type of house offered and the neighborhood within which it was located. Residents identify themselves as people who find urban environments more stimulating than suburban ones, feel they have more recreational and cultural opportunities in the city, and are able to interact with a more diverse group of people. The president of one of the private-street corporations claimed "Many young families, from various backgrounds, are moving onto the street because they like the urban feeling, the closed character, and the value of the houses for the prices . . . These people are committed—they want a particular way of life and are committed to a special kind of community."[1]

When questioned about the specific benefits of homeownership in the city versus the suburbs, residents consistently mentioned the greater range of styles in older urban housing. They also said that the older housing was far superior in construction, size, and materials to anything available in suburban areas. However, residents were quick to say that location in an urban setting and quality of construction and materials were not their only concerns: the soundness of their investment was also of great importance to them. Residents felt that investment in a house in the city required reasonable assurance that the value of the house would neither drop suddenly nor gradually diminish. They argued that many of the types of houses they preferred in the city of St. Louis were located in areas which had undergone or were undergoing significant racial and economic change. Residents were well aware that poor maintenance, demolitions, blockbusting, and conversions to multiple-family occupancy had diminished the value of housing on neighboring public streets and had served to wipe out entire blocks of housing that were sound only a few years ago. As a condition to their

Fig. 6.7: A child's bicycle left unattended on the sidewalk in front of a house on a private street.

purchase of a house within the city limits of St. Louis, residents felt they needed assurance that neighboring homeowners shared both their values and financial capacity to maintain the standards of homeownership. The private-street system appears to provide a mechanism for the self-selection and association of like-minded, economically similar, and committed residents. Our interviews show that concern for the security of their investment was a critical factor which led urban-oriented residents to the selection of a house on a private street. However, further questions revealed that most residents were not conscious of all the restrictive covenants of a private street before they moved onto it. Rather, it was the environmental feeling of the private street and its "status" which prompted their decision.

From a visual perspective, the private streets appear to the potential buyer to be stable and well-maintained residential environments (Figure 6.7). There is none of the physical deterioration prevalent on the surrounding public streets, nor are there any houses which give the unmistakeable sign of having been converted to multifamily occupancy (Figure 6.8). There is little pedestrian and vehicular traffic through the private streets and their physical seperation provides one with the distinct feeling that the closed streets can resist the change taking place around them.

Physical closure appears to provide both a real and symbolic demarcation which separates the private streets from their surroundings. In the residents' minds, closure is a necessary statement to the outside world that their street is different; it lessens their feelings of

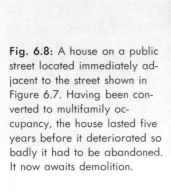

Fig. 6.8: A house on a public street located immediately adjacent to the street shown in Figure 6.7. Having been converted to multifamily occupancy, the house lasted five years before it deteriorated so badly it had to be abandoned. It now awaits demolition.

vulnerability to the change taking place in the city around them. "Those gates are not so much barriers as they are signs. We have a need for . . . symbols, signs, and arches which say our street is different," is the way one resident put it.[2] Closure also stands as a symbol to residents that they are cohesive in their resolve to maintain the ambience and stability of their street. "When I come through those gates onto Cabanne Place, it is like coming into another world. . . . There's a

Fig. 6.9: The closure of the private streets to automobile through traffic enables the street right-of-way to be gained as a play area.

spirit here to keep things going. Closing the street gives the area a different feeling. If it is closed, you have the feeling of control and that you are living on your own turf."[3]

The ultimate effect of this symbolic definition of the street is that residents come to think of the street as their neighborhood. When asked by our interviewers to delimit the boundaries of their neighborhood, residents of private streets almost invariably defined it as congruent with their private street. By contrast, residents on public streets rarely equated the boundary of their neighborhood with that of their street.

In addition to defining the street as separate and different from the outside world, closure appears to make the street a more desirable residential environment. Streets which previously carried through traffic were turned into culs-de-sac, reducing the presence of moving automobiles and their accompanying noise and pollution. The reduction of vehicular activity has, in turn, redefined residents' relationship to the street. With traffic flow limited to an occasional slowly moving car, the street has become an extension of the front yards of the abutting houses: an area that can be shared by all residents, a zone where children can play and adults meet and socialize (Figures 6.9 and 6.10).

Some residents expressed the feeling that closure gave the street an ambience similar to that found in suburbia. For young families, the safe area for the communal play of children right in front of their homes proved to be an important criterion in enabling them to choose an urban home.

Fig. 6.10: The closed streets create a sufficiently private atmosphere to allow residents to feel comfortable enough to visit their neighbors on the street in their bathing suits. The steps at the entry walks to each house provide a place to encounter one's neighbors casually.

Behavioral observations showed that residents of closed streets were more apt to use the street for casual social interaction than were residents of similar socioeconomic backgrounds who lived on open streets. Paired twenty-minute observations on socially similar closed and open streets in University City and St. Louis showed that the closed streets had lower levels of transient activity (people passing through) and considerably higher rates of visiting, group formation, and street interaction by residents.

The private streets of St. Louis and University City were also examined for the claim of residents that they have achieved low-crime, stable, middle-class communities in urban areas which have otherwise undergone a rapid transition to low-income areas. The nature of these achievements are claimed to be of two orders: (1) those of primary benefit to private street residents and (2) those of benefit to the surrounding community and city. The residents claim that the streets provide them with a desirable environment around the home for raising children; that they have a low crime rate; that they serve to maintain property values; that they provide an excellent housing buy for middle- and moderate-income residents; and, finally, that they provide the last opportunity in St. Louis for enjoying an urban life-style. As regards the benefits to the surrounding community, residents claim that the private streets achieve stable, long-term integration of middle-income residents with their low-income neighbors on surrounding streets; that together they create an integrated political community of rich and poor, white and black, which strengthens the power of the poor; that the higher taxes the residents of private streets pay provide the poor with a higher level of municipal services; and, finally, that the presence of middle-class residents helps to maintain quality shopping, entertainment, and recreational opportunities for lower-income groups as well as themselves.

It is claimed by Planning Commission staff in St. Louis that the private streets stem white flight and prevent the erosion of the urban tax base. Because middle-income private streets are located adjacent to low-income public streets, they are also said to serve as a mechanism for integrating different racial and economic groups. Integration does not occur so much at the scale of adjacent houses but at the scale of adjacent city streets. If there is any substance to these claims, they should be reflected in lower crime rates and higher sales prices for similar homes. The private streets should also prove immune to blockbusting, conversions to multiple occupancy, and the erosion of real estate values.

To determine whether this was so, our institute undertook an analyses of these factors by comparing public versus private streets. In the first set of comparisons we examined adjacent public and private

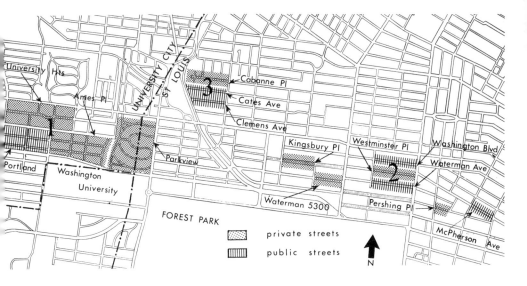

Fig. 6.11: Map locating the private and public streets examined in this study.

streets at the beginning of the cycle of socioeconomic change; in the second set of comparisons, we looked at adjacent public and private streets after the change had taken place. In the latter case, we were obviously not comparing variations in crime and property values between socially similar streets but rather the ability of private streets to withstand the change that had taken place around them.

The streets used in the comparison of crime and stability are shown on the accompanying map. Private streets are denoted by the dot screening; public streets by vertical hatched lines (Figure 6.11). Figure 6.12 shows the location of the study area shown in Figure 6.11 in the center of the greater St. Louis area.

A total of three sets of public and private streets were used: adjacent streets which have populations of similar socioeconomic characteristics and located in the southeast sector of University City and are labeled 1; adjacent streets which have populations with different socioeconomic characteristics are located in the central West End of St. Louis and are labeled 2 and 3. The streets labeled 2 consist of a white-populated middle-income private street and has adjacent low-income black-populated and white-populated streets. The streets labeled 3 consist of a black middle-income private street and has adjacent lower-income black-populated streets.

The reported crime rate in the Central West End of St. Louis, the sector containing two of our comparison areas, was the highest in the region: a rate of one thousand index crimes per one thousand population—nearly fifteen times the city-wide rate. By contrast, the total index crime rate of St. Louis County, of which University City is a part, was only twenty-three per one thousand population during the same period. It should be noted, however, that although University City has a lower crime rate than St. Louis, our comparison streets in University City are located adjacent to the central West End of St. Louis and are part of the continuum of the urban fabric of that area.

Our purpose in undertaking a comparison of crime rates between private and public streets in such divergent areas as University City and the central West End of St. Louis was to measure how private streets operate in resisting crime, and the fear of crime, in different circumstances. The analysis of private versus public streets in University City is closer to a true "control" comparison, in that the populations in both sets of streets are similar as are the physical form of the buildings and the street layouts.

In St. Louis the private middle-income streets composed of single-family houses are located adjacent to public streets with predominantly subdivided houses containing a low-income and, at times, racially different population. Previous research on urban crime has found that

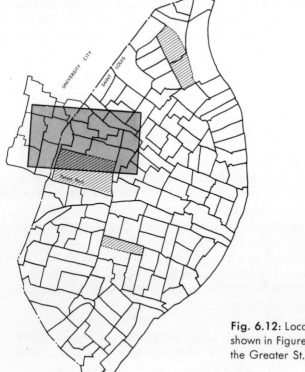

Fig. 6.12: Location of the study area, shown in Figure 6.11, in the context of the Greater St. Louis area.

such juxtapositions often produce areas with the highest crime rates in the city — and that it is often the higher-income group that experiences the higher crime rates.

Comparison 1: Ames Place Compared to West Portland Place

Ames Place, a private subdivision located in University City, consists of one hundred seventy-eight single-family houses and forty-four apartment units located on a total of ten city blocks. The single-family houses were built in the 1920s and are more modest in size and in construction than the houses on the private streets which we will be examining in St. Louis. The average lot size is 40′ × 20′. The forty-four apartment units are located in four three-story walk-up buildings. The residents of the single-family homes are middle-income and predominantly white, and the residents of the apartment buildings are of a similar racial and social status but are younger and, consequently, of lower income.

The comparison public streets are called West Portland Place and consist of one hundred eighty-nine single-family dwellings on a total of six blocks. This public subdivision is also in University City and is located adjacent to Ames Place and University Heights, two private subdivisions. West Portland Place has a population, buildings, and site characteristics similar to Ames Place.

In a comparison of crime rates over a five-year period, residents in the public subdivision reported having experienced 108 per cent more crimes per thousand population than those in the private subdivision (Table 6.1).

Table 6.1: Aggregate Burglary Rate per 1,000 Residents, Includes All Burglaries, 1968–73

University City Study Streets

Subdivision	Number of burglaries	Burglary rate[a]	Per cent difference[b]
Ames Place (private)	9	11	—
West Portland Place (public)	19	27	+108

[a] Rates computed using estimates of population derived from resident interview responses and U. S. Bureau of the Census, "Census of Housing, 1970, Block Statistics, Final Report HC(3)-137, St. Louis, Mo.-Ill: Urbanized Area."

[b] Per cent difference is computed using aggregate burglary rate for the three private subdivisions as a base and comparing it to the rate for West Portland Place, a public subdivision.

Comparison 2: Westminster Place Compared to Washington Place and Waterman Avenue

Westminster Place became a private street upon the petition of its residents in 1959. It is occupied by middle-income white residents. The street contains fifty-two good-sized homes on 40′ × 130′ lots. The houses were built in the 1920s and are characteristically brick with some stone and wood components. The residents formed a private-street association in response to the perceived decline of adjacent streets. Residents who have lived on the street since before it became private say that Westminster Place would have experienced decay similar to that of an adjacent street. Washington Boulevard, if it had not become a private street (see Table 6.2 for a comparison of conversions of single-family houses to multifamily occupancy on Washington Boulevard versus Westminster Place). For the older residents of Westminster Place who remember Washington Boulevard historically as having been a better place to live, the success of the privatizing process in maintaining a middle-class milieu and single-family houses has been more than proven.

Table 6.2: Conversions of Single-Family Structures on Street to Multiple-Occupancy Structures. Includes All Conversions, 1960–73

	Number of conversions	*Approximate per cent of total structures*
Westminster Place (private)	0	0
Washington Boulevard (public)	33	67

SOURCE: Building Permits Office, City of St. Louis, Permit Records for Structural Alterations.

Washington Boulevard is an immediately adjacent public street running parallel with Westminster Place. The housing on Washington is identical in physical form to that on Westminster, but the buildings have been converted to multiple occupancy over the past twenty years. In the past ten years the street has become occupied by a high percentage of low- and moderate-income blacks.

Waterman Avenue is a public street located immediately to the south of Westminster Place and contains a mix of both single-family and multiple-occupancy structures. It has recently begun to be occupied by lower-income blacks although there are still white families in residence. The building structures and lot sizes (40′ × 160′) are slightly larger than those on the other two streets, but the architecture and general appearance of the street is the same. All three streets receive city police patrolling. Westminster Place does not have a separate guard or security force. Although the differences in crime rates between the public and private streets in St. Louis are not as dramatic as those between the public and private streets in University City, they are still appreciable (Table 6.3).

Table 6.3: Aggregate Crime Rates per 1,000 Residents, Includes All Crimes, 1966–73

Central West End, St. Louis Study Streets

	Rate[a]	Per cent difference [b]
Westminster Place (private)	750	—
Waterman Avenue (5000-5200) (public)	944	+26
Washington Boulevard (public)	1,138	+52

[a] Rates based upon crimes of burglary, assault, vandalism, theft from auto, theft of auto accessories, and purse snatching. Computed using estimates of street populations derived from resident interview responses and U. S. Bureau of the Census, "Census of Housing, 1970, Block Statistics, Final Report HC(3)-137, St. Louis, Mo.-Ill.: Urbanized Area."
[b] Per cent difference is computed using private street crime rate as base.

Comparison 3: Cabanne Place Compared to Cates and Clemens Avenues

Cabanne Place was built in 1890 and was a private street from its inception. The lots are large, (60' × 160'), as are most of the original homes. Three of the very large lots were subdivided recently and now contain more modest-sized single-family homes (Figure 6.13). The street consists of thirty-nine homes and is almost exclusively occupied by black middle-income families. Some older white residents still remain on the street.

Cates Avenue is a public street located immediately adjacent to and south of Cabanne Place. It contains structures of a similar physical character to Cabanne but on smaller lots (50' × 120'). Cates Avenue was entirely composed of single-family houses until a few years ago. Recent conversions have made the street a mixture of multifamily and single-family dwellings. The street is occupied by a mixture of middle- and lower-income blacks.

Clemens Avenue is a public street located immediately adjacent to and south of Cates Avenue. Its physical and social characteristics are almost identical with those of Cates Avenue. Because the lots are five feet narrower than those on Cates, the houses are grouped somewhat closer together.

Fig. 6.13: The house on the right is a recent addition to Cabanne Place. The purchase price is about the same as the older houses on the left.

All three streets are located in a large black community composed of poor and working-poor families. The area has been undergoing extensive urban renewal in recent years.

The data in Tables 6.1, 6.3, and 6.4 indicate that the private streets experience less crime than do public streets. The comparisons in Tables 6.3 and 6.4 show that private streets nested amid socially dissimilar population in a high-crime community are not subject to the same level of crime as their neighbors.

To detail the differences in crime between public and private streets more fully, Table 6.5 presents a breakdown, by type, of the aggregate crime rates in Tables 6.3 and 6.4.

Table 6.4: Aggregate Crime Rates per 1,000 Residents, Includes All Crimes, 1966–73

	Rate[a]	Per cent difference[b]
Cabanne Place (private)	206	—
Cates Avenue (public)	498	+142
Clemens Avenue (public)	338	+64

[a] Rates based upon crimes of burglary, assault, vandalism, theft from auto, theft of auto accessories, and purse snatching. Computed using estimates of street populations derived from resident interview responses and U. S. Bureau of the Census, "Census of Housing, 1970, Block Statistics, Final Report HC(3)-137, St. Louis, Mo.-Ill.: Urbanized Area."
[b] Per cent difference is computed using private-street crime rate as base.

**Table 6.5: Comparative Crime Rates per 1,000 Residents
Includes All Crimes, 1966–73**

Central West End, St. Louis Study Streets

COMPARISON A

| | PRIVATE | PUBLIC | |
| | | | |
Crime	*Westminster Place rate^a*	*Waterman Avenue (5000–5200) rate^a*	*Per cent difference^b*
Assault	135	174	+ 29
Purse snatching	20	56	+180
Burglary	405	388	− 4
Vandalism	55	74	+ 35
Theft from auto	55	122	+122
Theft auto accessories	80	130	+ 63

Crime	*Westminster Place rate^a*	*Washington Boulevard rate^a*	*Per cent difference^b*
Assault	135	360	+167
Purse snatching	20	74	+270
Burglary	405	449	+ 11
Vandalism	55	98	+ 78
Theft from auto	55	80	+ 45
Theft auto accessories	80	77	− 4

COMPARISON B

| | PRIVATE | PUBLIC | |
| | | | |
Crime	*Cabanne Place rate^a*	*Cates Avenue rate^a*	*Per cent difference^b*
Assault	60	157	+214
Purse snatching	0	0	0
Burglary	100	199	+ 99
Vandalism	6	31	+416
Theft from auto	13	15	+ 15
Theft auto accessories	38	98	+158

Crime	*Cabanne Place rate^a*	*Clemens Avenue rate^a*	*Per cent difference^b*
Assault	50	62	+ 24
Purse snatching	0	7	—
Burglary	100	185	+ 85
Vandalism	6	22	+267
Theft from auto	3	22	+ 69
Theft auto accessories	38	40	+ 5

[a] Rates computed using estimates of population derived from resident interview responses and U. S. Bureau of the Census, "Census of Housing, 1970, Block Statistics, Final Report HC(3)-137, St. Louis, Mo.-Ill.: Urbanized Area."
[b] Per cent difference is computed using private-street rate as the base.

Table 6.5 shows that the crime differences between public and private streets found in Tables 6.3 and 6.4 are also valid when comparing specific types of criminal behavior. Even though each street shows some idiosyncrasies in the criminal behavior experienced in each comparison, the private street has less crime in almost every category than the public street.

Since the privatizing of streets involves not only a change in the physical character of the streets but in the nature of its ownership, it is not surprising that certain types of crime are more affected than others by the difference in the tenure status of the street. Of the crimes examined, private status appears to have had the greatest impact in deterring crimes against persons and crimes of opportunity—that is, those crimes which usually take place within the street: assault, purse snatching, and auto-related theft. Crimes which take place against the home, such as burglary, are not as significantly affected. It should be kept in mind that the rear yards of adjacent public and private streets abut.

"Crimes of opportunity" are those in which a criminal is presented with an unanticipated opportunity for gain with minimal chance of intervention. The physical closure and private status of the private street work to limit access primarily to those who have legitimate presence. Furthermore, residents of private streets tend to recognize their neighbors and are hence more likely to perceive a stranger on the street. The data indicate that potential criminals may be aware of both these characteristics and thus be deterred from entering a private street and undertaking a crime on the street for fear of being recognized or apprehended. The burglary statistics, on the other hand, indicate that premeditated crimes are not affected by private status to the same degree. The breakdowns of crimes (Table 6.5) show that burglary is in fact the largest single contributor to the aggregate of private-street crime. In our paired comparisons between public and private streets, the differences in crime rate are smallest for burglaries. Two explanations are proposed for this phenomenon. First, physical closure and institutionalized ownership may make a stranger more obvious and residents more watchful, but it may do little to limit clandestine entry into a structure from the rear alleys and yards, which, although privately owned, are often only minimally fenced. Second, the very status of the private streets (composed of middle-class single-family homes) compared with adjacent public streets (composed of lower-income multifamily homes) may serve to label the private streets as lucrative targets for burglary.

Perception of Security

The data presented so far suggest that while the private streets do not experience as much criminal activity as do the surrounding public streets, their rate is not so low that one would anticipate that the residents consider themselves safe from crime. In fact, the crime rates on the private streets are such that one would expect residents to be aware of, and possibly concerned about, crime. In order to gauge the effect of private status on residents' perceptions of crime and their own safety, our staff attempted to determine whether the private-street residents perceived their street to be safer than the surrounding area.

Residents were asked about the safety of their neighborhoods and streets at night; whether they or anyone in their family had been victims of a crime over a two-year period; whether they were aware of any crimes committed against their neighbors, along with the specifics of any such crime; and finally, what crimes they felt were most common in their area.

We also undertook unobtrusive measures of residents' feelings of safety. This was done by recording residents' propensity for leaving the doors and windows of their houses and cars open and their personal possessions unattended on their front lawns and porches.

Table 6.6 presents the responses of residents of three private streets and a socially comparable public street to questions regarding neighborhood and street safety.

Table 6.6: Residents' Perception of Neighborhood/Street Safety at Night

St. Louis Streets

Street	Neighborhood unsafe?		Street unsafe?	
	Yes	*No*	*Yes*	*No*
Street 1 (private)	72.2%	27.8%	22.2%	77.8%
Street 2 (private)	53.3%	46.7%	33.3%	66.7%
Street 3 (private)	92.6%	7.4%	44.4%	55.6%
Street 4 (public)	78.3%	17.4%	73.9%	26.1%

Residents of each of the private streets felt that their street was considerably safer than the surrounding area. Depending on the private street taken, from 53 to 93 per cent of the residents felt that their neighborhood was unsafe at night, while from 22 to 44 per cent of those same residents felt that their street was unsafe. On the one public street where these questions were asked, residents made no significant differentiation between their street and the neighborhood, with about three quarters of the residents feeling that both areas were unsafe at night.

Table 6.7 presents the totals of all observations of windows open, doors open, and cars open on selected University City Streets located in Ames Place, a private area, and West Portland Place, a public area.

**Table 6.7: Unobtrusive Measures of Security
(House Doors and Windows and Cars)**

University City Streets

House windows	Private streets[a]	Public streets[b]
No. observed open	513/668[c]	347/883[c]
Per cent of total	77	39
House doors		
No. observed open	147/628[c]	145/872[c]
Per cent of total	23	17
Car doors or windows		
No. observed open	177/314[c]	177/648[c]
Per cent of total	56	27

[a] Based upon twenty-eight tours, taken on six different streets during fifteen different days.
[b] Based upon twenty-four observations, taken on three different streets, during fifteen different days.
[c] Numerator is number of houses or cars observed to be open; denominator is the total number of houses or cars observed.

The data show that automobiles parked on the private streets were left open with much greater frequency than those on the public streets. Additionally, first-floor windows facing the street were left open (with at least half of the window uncovered by draperies or curtains) more often on the private streets than on the public. The data for doors are inconclusive, as the doors on the private streets were left open only 6 per cent more frequently than those on the public streets.

The results of twenty-six separate tours undertaken in each of two sets of streets in University City — Ames Place and West Portland Place — to determine the variation in residents' tendencies to leave possessions unguarded on their lawns show that private street residents are 50 per cent more likely to leave possessions lying on their front lawns, porches, or sidewalks than are public street residents. The data also indicate that residents of private streets do engage in activity which reflects their overt statements about their feelings about safety and crime. Whether we examine a low-crime area like University City or a high-crime area like the Central West End of St. Louis, the results are similar: private-street residents do not greatly fear auto-related thefts, thefts of possessions left outside, or even residential burglary. Given the significant amount of burglary and petty theft which does occur on the private streets, it would appear that privatizing and physical closure work to create an aura of security from crime in spite of actual occurrence.

Comparison of Property Values

To determine whether closure and privatizing produced stability in property values we undertook a comparison of sale prices and property taxes in private versus public streets.

The two measures used to determine property value were: the prices asked by residents when they first put their homes on the market and the actual sale prices. For the Central West End study area two sources were used to obtain the sale price data: interviews with residents and federal sales-tax stamps affixed to the deeds of properties located on our study streets. As the stamps were not employed after 1968, resident interview responses were used to supplement and update the sample set.

Comparisons of housing sale price in the Central West End study areas are shown in Table 6.8.

Table 6.8: Comparison of Housing Sale Prices, St. Louis, 1960–73

Street	*Average price/room 1967 dollars*		*Per cent difference*[a]
Westminster Place (private)	2,089	(17)	+35.4
Washington Blvd. (public)	1,543	(7)	—
South side, adj. to Westminster Place	1,974	(3)	+61.9[b]
North side, adj. to Delmar Blvd.	1,219	(4)	—

[a] Per cent difference calculated with the public-street average price as a base. The number in parenthesis is the sample size, derived from all available data.
[b] Per cent difference calculated using Delmar Blvd. side of Washington Blvd. as a base.
SOURCE: Sale price sample derived from real estate sales tax stamps affixed to copies of deeds kept on file at the St. Louis City Hall and resident interviews.

To make comparison of sale prices on a street or between different streets meaningful, all sale-price data was converted to a common base year to eliminate distortions caused by inflation. A standard conversion was made to 1967 dollars, using the Consumer Price Index for homeownership.[4]

Although the homes on the public streets were similar to the homes on the private streets, it was realized that even a slight variation in size might make a difference in a property's market value. Several techniques were considered to take these variations into account. Pretesting showed that a per-room price conversion method was the most accurate because, according to real estate appraisers, the total number of rooms in a house proved a more important determining factor in a purchase than the over-all square-footage.

The table shows that houses on Westminster Place sold for more than structurally similar houses on adjacent public streets in spite of the fact that many of the dwellings on the public street were converted to multiple occupancy. Multiple-family structures, as income-producing properties, normally command higher prices than the single-family dwellings.

The variation in sale prices becomes even more interesting when broken down for either side of Washington Boulevard. The average price is considerably higher on the south side of the street abutting the rear of the homes on Westminster Place than on the north side of the street which backs on to the structures facing Delmar Boulevard, a decaying, although still active, commerical street. Whether Westminster is exerting a positive influence or Delmar a negative one is uncertain.

Table 6.9 below presents a comparison of housing sale prices in subdivisions in University City which are both socially and physically comparable.

The small differences between average prices per room for houses on private versus public streets may be due to the fact that the public subdivision, West Portland Place, is nested among the private subdivisions. This location may benefit from the protection buffer zones against encroaching change and heavy traffic. One West Portland resi-

Table 6.9: Comparison of Housing Sale Prices, University City, 1968–73

Socially and Physically Comparable Subdivisions

Subdivision	Average price/room 1967 dollars[a]		Per cent difference
Ames Place (private	2,802	(32)	—
West Portland Place (public)	2,495	(36)	−12

[a] The number in parentheses is the sample size, derived from all available data.

dent put it this way: "West Portland is in a desirable location; it's surrounded by private streets . . . For the money, it was the best place for us to buy even though it's a public street."

A year-by-year analysis of sale prices in the University City study area showed that average sale prices in private subdivisions, like public subdivisions, are not free from the effects of change. During the late 1960s, University City experienced a large influx of black residents from neighboring St. Louis. During this period (1970–71) a change in the school system was also under consideration. The combination of events led to a rapid loss of confidence in University City and a corresponding decline in property values in both the private and public subdivisions. After months of debate, the proposed change in the school system was defeated. Real estate prices in the private-street subdivisions have since experienced a significant upturn, whereas those in West Portland Place have remained comparatively low.

In order to obtain a measure of residents' perception of the worth of their homes in University City, we compared the residents' asking prices with actual sale prices. We assumed that the residents of private streets would place a higher value on their property than residents of public streets owning comparable houses. The comparison revealed that residents of private streets not only perceived their homes as being

Table 6.10: Incremental Comparison of Average Asking and Sale Prices, University City, 1968–73

Socially and Physically Comparable Subdivisions

PRICES EQUATED TO 1967 DOLLARS

Average final asking price/room[a]	Average actual sale price/room	Per cent difference
AMES PLACE (private)		
3,405 (6)	2,865	18.8
2,943 (11)	2,657	10.7
2,651 (13)	2,572	3.0
2,881 (6)	2,597	10.9
2,402 (1)	2,180	10.2
	Average percent difference	10.7
WEST PORTLAND PLACE (public)		
2,641 (6)	2,465	7.1
2,573 (16)	2,436	5.6
2,531 (12)	2,462	2.8
	Average percent difference	5.6

[a] Houses are grouped together by similarity in number of rooms/house. The number in parenthesis is the number of houses used to obtain the average in each category. Data were obtained through the files and published weekly reports of the Real Estate Service Corporation (RESCO), a local company founded in 1976, which maintains listings of most homes on the market handled by realtors.

worth more than equivalent properties on public streets, but more than
the market would actually bring. The residents of private streets are
clearly confident about the stability of their property values, even to
the point of being unrealistic in their estimation of their property's
worth. The private streets obviously breed a feeling of security and op-
timism in residents not found on public streets.

Table 6.10 presents a comparison of average final asking prices
with actual sale prices in a subdivision of private streets versus a subdivision of public streets in University City.

Comparison of Assessed Valuations

As a further check on our data concerning the market value of
homes on private and public streets, we examined how the municipalities themselves assessed comparative properties. Using the record
ledgers kept by the appropriate tax assessor's office as our source of
data, we compiled random samples on assessments of properties on
comparable public and private streets.

Without exception, the St. Louis properties on the private streets
were found in 1971 to have a higher average assessment than those on
adjacent public streets. A comparison of these findings is made in
Table 6.11

These differences are even more remarkable when one considers
that multifamily profit-producing housing is normally assessed at a
higher rate than single-family private residences. The single-family
structures on the private streets have the higher assessed value in spite
of the fact that the public streets used in these comparisons have
houses in good condition which have been converted to multiple-family
occupancy.

Table 6.11: Property Assessment Comparisons, St. Louis, 1971

Street	Average assessment[a]		Per cent difference[b]
Westminster Place (private)	$8,307.69	(26)	—
Washington Boulevard (public)	$7,782.80	(25)	−6.3
Cabanne Place (private)	$7,003.70	(27)	—
Cates Avenue (public)	$5,334.00	(25)	−23.8
Clemens Avenue (public)	$5,844.83	(29)	−16.6

[a] "Assessment" represents the combined value of both the land and the improvement on the land. The number in parenthesis is the number of houses
used to obtain the average.
[b] Per cent difference computed using the average private-street assessment in
each grouping as the base number.
SOURCE: Data obtained from the City Tax Assessor's Office, St. Louis.

Table 6.12: Property Assessment Comparisons, St. Louis, 1971–73

Street	Average 1971 assessment[a]		Average 1973 assessment		Per cent change
Westminster Place (private)	$8,307.69	(26)	$7,120.77	(26)	−14.3
Washington Boulevard (public)	$7,782.80	(25)	$6,091.60	(25)	−21.7

[a] "Assessment" represents the combined value of both the land and the improvement on the land. The number in parenthesis is the number of houses used to obtain the average.
SOURCE: Data obtained from the City Tax Assessor's Office, St. Louis.

Between 1971 and 1973, average assessments had decreased on both public and private streets, but, as Table 6.12 indicates, this decrease was greater for the properties on the public street.

An interview with the assessor revealed that this difference was the result of better maintenance and a higher level of stability on the private street, Westminster Place. According to the assessor, assessments were reduced on the private street as well because the total area was suffering deterioration.

Comparison of Rented Versus Owner-Occupied Property

Although our analysis of real estate data was primarily concerned with property values and market behavior, attention was also given to differences in dwelling utilization on private and public streets. We were interested in the degree to which those homeowners in threatened areas who could not sell their homes at a good price would rent them as income-producing property. Any property whose owner was found to have a mailing address different from that of the property was assumed to have an occupant other than its owner and was therefore considered a rental property. The resulting data showed that the private streets in the Central West End of St. Louis have a lower rate of nonowner occupancy than their adjacent public streets (see Table 6.13). It should

Table 6.13: Nonowner-Occupied Structures, St. Louis (1973)

Street	Nonowner-occupied structures	Per cent of total no. structures on street
Westminster Place (private)	1	1.9
Washington Boulevard (public)	8	16.3
Waterman Avenue (public)	20	41.7
Cabanne Place (private)	1	2.5
Clemens Avenue (public)	6	11.3

SOURCE: Data derived from 1973 property assessment records, City Tax Assessor's Office, St. Louis.

be noted that there are no deed restrictions on the private streets preventing the rental of dwellings.

A similar analysis was completed for the University City study area which compares socially as well as physically similar streets. A count of house rentals was extracted from the University City occupancy permits; the data is presented in Table 6.14. The differences between private and public streets were not as dramatic as in St. Louis but the public subdivision, West Portland Place, was still shown to have more than twice the percentage of rentals of the three comparable private associations.

Table 6:14: Rented Structures, University City, 1968–73

Subdivision	No. rented structures during six-year period	Per cent of total no. structures on street
Parkview (private)	12	7.3
Ames Place (private)	12	6.7
University Heights (private)	4	3.6
West Portland Place (public)	28	15.2

SOURCE: Data obtained from University City occupancy permit files.

Extent of Demolitions

The consequences of social change and real estate speculation in St. Louis have been deterioration, noninvestment, and, ultimately, abandonment. As structures have been abandoned, the city of St. Louis has demolished them. We expected that there would be few such demolitions on the private streets. From records in the St. Louis Department of Building Permits, we were able to determine the total number of demolitions executed by the city. A comparison of demolitions (Table 6.15) shows that the private streets in St. Louis have not experienced the extent of deterioration or abandonment of adjacent public streets.

In summary, property values on private streets have been found to be comparatively stable, but it must be said that they do not rise as rapidly as property values in the suburbs. A very important attribute of the private-street system is that it creates a covenant among residents to restrict the zoning of the street to single-family dwellings. The erosion which normally attends the multiple-family rezoning is thus avoided. For this reason, houses on private streets in neighborhoods undergoing rapid change take longer to sell. Some private-street cor-

Table 6.15: Structures Demolished,
St. Louis, 1937–73

Street	No. of demolitions
Westminster Place (private)	0
Washington Boulevard (public)	10
Cabanne Place (private)	3
Clemens Avenue (public)	9
Cates Avenue (public)	12

SOURCE: Data obtained from the St. Louis Department of Building Permits.

porations have been known to purchase a home from a departing resident who has had to sell quickly rather than allow the resident to sell to a family who would not be able to keep up the property. The street association then resells the house at a more leisurely pace and is able to attract both a higher-income family and a higher price.

The Benefits of the Private Streets to Their Surrounding Communities

The private streets are alleged to facilitate racial integration at two levels: at the level of neighboring houses within a street and at the level of neighboring streets within the neighborhood. At the level of the neighborhood, the private streets create a sufficient sense of security and aura of stability to allow middle-class residents, white and black, to remain in the neighborhood. At the level of the individual private street, closure in combination with the legal association provides a strong enough mechanism to prevent residents from panicking when a few additional black families move onto a street. Private-street residents do not fear that there will be a sudden rush of selling by their neighbors and that they will be left with deflated property values.

In most neighborhoods the influx of black residents is regarded as the prelude to higher crime, conversion to multiple occupancy, poor maintenance, and the decline of housing values. On the private street, the theory goes, this equation is nullified because residents feel secure enough in their ability to control activity on their street and to prevent conversion to multifamily occupancy and the physical decay which accompanies it. The private-street association is said to provide a vehicle for protecting the community interest with regard to the maintenance of housing values and the quality of the street environment. It can provide for integration without panic and can serve as an instrument for community acceptance.

Many of the white-populated private streets do in fact have a few black households, but very little integration actually occurs at the street level. Estimates of the percentage of black-occupied dwelling units on private streets included in this study (derived from interviews and census data) show that in St. Louis, Pershing Place has 2 per cent black residents; Kingsbury Place, 5 per cent; Westminster Place, 0 per cent; Waterman Place, 20 per cent; Cabanne Place, 90 per cent; Lewis Place, 100 per cent. In University City the figures are Ames Place, 2 per cent; Parkview, 2 per cent; University Heights, 0 per cent.

If we examine the claim that the private streets help to maintain community amenities, we find that in St. Louis the public schools are not educational environments to which middle-income families send their children. In University City, however, because of the large concentration of private streets and the general middle-class character of some public streets, many of the public schools are still used by the children of middle-income families. Residents of the private streets in St. Louis send their children to private school, and can afford to do so, for the following reasons. The homes on the private streets located within the city of St. Louis now sell for about $30,000, with some of the better, remodeled homes occasionally selling for as high as $40,000. An equivalent home of the same general age and condition located in one of the white suburbs of St. Louis would sell for from $55,000 to $90,000. This explains one of the key attractions of purchasing a house within the private streets of St. Louis. The value of the purchase, as an item for immediate use, is excellent. But a family with children living on a private street in St. Louis must also include in their monthly accounting the cost of sending their children to private schools. Furthermore, the resale value of their home is not likely to increase as rapidly as a home in the suburbs. The difference in monthly payments between a $30,000 home on a private street in St. Louis and a $55,000 home in the suburbs must be supplemented by the residents of the private street in monthly tuition fees for their children in private schools. The suburban purchaser may be getting less of a home for his larger monthly payments, but he has the use of public schools and a home which will increase in value more rapidly because of its location —assuming it was reasonably well built (Figure 6.14).

It is not surprising, therefore, that the people who are attracted to the private streets of St. Louis (as distinct from those in University City) have a tendency to be families with few or no children. Residents are either older families who have lived there before the changes in their neighborhood took place, or families with few children or with young children who are not of a school age. Some religious Catholic

Fig. 6.14: Private house, at left, and school, at right, in a suburb of St. Louis. The modest one-story house sells for the same price as older two- and three-story stone houses on the converted private streets in St. Louis. However, the suburban middle-class residents are able to use the public schools their taxes pay for and so do not have the additional expense of private schooling for their children.

and Jewish families who would send their children to private parochial schools no matter where they lived are also found on the private streets.

The children of public-street residents in St. Louis may not attend public schools with the children of private street, but they do benefit from the school taxes paid by the middle-income private-street residents.

The Possibility of Closure Without Privatizing

The physical closure of the private streets has been shown to create a sense of place for its residents; it serves to redefine the street as a social space and encourages interaction among residents. But must the physical closure of the street be tied to street ownership to provide these benefits? There are some streets in St. Louis that are closed to through traffic but that are not private. The evidence indicates that closure can be of benefit without privatizing in that it creates a more amenable residential environment, allows the street to be utilized as a communal space, facilitates recognition among neighbors, and increases social interaction; however, if it is employed as a mechanism to counteract declining property values, blockbusting, zoning changes, and abandonment, it is unlikely, in itself, to provide the social and legal reinforcement necessary to resist change. Physical closure without privatizing will be found to be more convenient to some municipalities because it enables them to maintain the right to rescind closure should they choose to do so at some future date. A street which is closed but not private remains dependent upon municipal action to protect it from changes in zoning; there are no legal restrictions which the residents of the street can apply to protect themselves.

The Possibility of Association Without Privatizing

If the private-street association acts as a vehicle for residents' self-determination, might it not be possible that a simple street or block association, not tied to private status, could serve the same purpose? The evidence indicates that public-block associations do not provide residents with the same protections as private associations. Public-block associations are voluntary organizations with no legal standing. They are normally ill-defined with no specific corporate structure, rights, or responsibilities. They have no sanctions they can apply to prevent deleterious actions on the part of individual residents and must depend upon the municipal authorities to protect their environment. The effectiveness of a public-block association is directly tied to the level of involvement of its members on a day-to-day basis. When there are no important issues facing a block association, interest wanes and the association becomes relatively dormant. During these periods of low interest, the association rarely acts as an overseer of street affairs. It a particular issue threatening to the stability of the street arises at some later time, there is usually considerable time lag before the association can confront the problem by which time it may be too late to do very much about it. Private associations, on the other hand, can act immediately through their trustees because they have a legally defined mandate to allow them to do so.

The Replicability of the St. Louis Model

Before drawing any conclusions about the ability of other cities to replicate the private streets of St. Louis, we must ask whether there is anything peculiarly unique to the private-street areas of St. Louis and University City which make them continually attractive to middle-income families and provide sufficient incentive for such families to purchase homes in areas of rapid transition.

There are two magnets, peculiar to this area of St. Louis, which have served to make the private streets of both St. Louis and University City attractive over time: the proximity of two major universities (with their medical complexes) and a major park (Forest Park). Both provide the residents with stabilizing elements and cultural, recreational, and job opportunities. Forest Park, a two-square-mile area containing the St. Louis Zoo, an open-air amphitheater, a planetarium, two golf courses, lakes, picnic grounds, and ball fields, is located less than one mile from most of the white-populated private streets. Forest Park, in fact, serves as a regional resource for cities more than one hundred miles from St. Louis. Abutting the western side of the park is Washington University, one of the better private universities in the Midwest. Adjacent to it is Concordia Seminary University, a Roman Catholic institution of higher learning of good quality. On the east side of the park is a complex of hospitals associated with Washington University and providing some of the best medical services in the Midwest. Many of the faculty and staff members of these institutions desire to live close to their place of work. Not surprisingly, the private streets serve as neighborhoods for university and hospital employees. These institutions are stabilizing elements in that they represent substantial investments which are not likely to disappear overnight. They are also staffed and occupied by professionals, making them status institutions.

Such a juxtaposition of older, quality residential streets with institutions or large scale recreational amenities is not unique to St. Louis: they occur in most American cities as do the stabilizing benefits that accrue to surrounding residential streets. The mechanism of the privatizing of streets provides an additional stabilizing element necessary to making these institutions and their surrounding neighborhoods viable over time.

Privatizing has been shown to be a successful technique for stabilizing streets located in transitional urban areas. While the character of the St. Louis environment is not unique in America, the magnitude and rate of the changes that have occurred there is somewhat atypical. The success of the private streets in so rapidly changing an environment suggests that the concept will certainly be equally successful if applied to a less rapidly changing urban area. In implementing the concept in another city, however, certain qualifications should be kept in mind. Implementation of the private-street concept in a city which has no previous experience with private streets may prove difficult. Privatizing is not a unilateral action which can be mandated by the municipal authorities — it requires the active co-operation and initiative of the residents of that street. Originally, the process of returning streets to private ownership required that all of the residents of a street (literally 100 per cent of the households) agree to change its status from public to private. Most recently, the City of St. Louis has begun to consider petitions for privatizing requiring only 95 per cent of the residents' signatures.

In addition, privatizing requires the residents' corporation to accept financial responsibility for maintaining their street. This financial burden takes the form of a yearly assessment of from $50 to $100 per household for the general maintenance of the street. On occasion it may also include special assessments for major repairs. Additionally, upon their street's becoming private, residents are required to share the cost of purchasing the underground service lines from the city — a considerable expense — although some cities may choose not to make this a requirement. While these financial responsibilities may not represent a burden to middle-income families, a moderate-income family may find them prohibitive. This problem could be solved by developing an alternative whereby moderate-income residents contributed a portion of their own labor to maintain the street.

But for all this to happen, residents of a private street must recognize the utility of the concept and agree to the covenant transferring ownership of and responsibility for the street to them. Without the ready examples of a number of successful private streets, this may prove difficult to achieve. If this type of program is to be encouraged in a particular city, an educational program or experiment may be required, and the city will have to devise a privatizing procedure which will make the attainment of that status as easy as possible. In such experiments, physical closure alone may be undertaken as a first step in displaying some of the benefits.

VII

Design Principles for Different Housing/Resident Type Combinations

In the previous chapter I demonstrated that communities of interest could be created in streets composed of single-family houses; in Chapters IX and X I will demonstrate how they can be created in new and existing housing developments. However, prior to embarking upon the programming and design of entire developments it is essential to describe the principles employed in building design and site planning to facilitate the creation of communities of interest.

The first and most critical step in creating a housing development with community of interest is to select building types which are most suited to the life-styles and needs of the occupant groups. This is a rule that, in housing practice, is more often honored in the breach. All the other design guidelines are secondary and supportive of this basic requirement.

Unfortunately, each building type has a narrow density (units per acre) range at which it can be built, so that the density requirement of a particular development, as determined by land costs, itself dicates the use of certain types of buildings. As each building type varies in its suitability for the housing needs of different types of families, the dictates of density and suitability at times come into conflict — particularly at the high end of the density range. Later in this chapter a comparative set of drawings is provided illustrating, at a glance, the density limitations of different building types but, starting with the more important requirements, the following summarizes previous discussion of the suitability of different housing types to the needs of various types of families and life-style groups.

There are many different ways of classifying families and life-style groups just as there are many types of residents who avoid classification. Every classification system suffers from simplification. However, our desire to avoid simplification often results in reaching no conclusions. There is much of immediate utility that can be learned from a classification of life-style groups, even though this may require that we gloss over interesting complexities. For our purposes, we will use two criteria in classifying residents: income and life-style. The income of the resident population is critical in evaluating the suitability of different building types because high incomes and rents can buy the presence of a doorman and porters, who, in turn, can make an otherwise unsuitable building type workable. For the purposes of this discussion, I have identified three life-style groups: families with children, working adults, and retired elderly. These three life-style categories, although sometimes including people of different ages within the same group, serve to identify the primary pursuits of the individuals within the group and their resultant demands from their residential environment.

The "families with children" category contains two distinctly different age groups: children and adults. Where the requirements of home for each age group within such a family are, on occasion, different, they are rarely in irresolvable conflict in that all members in a family with children are supposed to be united in a common purpose. At times, though, one suspects that the tolerance of one age group of the demands of the other is just barely sustained by the fact of their being related. The superior bargaining position of the adults is probably the factor that deters most potential conflicts.

The "working adults" category contains people of different ages who, whether married or single, young or old, spend the greater part of their day at work. As a consequence, these households' members' activities are centered away from home. Their evening and weekend activities follow similar patterns in that evening meals are often consumed away from home and weekends are often spent in travel. The "working adult" category contains everyone from young adults fresh out of school to older adults whose children have grown and left home.

The "retired elderly" category contains people of a distinct age group, even though the range in ages may vary by as much as twenty years.

(College students form a further category and will not be considered in this study, except that they can normally be classed as working adults.)

The three life-style groups identified above use their homes in different ways. Families with children and the retired elderly tend to occupy their homes environments continuously, while working adults tend to use their home environments in the evenings and on weekends.

Families with Children

For families with children, the home and its environs is where much of the daily activity is centered. When not at school, children play in and around the home continuously. They also seek out companionship and interactions with children and adults in neighboring homes. The adult that stays at home to raise the children occupies the family's home environment even more fully. Children are so much the focus and purpose of a family with children that much of the form of the home environment and its surroundings is directed toward satisfying their needs. Even the interaction among adult neighbors is often generated by children in that children introduce their parents to each other and parents will occasionally share in the chores and responsibilities of caring for each other's children.

For children, the home environment must be designed to facilitate access to outside grounds and play areas. These grounds and play areas are best located in close proximity to the interior of the dwelling unit to facilitate the supervision of the children by adults within the home. The younger the children, the closer to home they will want to play. Teen-age children, on the other hand, prefer to play some distance from the home environment. Their play facilities should not, however, be placed so far away that the activities of the teen-agers cannot be supervised.[1]

Children are in and out of the house on a continuing basis all day long. They cannot be counted on to be conscientious about rules involving the use of elevators, entry doors, and exits. They are easily frustrated by intercoms, and their parents will not always entrust them with door keys, particularly in a high-crime neighborhood. To facilitate their access to multiple dwellings, children will often vandalize locking hardware on entry and exit doors and inactivate the intercoms. They will place chewing gum in the latch portion of the lock, twist doors on their hinges, and break the glass panels in a door to gain access to the interior knobs of the common entry doors controlled by the intercom.[2]

The occupation of a high-rise building by many families with children but with no funds for doormen will result in the interior common circulation areas' becoming virtually public in nature. The use of doormen in such a circumstance can help to reduce security and vandalism problems but this is by no means as effective as it would be if the same building was occupied exclusively by elderly or working adults. It is clear that families with children are best placed in walk-up environments with play facilities located as close to a building entry as noise will permit.[3]

Buildings designed with as few apartment units as possible sharing a collectively defined territory—both within the building and on its outside grounds—are a critical requirement for the successful creation of a satisfactory and controllable environment for families with children. Families with children who cannot afford the use of doormen and elevator operators should be placed in nonelevator buildings with as few families as possible sharing a common entry. Single-family row houses are the preferred solution, followed by walk-ups. The cost of the land will be critical in determining the density required and, as a consequence, the height of the walk-up. This is particulary true if there is no demand for high-rise housing for the elderly or for working-adults in the same development. As will be demonstrated later, a three-story walk-up can produce a density of thirty-five units to the acre, while a five-and-a-half-story walk-up will produce a density of seventy-two units to the acre. However, where the three story walk-up can be designed to have only six families sharing an entry, the five-and-a-half-story walk-up will have twelve families sharing an entry.

The Retired Elderly

The retired elderly, like families with children, tend to center much of their daily activity in and around the environs of their home. This proves to be even more the case with elderly of low or moderate income who have little in the way of disposable income for travel. However, where families with children are inwardly oriented (that is, they spend much of their time with other members of the nuclear family), the elderly, by contrast, tend to seek out the companionship of other families—most often, other elderly. It is not surprising that many elderly seek residential environments which are occupied by other elderly and that they place much importance on this criterion in the choice of the environment to which they move.[4] The building type selected for elderly residents should therefore be one which facilitates the interaction of neighbors.

There are no types of residential buildings which are not suitable for use by the elderly; the only type which produces any difficulty at all is the walk-up, but here the problem is one of ease of access rather than of interaction between neighbors or of control of public areas. As the retired elderly grow still older, the problem of climbing a flight or two of stairs — particularly with groceries — can become severe. Although row-house environments facilitate easy access to the grounds and neighboring families, the building type which is most conducive to the interaction of gregarious elderly is the high-rise elevator building. In a high-rise there are no stairs for the elderly to climb to reach their apartments and, with a push of an elevator button, each resident has access to hundreds of other residents.

Although elderly who have never lived in a high-rise building may be reluctant to consider doing so upon retirement, once having had the experience they show a marked preference for elevator buildings over walk-ups because they can then avoid the use of stairs completely. The elderly also benefit by having a large group of like people housed together under one roof, in that ancillary services can be provided by management which would not be possible in buildings where the elderly are few. The inclusion of a health clinic, a meal service center, and other special amenities can be economically justified in even low-income elderly high-rise buildings serving two hundred or more units. One final reason for advocating the housing of the elderly exclusively in their own building is that in buildings where the low-income elderly are mixed with families with teen-age children the crime rate suffered by the elderly climbs as high as five times that experienced by the average project resident.[5]

Assigning all elderly to one building need not result in the creation of communities composed solely of the elderly. An all-elderly building can be placed adjacent to buildings housing families with children, with the elderly building and its outside grounds distinctly defined for the use of its residents only. Those elderly who desire contact with young families can find it in common park areas provided for the use of all residents in the larger development. In interviews conducted by several study groups, it was found that many elderly express a clear preference for living among other elderly and having contact with younger families only at their own choosing.[6] Other elderly, however, find such environments stigmatize them as old and the limited contact of other elderly boring.[7] This latter group might well be placed in high-rises which are also occupied by working adults, both young and old.

Buildings occupied entirely by elderly residents do not always require doormen. Many low-income, all-elderly high-rise buildings exist which comfortably house two hundred to three hundred families to the acre and are perfectly secure without the benefit of doormen, despite the fact that they are located in low-income areas. The fact that low-income retired elderly have few financial resources results in their spending much of their time in and around their building socializing with each other. It is common for them to set up tables and chairs in the building lobby for community activities. Such groupings also serve as control stations. In an all-elderly building, the uniform physical characteristics of old people differentiates them from all potential intruders who are likely to prey upon them. Most importantly, the elderly, as a group, are conscientious about security and will, without being continually asked, keep emergency exit doors locked and unused. By 11:00 P.M. a community of retired elderly will normally all be in bed, and the main entry door to their building can be locked and the building secured.

Working Adults

Working adults do not perceive their home environments as their living milieu, but rather like a base of operations. Young working adults tend to use their home environments much as travelers use hotel rooms—as a place to sleep, shower, and change clothing. They do, on occasion, use their homes for entertainment, but this use is usually limited to the interior confines of the apartment unit.

Some high-rises designed for occupancy by working adults provide communal recreation facilities—such as tennis courts and pools—on the grounds of the development as an added attraction, but their use is intermittent and has been found to be largely confined to particular residents.

This minimal presence of working adults in their apartments and their sparse use of the areas outside them combine to make the public areas of their buildings and grounds difficult to control. The dwelling units of working adults, whether apartments or row houses, are highly vulnerable to burglary when the residents are away at work. Not surprisingly, residential environments without doormen (i.e., row houses and walk-ups) occupied by working adults have been found to experience more burglaries than row houses or walk-ups occupied by families with children or the retired elderly. For all of the above reasons it is strongly recommended that working adults be provided with housing in high-rise elevator buildings which are provided with round-the-clock doormen and a custodial staff to control the interior public areas of the building. Such environments can be built and maintained for this life-style group with great economy. As working adults have little desire or need for living areas immediately outside their apartments, the provision and maintenance of such spaces need only be minimal. The provision of doormen in high-rises occupied by moderate-income working adults is therefore economically feasible. Thus for one type of low-income resident, the elderly, and one type of moderate-income resident, the working adult, it is possible to duplicate the safe high-rise building that is provided for upper-income residents.

Such use of high-rise buildings provides much of the solution to the problem of building high-density urban housing for low- and moderate-income residents while still providing walk-ups for families with children. The upper density limit for three-story walk-up buildings for families with children is about fifty apartment units to the acre, but in the heavily built up areas of many major U.S. cities the high cost of land requires that we build at one hundred units to the acre and more. By designing a development as a mixture of walk-ups for families with children at fifty units to the acre and high-rises for the elderly or working adults at from one hundred fifty to two hundred fifty units to the acre, we can achieve an average density of about one hundred units to the acre, depending on the percentage of units assigned to each family type.

Table 7.1 summarizes the recommendations of this chapter regarding the suitability of various building types to the needs of different types of residents. The table lists the four main categories of building types and juxtaposes them against the three basic family types identified by life-style. The two categories of elevator buildings (3) and (4) have, in turn, been further broken down into doorman and nondoorman buildings. These are the only two building types in which the use of doormen is considered economical. Because of the low rents paid by moderate- and low-income groups, the only building type which can have a doorman assigned to it is the elavator high-rise.

For families with children, single-family houses, walk-ups, and medium high-rise buildings with doormen are recommended. Medium

Table 7.1: The Assignment of Family Types to Building Types

Family Type	Building Types					
	1. Single-family	2. Walk-ups	3. Medium High-Rise		4. Elevator High-Rise	
			Doorman	Non-doorman	Doorman	Non-doorman
Families with children	**	**	*	●	●	■
Elderly	*	■	**	*	**	*
Working adults	■	●	**	■	**	■

** strongly recommended   ● barely acceptable
 * recommended   ■ not recommended

high-rise buildings without doormen (fifty dwelling units per entry, maximum) are considered barely acceptable and even then, only for two-parent families.

For the elderly, virtually every building type is recommended except walk-ups, as long as the buildings are kept exclusively for the elderly. The high- and medium-rise elevator buildings with doormen are the ones most strongly recommended for the elderly.

For working singles and couples, the ideal environment is the high-rise building provided with round-the-clock doormen. Single-family homes and high-rise buildings without doormen are not recommended for working adults. Walk-ups are considered barely acceptable.

Unfortunately, even though we may recognize the comparative suitability of different building types, the provision of the best type may not always be possible because of the density requirements of the site — that is, the land may be too costly to allow the construction of a low-density development. However, some types of walk-up developments can be built at a high density. The following set of drawings were prepared to provide a quick guide to the density limits of different housing types.

Figures 7.2 through 7.13 together frame a synoptic view of the density that can be achieved by different housing types on the typical acre of urban land illustrated in Figure 7.1. In this set of illustrations the density range is from six units to the acre for the single-family house in Figure 7.2, to one hundred three units to the acre for the high-rise in Figure 7.13. The most important point revealed by these diagrams is that at the middle-density range at which most urban housing is built —

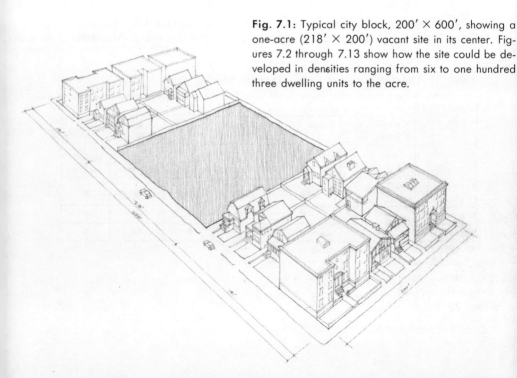

Fig. 7.1: Typical city block, 200′ × 600′, showing a one-acre (218′ × 200′) vacant site in its center. Figures 7.2 through 7.13 show how the site could be developed in densities ranging from six to one hundred three dwelling units to the acre.

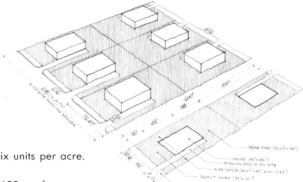

Fig. 7.2: One-story detached houses, six units per acre.
— Detached houses on 1-acre site
— Site dimensions: 218' × 200' = 43,600 sq. ft.
— 3 units per side = 6 units per acre
— Typical interior unit dimension: 30' × 40' = 1,200 sq. ft.
— 1,200 sq ft. = 3-bedroom unit
— Parking: 6 on-site spaces

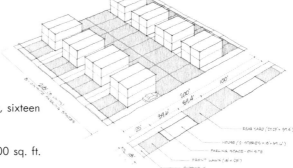

Fig. 7.3: Two-story semidetached houses, sixteen units per acre.
— Semidetached houses on 1-acre site
— Site dimensions: 218' × 200' = 43,600 sq. ft.
— 8 units per side = 16 units per acre
— Typical anterior unit dimension: 17' × 37.6' × 2 stories = 1,280 sq. ft.
— 1,200 sq. ft. = 3-bedroom unit; + 40 sq. ft. of stairs per floor
— Parking: 16 on-site spaces

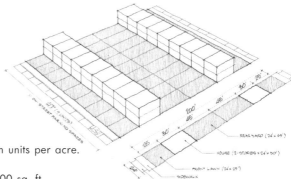

Fig. 7.4: Two-story row houses, eighteen units per acre.
— Row houses on 1-acre site
— Site dimensions: 217' × 200' = 43,400 sq. ft.
— 9 units per side = 18 units per acre
— Typical interior unit dimension: 23' × 28' × 2 stories = 1,288 sq. ft.
— 1,200 sq. ft. = 3-bedroom unit; + 40 sq. ft. of stairs per floor
— Parking: 22 on-street spaces

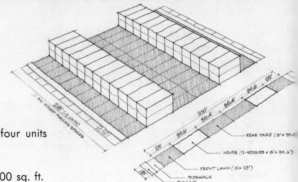

Fig. 7.5: Two-story row houses, twenty-four units per acre.
—Row houses on 1-acre site
—Site dimensions: 217′ × 200′ = 43,400 sq. ft.
—Typical interior unit dimensions: 17′ × 37.6′ × 2 stories = 1,280 ft.
—1,200 sq. ft. = 3-bedroom unit; + 40 sq. ft. of stairs per floor
—Parking: 22 on-street spaces.

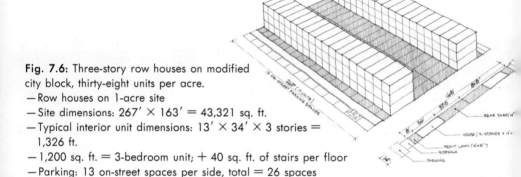

Fig. 7.6: Three-story row houses on modified city block, thirty-eight units per acre.
—Row houses on 1-acre site
—Site dimensions: 267′ × 163′ = 43,321 sq. ft.
—Typical interior unit dimensions: 13′ × 34′ × 3 stories = 1,326 ft.
—1,200 sq. ft. = 3-bedroom unit; + 40 sq. ft. of stairs per floor
—Parking: 13 on-street spaces per side, total = 26 spaces

Fig. 7.7: Three-story garden apartments, thirty-six units per acre.
—Garden apartments on 1-acre site, 6 units per entry
—Site dimensions: 218′ × 200′ = 43,600 sq. ft.
—18 units per side = 36 units per acre
—Typical interior unit dimensions: 29′ × 41.4′ = 1,202 sq. ft.
—1,200 sq. ft. = 3-bedroom unit
—Parking: 10 spaces per side on street = 20 spaces; + 16 on-site spaces in interior; total = 36 spaces

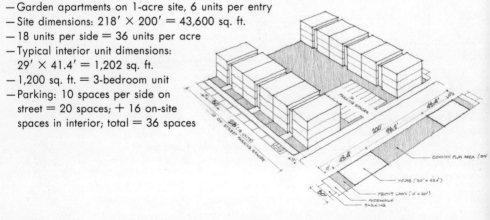

Fig. 7.8: Six-story medium high-rise apartment house, thirty-five units per acre.
— Medium high-rise apartments on 1-acre site, 35 units per entry
— Site dimensions: 218' × 200' = 43,600 sq. ft.
— 6 apartments per floor
— Typical interior unit areas per floor: 2 apartments
  @ 1,200 sq. ft. + 4 apartments @ 1,280 sq. ft.
— 1,200 sq. ft. = 3-bedroom unit
— Parking: 44 on-site spaces

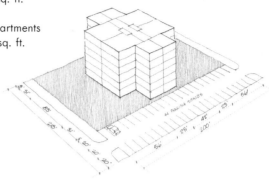

Fig. 7.9: Seven-story medium high-rise apartment house, fifty-five units per acre.
— Medium high-rise apartments on 1-acre site, 55
  units per entry
— Site dimensions: 218' × 200' = 43,600 sq. ft.
— 8 apartments per floor
— Typical interior unit areas per floor: 4 apartments
  @ 1,202 sq. ft. + 4 apartments @ 1,227 sq. ft.
— 1,200 sq. ft. = 3-bedroom unit
— Parking: 44 on-site spaces

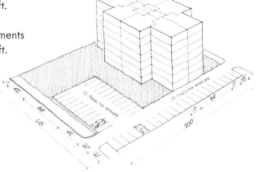

Fig. 7.10: Four-story European-style walk-up, fifty-six units per acre.
— Walk up apartments on 1-acre site, 28 units/entry
— Site dimensions: 218' × 200' = 43,600 sq. ft.
— 28 units per side = 56 units per acre
— Typical interior unit dimensions:
  27.7' × 43.4' = 1,202 sq. ft.
— Typical interior unit dimensions,
  duplex: 13.35' × 48.8' × 2
  = 1,282 sq. ft.
— 1,200 sq. ft. = 3-bedroom unit;
  + 40 sq. ft. of stairs per floor
  for duplex
— Parking: 22 on-street spaces per side;
  total = 44 spaces

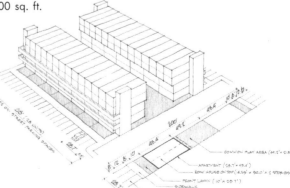

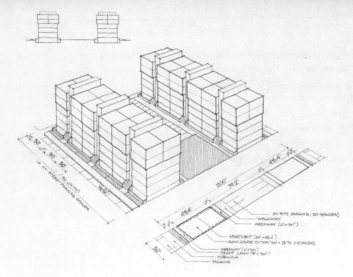

Fig. 7.11: Five-and-a-half-story high-density walk-up, seventy-two units per acre.
—Walk up apartments on 1-acre site, 12 units/entry
—Site dimensions: 218′ × 200′ = 43,600 sq. ft.
—36 units per side = 72 units per acre
—Typical interior unit dimensions, duplex: 29′ × 22.2′ × 2 = 1,288 sq. ft.
—1,200 sq. ft. = 3-bedroom unit; + 40 sq. ft. of stairs per floor
—Parking: 30 on-site spaces + 20 on-street spaces: total = 50 spaces

twenty-five to seventy units to the acre—there is sufficient variation in the types of housing available to allow the designer to pick the housing type most suitable for the resident group who will be occupying it.

With a density of fifty-five units to the acre, one can either opt for the high-rise solution shown in Figure 7.9 or build a four-story walk-up, as shown in Figure 7.10. The upper two stories of the four-story walk-up form a maisonette that residents have to walk up two floors to gain access to.

Figure 7.11 illustrates the maximum density that can be achieved in a site plan composed of walk-up units. This building type is five-and-a-half stories in height. The upper two stories form a maisonette unit, and the lowest story is sunk half a floor below the ground to keep the over-

Fig. 7.12: Twelve-story twin-tower apartment house, ninety-four units per acre.
—High-rise apartment house on 1-acre site, 2 buildings, 47 units per entry.
—Site dimensions: 218′ × 200′ = 43,600 sq. ft.
—47 units per tower, 4 units per floor = 94 units per acre
—Typical interior unit dimensions: approx. 40′ × 32′ (unit actually 1,194 sq. ft due to corners)
—Parking: 20 on-site spaces per side; total 40 spaces

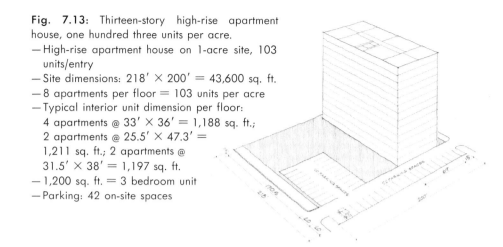

Fig. 7.13: Thirteen-story high-rise apartment house, one hundred three units per acre.
— High-rise apartment house on 1-acre site, 103 units/entry
— Site dimensions: 218' × 200' = 43,600 sq. ft.
— 8 apartments per floor = 103 units per acre
— Typical interior unit dimension per floor:
  4 apartments @ 33' × 36' = 1,188 sq. ft.;
  2 apartments @ 25.5' × 47.3' =
  1,211 sq. ft.; 2 apartments @
  31.5' × 38' = 1,197 sq. ft.
— 1,200 sq. ft. = 3 bedroom unit
— Parking: 42 on-site spaces

all height down for the families living in the unit on the top two floors. These families must walk up a total of three-and-a-half floors to get to their apartments: half a floor outside the building and three floors inside the building. This building type achieves a density of seventy-two dwelling units to the acre but is often considered too high to climb to be acceptable as a walk-up by American families.

Beyond seventy-two units to the acre, one must resort to elevator buildings. Figure 7.12 illustrates a twelve-story twin-tower point-block scheme that can be built at a density of ninety-four units to the acre (a point-block is a high-rise tower with a small number of apartments per floor). Figure 7.13 illustrates a thirteen-story double-loaded corridor scheme at one hundred three units to the acre. The twin-tower scheme contains four families per floor for a total of forty-seven families per building and is therefore preferable to the double-loaded corridor scheme which houses six families per floor for a total of one hundred three families per building. However, it should be noted that the double-loaded corridor building is less costly to build than the twin-towered point-block scheme because it has less peripheral wall, less foundations, and a less costly elevator and service core than the two towers combined.

Subsequent Design Principles in Creating Communities of Interest

The second design principle for creating communities of interest requires that the collective public areas of a housing development be designed to serve the needs of residents. It is far easier to tailor these collective areas to the needs of residents if residents sharing similar needs are grouped together, to the exclusion of families with different life-styles and correspondingly different needs.

The third principle requires that the site and the buildings be designed so that the grounds and interior common circulation areas be defined as belonging to specific groups of residents. This should be accomplished in the most clear and unequivocal way possible: each building entry should provide access to a particular group of units and to that group only; access to that building entry should be across grounds that are clearly defined as belonging to that building and its group of residents.

The fourth design principle requires the assignment of the nonprivate areas of buildings and grounds to as small a group of residents as possible. Interior and exterior areas that cannot be made private by being assigned to individual families should be assigned to small groups of families to make them semiprivate as opposed to public. In large buildings the third and fourth principles can be realized either through subdivision or through the use of doormen, depending on the life-styles and socioeconomic characteristics of the resident population.

To illustrate how to integrate the four design principles with the dictates of density, five model designs for different building type/family type combinations are presented below:

1. Single-family houses, for families with children or for the elderly.
2. Walk-ups, for families with children.
3. Medium high-rises without doorman, for families with few children.
4. Elevator high-rises with doorman, for working singles and couples.
5. Medium high-rise and elevator high-rise without doorman, for the elderly.

In explaining the design process used in developing each solution, I will summarize the key elements that had to be addressed in each case.

Single-Family Houses, for Families with Children or for the Elderly

A single-family building, whether detached, semidetached, or row house, is very easy for residents to control provided the house is occupied on more or less a continuing basis—that is, by a family with children or retired elderly. By its nature, the interior of a single-family house and the grounds upon which it sits are for the private use of one family. If positioned so that the entrance faces the street and the private grounds abut the sidewalk, the zone of influence of the private single-family house can be made to extend to and encompass a portion of the adjacent public street.

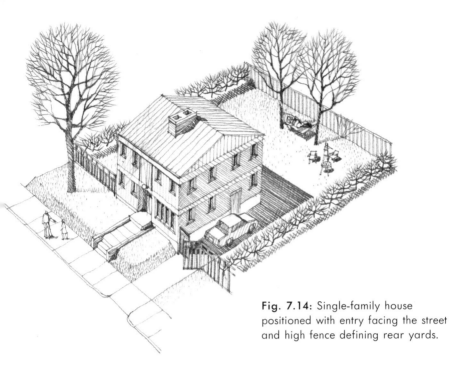

Fig. 7.14: Single-family house positioned with entry facing the street and high fence defining rear yards.

A single-family house, therefore, should be designed and positioned so that the main entry to the dwelling faces onto the public street. This front portion of the house should be designated and designed as the primary area of public access to the unit and its grounds. The remaining portion of the dwelling and its grounds should be defined as being distinctly private — and should be made correspondingly inaccessible. The front portion of the house should therefore contain high-intensity activity areas, such as the kitchen, dining room, and family room. The windows looking out from these rooms should face onto the street to provide it with surveillance. The positioning of the front part of the house as close to the street as possible serves to set up a strong association between the dwelling unit and the street. It facilitates both the surveillance of the street from the unit and the surveillance of the unit from the street.

Single-family buildings should not be set back much more than twenty-five feet from the street. If a private buffer area between the dwelling and the street is desired in the form of a front lawn, the landscaping should be designed so as not to interfere with the visibility from the windows and doors facing the street and the dwellings opposite. Shrubs and trees should be placed on the front lawn so that they do not screen the windows and doors to the units (Figures 7.14, 7.15, 7.16).

By designing a house with only front-door access, residents are

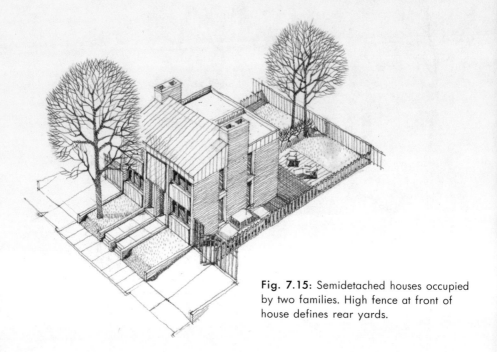

Fig. 7.15: Semidetached houses occupied by two families. High fence at front of house defines rear yards.

Fig. 7.16: Row houses. The buildings themselves define rear yards.

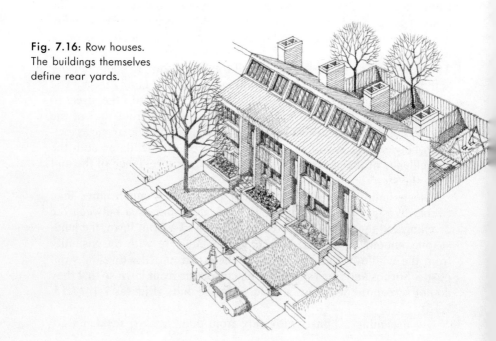

required to come and go from their dwellings via their front lawns. The front zone of the house is, as a consequence, heavily trafficked. It is also surveyed by neighbors on the opposite side of the street. With continual use of the street to gain access to their homes, residents quickly learn to distinguish their neighbors and each other's patterns of movement.[8]

The side and rear walls of a single-family dwelling and their abutting grounds are not as readily visible from the streets as the front of the house. As a consequence, these side and rear yard areas are difficult to supervise and control. Most single-family house residents use the rear grounds of their homes as private outdoor extensions of their dwellings. This is in part a convention that has arisen because the rear yard is less trafficked and less visible than the front of the house. Convention reinforces use, just as use reinforces convention. Many residents, in an effort to ensure the privacy of the rear-yard area, screen it from view with high shrubs or wood fences, thus further diminishing their visual contact with their neighbors to the rear. Ironically, the higher the rear fence, the greater is the need for the fence. That is to say, the more the area at the rear of a dwelling is hidden from the view of one's neighbors — who might provide a natural form of surveillance — the greater is the need to make this area truly inaccessible. It is important to keep in mind that even with low fences, rear yards never receive the intensity of surveillance that front yards do.

In summary, if residents of a single-family house desire to maintain their rear yards as private outdoor spaces, partially or totally screened from view, the yards should be fenced off by real barriers so as to make access by outsiders impossible. Ideally, these real barriers should enclose the side yard areas as well. The most effective and least costly means of fencing side yards in detached or semidetached houses is to run a six- to eight-foot-high fence between neighboring houses parallel with and close to the front face of the buildings (Figures 7.17 and 7.18). (This is not required in a row-house complex, as the neighboring buildings themselves prevent access to the rear yards [Figure 7.16]). The short lengths of fence running between each dwelling unit together form a collection restriction of access to the rear-yard areas of the homes in the entire city block. With this in place, the fencing defining the individual rear yards need not be anything more than symbolic. It should be remembered, however, that a collective rear-yard area subdivided into individual rear yards by symbolic barriers will not be totally private. The success of the common high fence in keeping the collective rear-yard area secure and vandal-free is still dependent on the number of private yards that are linked together and the degree to which residents share a community of interest. However, the principle behind the clustering of small numbers of units to share a collective

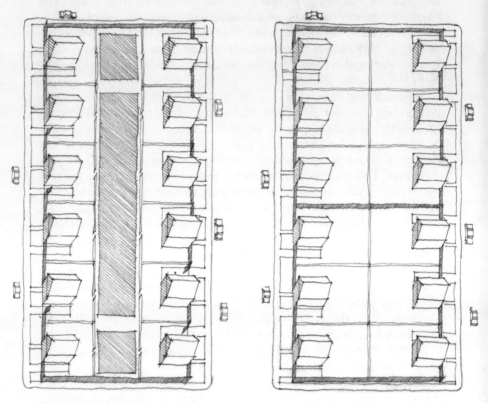

Fig. 7-17 (Left): Block of single-family houses with common rear play area serving all residents of the block.

Fig. 7-18 (Right): Block of single-family houses in which a common high fence, running along the front of the houses, defines the rear-yard areas. An additional high fence has also been run across the block so as to further subdivide the number of families combined in a cluster.

area still holds, and in the case of a long city block, residents may desire to run a high fence across the block at one or two places so as to cut the collective rear-yard area defined by the high fence in half or in thirds (Figure 7.18). The greater the degree of commonality of interests among neighbors, the larger the number of units that can be grouped together within the same fenced-off area.

Some developments composed of single-family houses have been designed with communal paths or play areas running between two juxtaposing rear yards, and to this extent the rear yards receive some additional traffic and surveillance (Figure 7.17). However, from a control point of view, it is not recommended that a pedestrian path or communal area serving the rear yards of neighboring dwellings connect with public streets. In the block of housing that has been developed with a collective recreation area at the rear (Figure 7.17), the communal area should remain sealed off from access to the public street. In a row-house scheme, the judicious placement of a very small stretch of common high fence at the four corners of the city block succeeds in limiting access to the rear-yard areas of an entire block of houses (see Figure 7.19).

Walk-Up Buildings, for Families with Children

The interior circulation areas of walk-up buildings—the lobbies, corridors, stairs, and landings—are not private but are for the common use of all famiies that share the entrance to a particular building. If the number of families—in particular, the number of children—is kept small, these common circulation areas will function as semiprivate spaces. However, if the number of units that share an entry exceeds fifteen, these areas will be semipublic in nature. The fewer the children and the more uniform the concern for security and control, the larger

Fig. 7.19: City block developed as row houses. Four small sections of high fencing, placed at the four corners of the block, define all the rear-yard areas as private.

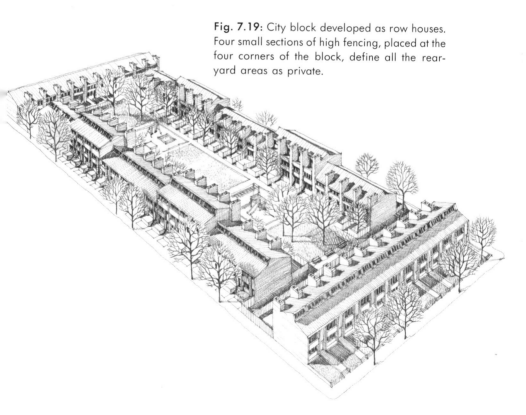

the number of families that can be grouped together while still having these areas function as semiprivate spaces.

Walk-up buildings are normally designed either as large entities with a common circulation system, a central corridor, and end stairs serving one large building (Figure 7.20) or are subdivided into distinct sections with separate stairs and entries serving only a limited number of units (Figure 7.21).

The walk-up buildings illustrated in Figures 7.20 and 7.21 have exactly the same volume and contain the same number of dwelling units, but one building (Figure 7.20) serves forty-eight families through a common circulation system while the other (Figure 7.21) serves only twelve families. In many localities across the country, the building codes which permit three-story buildings to be designed using the principles illustrated in Figure 7.21 require an additional set of fire escape stairs from each apartment.

A limited number of apartments per floor (from two to four), grouped around a shared staircase, facilitates the development of territorial and proprietary feelings in residents. This increases residents' sense of responsibilty for ensuring the safety and maintenance of the

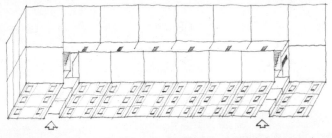

Fig. 7.20: Walk-up building with central double-loaded corridor, stairs, and two common entries serving all forty-eight apartments.

Fig. 7.21: Walk-up building with external dimensions identical to those of the building shown in Figure 7.20, but with four separate entries and stairs, each serving only twelve families.

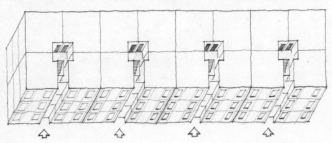

interior areas of their building. The floor plan of the long, double-loaded corridor building shown in Figure 7.20 should be avoided; this prototype has a history of being unsafe and evokes little enthusiasm among residents for assisting management in the maintenance of corridors and stairs (see the discussion of Greenwood Gardens/Martha Manor complex in Chapter X). In general, the increased cost of additional stairs required in the solution shown in Figure 7.21 is offset by the savings resulting from the elimination of portions of the long corridor seen in Figure 7.20.

In the southern and western portions of this country, local weather permits designs for three-story walk-ups with vertical access stairs and landings which are open rather than enclosed. This increases the surveillance potential, but also complicates the task of defining the vertical circulation area as semiprivate. One way to compensate for this lack of definition is to place amenities on the landings at each level. This helps to further designate the landings as extensions of the private space of each dwelling. For example, the landing, if large and secure enough, can be used as a play area for very young children and as an outside dining area (Figure 7.22).

Fig. 7.22: Outdoor landings extend the private space of dwelling units.

If a walk-up unit is large (approaching one thousand square feet), then it is desirable to design the vertical circulation stairs with only two units per floor rather than four. This not only limits the number of persons sharing an entry but also provides each apartment with cross ventilation.

It is important to note that building codes that permit the use of only one access stair, as in the subdivided walk-up we are advocating, seen in Figure 7.21, also limit the height of a building to three stories, or a total of forty feet.[9] Three-story walk-ups have an effective density limitation of forty-five units to the acre for apartments of six hundred square feet (one-bedroom units), and a density of thirty-five units to the acre for apartments of twelve hundred square feet (three-bedroom units). If, however, a developer decides to increase the building height, most codes will then require the provision of a second set of indoor stairs for egress from each dwelling unit.

The solutions shown in Figures 7.23 and 7.24 are both acceptable ways of answering the code requirements for walk-up buildings over three stories in height. The solution illustrated in Figure 7.23 provides two separate means of egress with accompanying sets of stairs, from each apartment dwelling; the building code requirement satisfied by this design states that the two exits from each apartment be no less

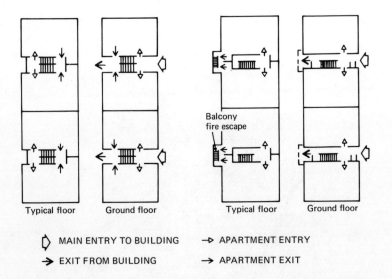

Typical floor   Ground floor   Typical floor   Ground floor

�‍⬠ MAIN ENTRY TO BUILDING   →◦ APARTMENT ENTRY

→ EXIT FROM BUILDING   → APARTMENT EXIT

Fig. 7.23: Typical floor and ground floor of four- to five-story walk-up, using scissor stairs.

Fig. 7.24: Typical floor and ground floor of four- to five-story walk-up, using exterior balcony fire escape.

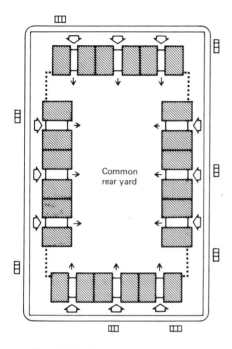

Fig. 7.25: Site plan of walk-up with rear entries exiting to a common rear yard.

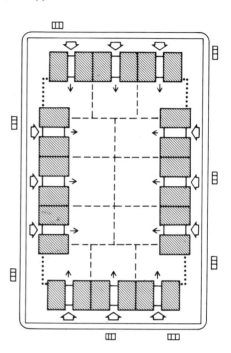

Fig. 7.26: Site plan of walk-up with rear entries exiting to semiprivate rear yards.

than fifteen feet apart. To conserve space, the two sets of stairs have been arranged in a scissor-stair configuration. One stair leads out to the main entry door in the front of the building; the second stair leads to the door at the rear of the building. This scissor-stair solution provides an important additional benefit in that once a person has entered either stair he must follow it out to its specific exit. If, for instance, it is desired to limit access to the yard area at the rear of the building to residents only, then residents can use one door in their apartment to get out the front door of their building and the other door in their apartment to gain access to the semiprivate yard at the rear of their building. In the site plans illustrated in Figures 7.25 and 7.26, the exit system would make the interior rear-yard areas accessible to residents only. The system has one drawback: visiting friends whom residents want to invite into the rear-yard area will have to come up to their apartments, through them, out the other door, and down the rear stairs in order to gain access to the rear-yard. As most visitors are invited into an apartment first and then out to the yard, this is seldom a problem.

The solution illustrated in Figure 7.24 allows for direct access to the rear of the building at the ground level. However, this solution makes it possible for anyone who has gained access to the front door of the building to have automatic access to the rear of the building and the interior grounds at the back. This has some security drawbacks.

In this latter solution the second means of egress from each apartment is provided via a balcony on which there is a fire escape leading down to the rear of the building. In designing the fire escape, the last run of steps should not descend all the way to the ground level but be provided with a counterweighted set of stairs that descends under human weight to provide access to the ground below. This will keep the fire stair from being used to gain access to the second and third floor balconies.

As in a row-house scheme, large portions of the grounds of a walk-up development can be removed from the public domain and be designated for the semiprivate use of particular residents. This requires that the buildings be positioned to encompass interior grounds areas and that secondary exits be provided from the interiors of buildings to the contained areas at the rear of the building (Figures 7.25 and 7.26). These interior grounds can be designed to serve either the collective needs of the residents sharing a group of entries, as shown in Figure 7.25, or can be subdivided to serve the residents of single building entries, as shown in Figure 7.26. The first solution allows for the provision of large play facilities, such as ball fields and basketball courts, which clearly cannot be accommodated within the limited space available in the subdivided grounds. The large common play area in Figure 7.25 will, however, require a maintenance staff, whereas the subdivided grounds of Figure 7.26 are more likely to be cared for by individual residents, particularly if the buildings are co-operatively owned or occupied by the owner.

Elevator Buildings

In general, high-rise buildings should be designed so that as few families as possible share an entry, elevator, and corridor. This rule is particularly important when high-rise buildings cannot be supplied with a doorman. When a doorman is a certainty, the opposite rule governs: that is, the economics of using doormen requires that as many families as possible be grouped together to share a common entry. But the basic rule of limiting the number of families sharing a corridor and building lobby should predominate, and a compromise should be reached between the cost of the doorman and the minimization of maintenance costs for the interior circulation areas of the building resulting from fewer families sharing an entry. Many of the older high-rise apartment buildings are subdivided into two wings, each with its own elevator. Both wings share a common lobby, entry door, and doorman. With this design the elevators and corridors at each level are shared by a small number of families and both wings profit from sharing a common doorman.

There is one important factor that makes it difficult to limit the number of families that share an entry to a high-rise building: the economics of operating elevators efficiently and of providing emergency stairways. First, a minimum of forty to fifty families must be serviced to justify the provision of an elevator. Second, elevators operate most efficiently if two or more are banked together. This banking reduces the waiting time, even when the number of families per elevator remains the same; for example, three elevators grouped together to serve a high-rise building with one hundred fifty families will provide faster service than the three elevators placed separately, each to serve fifty families (Figures 7.27a and b).

Nevertheless, if the economics of building management do not allow for a doorman, the solution that separates the elevators is preferable. By cutting the building into three sections vertically, three distinct entrances are created, each serving only fifty families and each provided with its own elevator. The buildings in this comparison have

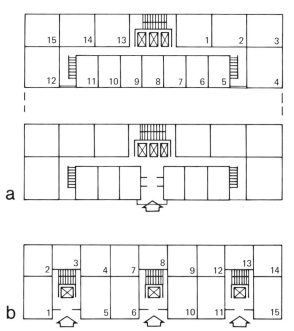

Fig. 7.27: (a) Typical floor and ground floor plan of high-rise building: three elevators banked in a ten-story building serving one hundred forty-nine families, at fifteen families per floor (fourteen families on the ground floor).

(b) Ground floor plan of high-rise building: three elevators, each serving only one third of the building, or a total of fifty families per entry. The entire building serves one hundred fifty families.

almost the same number and size of apartments (one hundred forty-nine versus one hundred fifty), within the same three-dimensional envelope. However, the building with three separate entrances must provide additional emergency fire stairs and additional incinerator shafts. The vertically subdivided building shown in the solution in Figure 7.27b employs scissor stairs behind the elevators in each vertical block. The cost of the extra set of stairs is counterbalanced by the fact that this solution produces one extra apartment in the building. At each floor level in solution (b) only five families share an elevator and com-

Fig. 7.28: As much of an elevator building's lobby area as possible should be visible from the street or entryway.

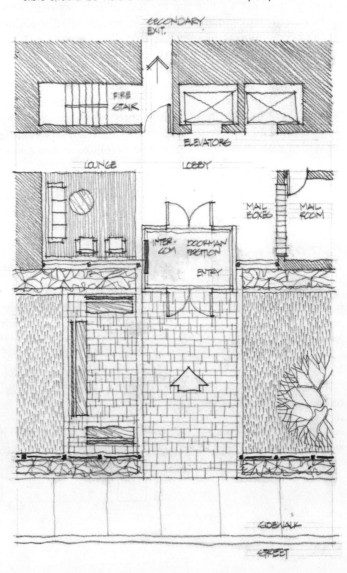

mon corridor, while in solution (a) fifteen families must share a corridor with much more resulting anonymity. If a doorman is possible for the residents of solution (b), then the ground floor could be designed with a single entry and a common lobby but still have three separate elevators, each serving only five families per floor. Not all municipalities have fire codes that allow the use of centrally located scissor stairs as shown. Some codes require that fire stairs be placed at the end of each corridor to avoid entrapment.

The lobbies of elevator buildings should be designed and positioned so that as much of the interior of the lobby as possible, including the vestibule, mailroom, and elevator waiting area, is clearly visible from outside the building (Figure 7.28). The entry to the building and the lobby area should be located parallel to and a short distance from a well-trafficked public walkway or street. In such buildings, designed with elevator waiting areas hidden from view, residents are required to enter with no knowledge of what awaits them and are visually isolated from observation by persons outside the building while waiting for an elevator.

When the provision of a doorman is possible, the positioning of the elevator waiting area and mail room adjacent to the entry vestibule allows these areas to be supervised by the doorman at the entry. For the same reason and also to facilitate casual control by the residents, emergency exit doors and fire stairs are best located where they can be seen from a position as close to the main entry door as possible. When the codes allow it, secondary fire stairs should be designed to exit on the same side of the building and as close as possible to the main entry. This will discourage residents from substituting secondary exits for the main entry door (Figure 7.29). The frequent use of secondary exit doors results in their remaining open continually.

When codes require that a secondary exit door be positioned on the opposite side of a building, the grounds at the rear of the building should be fenced off and provided with only one exit. This exit should be positioned in front of the main entry to the building, requiring those who use the secondary exit door to walk around the building to the

Fig. 7.29: Ground-floor plan of a high-rise elevator building in which the secondary exit from the building has been placed fifteen feet from the main entry. This is only permitted by building codes in some municipalities.

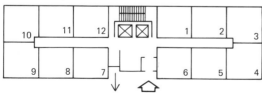

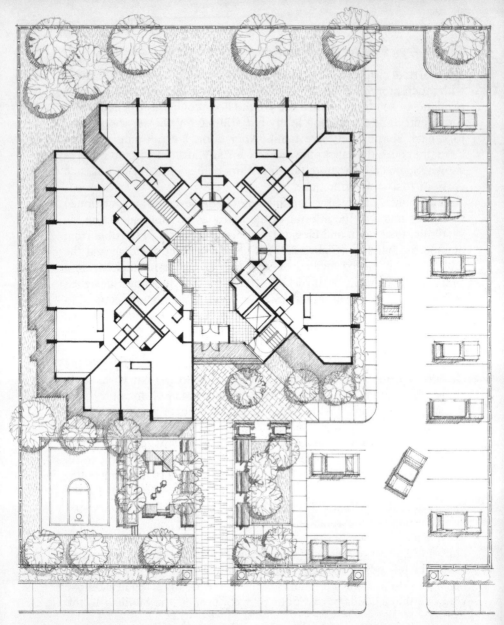

Fig. 7.30a: Ground floor and site plan of seven-story elevator high-rise for families with children. The grounds have been fenced except for two entries.

main entry where they can be scrutinized by other residents and by a doorman (Figure 7.30a).

If parking is provided on the grounds adjacent to the building, the entry to the parking area should be placed near the building entry to facilitate surveillance (Figure 7.30b).

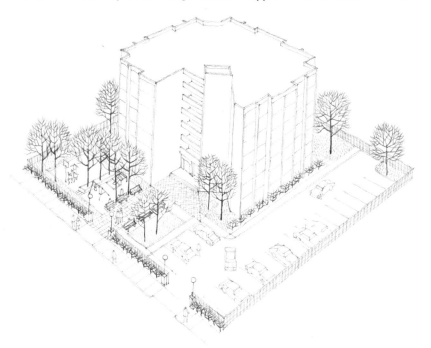

Fig. 7.30b: Aerial view of medium high-rise elevator building for families with children. Both entries to the grounds have been placed within view of the main building entry.

Medium High-Rise Buildings, for Families with Few Children

Medium high-rise elevator buildings used by families with children should be designed so that as few families as possible share an entry. A total of no more than fifty families is recommended. Apartments should be small (two-bedroom units), to discourage occupancy by large families, and two-parent families should be selected over one-parent families to increase the ratio of adults to children.

The entry of the building should be controlled by doormen, if possible. Six- and seven-story elevator buildings may be acceptable without doormen if the number of bedrooms (and children) is kept low. Single-loaded corridor buildings with open stairwells are preferred to double-loaded corridor buildings with sealed off fire stairs.

Figures 7.30a and b illustrate a ground floor and site plan of a seven-story elevator building designed for families with children. The apartments have been laid out so that only seven families share a floor,

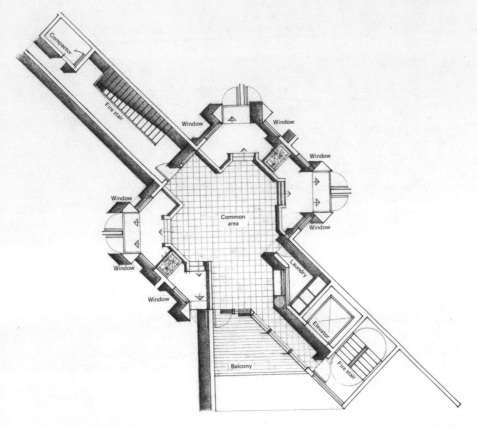

Fig. 7.30c: Common circulation area of a typical floor of building shown in Figures 7.30a and 7.30b.

and the entrance to each apartment faces other apartment entrances across a common interior area. This square area replaces the traditional long, double loaded corridor common to long, tall buildings. The interior area leads to small landings, each of which serves one or two apartments (see Figure 7.30c). Each apartment has also been provided with a fireproof, one-inch-thick unbreakable plastic window which looks out from the kitchen of the unit into the common central square.

At the ground level, the entry doors, lobby, and elevator waiting area are in close proximity to each other and are visible from the street.

In this particular plan the two fire stairs have been separated from each other to meet the more typical of code requirements. One of the stairs has been placed adjacent to the elevator and access to and egress from it are past the main entry to the building. The second fire stair, leading to an exit at the opposite side of the building from the first, is also visible from the main entry door.

The entire site has been surrounded with a six-foot fence, so that the only access to the grounds — both pedestrian and vehicular — is opposite the main entry door. All entrance points to the building and its grounds have thus been placed under resident surveillance and control. A doorman, if available, would be most effective if positioned in the vestibule of the building, adjacent to the intercom connected to each apartment. From this vantage point he can visually survey all access and egress points from the building and its grounds. The central mailbox is positioned on the opposite side of the intercom.

Play facilities for young children and teen-agers are placed immediately in front of the building, as are sitting areas for adult residents (Figures 7.30a and b).

High-Rise Buildings with Doormen
for Working Singles and Couples

Because of their life-styles and security needs, working singles and couples are very reasonably accommodated in high-rise buildings. As was stated earlier, this population normally shows little desire for or interest in maintaining grounds or interior communal areas. They also prefer housing located adjacent to high-intensity urban activity areas, which usually necessitates the construction of a high-rise building. Not only do working adults tend to use their apartments like hotel rooms, but the amenities they prefer within and around their buildings are also characteristic of a hotel: cafeterias, swimming pools, shops, dry cleaners, hairdressers, recreation areas, and theaters.[10]

It is therefore essential, in designing a high-rise for working singles and couples, to operate under the assumption that such a building is critically dependent on round-the-clock doormen to achieve any form of security. All access to such a building, whether from the street, garage, or parking areas, should be past a doorman who is always present. In this case, the larger the number of apartments that can be grouped together to share a common entry, the more economical will be the use of the doorman. There is an upper limit, however — somewhere around a hundred units — beyond which number the doorman will not be able to effectively recognize and remember residents by sight.

In that situation, all residents and their frequent visitors will have to be identified by credentials or intercom each time they enter the building. This can become unworkable. Between 5:30 P.M. and 7:00 P.M., when most residents are returning home from work and guests are coming to dinner, the lines of people waiting at the entry to be recognized and admitted will become very long — and tempers will become correspondingly short. Doormen function best in situations where they are able to recognize most residents and their guests and can admit them with a nod.

If there is a basement garage provided in the building and no attendant in the garage, the elevators should *not* be designed to operate so that they go directly from the garage to each floor of the building. Rather, the garage elevator should be designed to come up to the lobby of the building, requiring residents to transfer at lobby level to the elevators that will take them to their apartments. The transfer in the lobby should take place in full view of the doorman. A compromise, which admittedly is open to a degree of failure, is to have the door in the garage that leads to the elevators locked and under the surveillance of the doorman via closed circuit TV. The door can then be opened electrically by the doorman upon his recognition of residents or their guests.

If genuine security is desired in a high-rise building occupied by working singles and couples, a policy should be adopted whereby all guests are admitted on the approval of residents only — through intercom communication with the doorman. This requires the installation of a two-way intercom connecting each apartment to the lobby (and to the garage entry to the building). The main panel of the intercom should be positioned adjacent to the doorman at the main entry door (see Figure 7.28). It should be kept in mind that it is a time consuming procedure for residents in their apartments to give approval to the doorman to allow in guests waiting in the lobby. This puts a limit on the number of apartments that can be handled effectively by one doorman. The normal remedy is to schedule two doormen during the hectic evening hours, and this is usually accomplished by overlapping the shifts of two doormen during the critical 5:30 P.M.-to-6:30 P.M. hour.

Medium and Tall High-Rise Buildings Without Doormen, for the Elderly

A high-rise for the elderly, unlike one for singles and working couples, can be designed with the knowledge that many of the residents will be either fully or partially retired and will, as a consequence, spend a good deal of their day engaged in activities around their place of residence. Different from families with children, who tend to be inwardly oriented, the elderly are usually gregarious and tend to spend more time seeking out the companionship of other elderly living in the build-

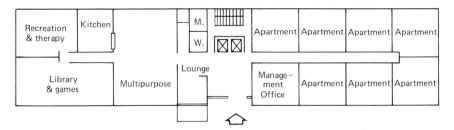

Fig. 7.31a: Ground floor of high-rise for the elderly, showing the location of the lounge area, multipurpose room, and library in relation to the entry, elevators, and mail room.

ing with them. It is quite common in an all-elderly high-rise to find that the residents know virtually all the other people living in the building.

High-rise buildings for the elderly should be designed to facilitate the gathering of residents in the common circulation areas. Areas within the vicinity of the main entrance, both inside the building and out, should be provided with seating and tables. An excellent position for a lounge area is on the ground level off the main entry and facing the elevators and mail rooms (Figure 7.31a). In this way the lobby of the building and the more traversed areas at the ground level will be under continual observation by residents. The positioning of lounge facilities near the main entry is particularly important if the building cannot afford doormen and the residents are required to provide the screening function themselves.

At each level of the building above the ground floor, the architect should provide a small lounge area near the elevator (Figure 7.31b). This space is intended to function, in part, like the larger lounge area provided at ground level—that is, as a place for residents to gather informally. In a double-loaded corridor building, the quality of the lounge area on each floor can be greatly enhanced by being related to an out-

Fig. 7.31b: Typical floor of high-rise for the elderly, showing location of a lounge area adjacent to the elevators.

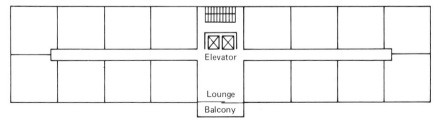

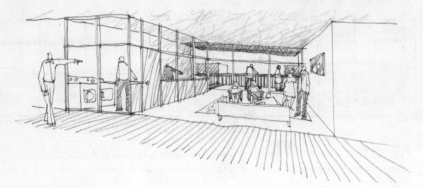

Fig. 7.31c: Lounge and laundry room located opposite elevator area on typical floor of high-rise for the elderly.

door balcony or at least to a glazed area with a view and looking out to the area on the grounds around the entry of the building (Figure 7.31c).

An alternative, preferable to the double-loaded corridor high-rise building for the elderly is the single-loaded corridor building (see Figure 7.32). This design has proved somewhat dangerous for families with children in the public housing projects of our country, but has been found highly desirable in all-elderly buildings. (Housing authorities with single-loaded corridor buildings occupied by families with children have fenced off the open balcony areas from floor to ceiling [Figure 7.33]. European experience with single-loaded corridor high-rise buildings occupied by families with children has not been so drastic as the American experience, but their buildings are rarely higher than six floors, [see Figure 7.34].)

In single-loaded corridor buildings, fire codes usually allow standard windows to be placed in the dwellings looking out into the corridor. This provides a natural and effective means for residents to survey activities taking place in the corridors. It is effective as a security mechanism only when the average resident is home a good part of every day. If more residents than not are off at work, their apartments are made even more vulnerable by the presence of corridor windows. This suggests that single-loaded corridor buildings are ideal for the el-

Fig. 7.32: Typical plan of single-loaded corridor high-rise building.

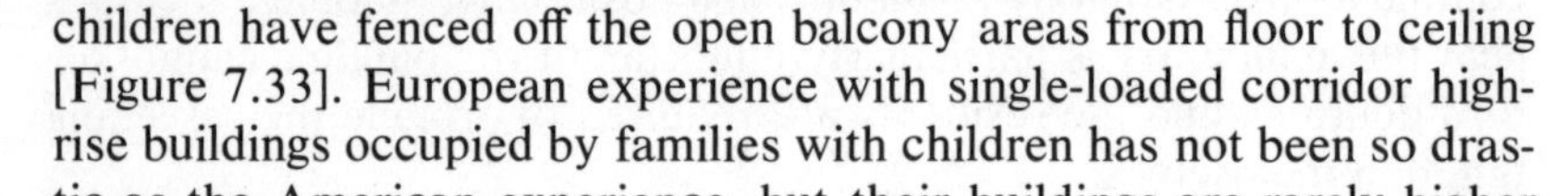

Fig. 7.33: A fence has been added between the balcony rail and the ceiling on each floor of the Schuylkill Falls housing project in Philadelphia to keep children from falling or being thrown over.

Fig. 7.34: A single-loaded corridor of a British medium high-rise project occupied by moderate-income families with children.

Fig. 7.35a: View of a single-loaded corridor in a high-rise for the elderly.

derly, usable for families with children as long as the buildings are no more than seven stories in height, and not recommended for working singles and couples who are away from home most of the day.

Some designers of single-loaded corridor buildings for the elderly have made an effort to individualize the entrances to each apartment by providing setbacks from the corridor. These setbacks can accommodate occasional lounge chairs. This encourages residents to use the corridor and actually enables them to extend the private domain of their apartments into the corridor (Figures 7.35a, b, and c).

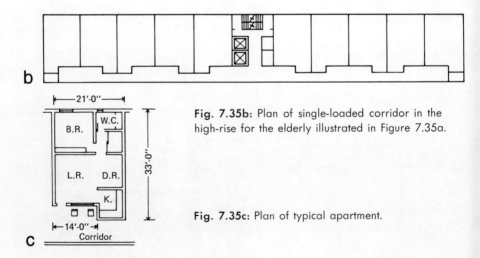

Fig. 7.35b: Plan of single-loaded corridor in the high-rise for the elderly illustrated in Figure 7.35a.

Fig. 7.35c: Plan of typical apartment.

VIII

Site-Planning Guidelines for Housing

In laying out the site of a housing development, buildings should be positioned so that the grounds can be subdivided and allocated to particular buildings. Residents should, as a result, be able to perceive particular areas of the project as being under their specific sphere of influence. The entries to buildings and the paths approaching them should them be placed within the grounds areas assigned to particular buildings. Recreation and parking areas should also be placed within these defined zones, as this will further assist residents in perceiving the grounds as their own and will aid them in exerting control over the grounds. Residents' supervision and control of the grounds surrounding their buildings is the most effective form of deterrent to crime and vandalism.

A resident's "zone of influence" in a housing development is an area within the immediate vicinity of an apartment that is perceived as an extension of that apartment for the use of the resident. As such, the zone will experience more use, surveillance, and maintenance by the resident.

However, the assignment of a particular ground area to a building's inhabitants will not in itself guarantee that residents will assume proprietary attitudes toward it. The number of residents sharing a building and its grounds are critical in determining their attitude toward it, just as is the suitability of the building type to residents' needs and the degree of community of interest among residents. However, of all the mechanisms that contribute to the creation of zones of influence, the *number* of residents is of the most critical importance. The fewer the families that share the entry to a building and its grounds, the greater will be each family's association with the grounds. The greater, too, will be their desire and willingness to participate in the maintenance and control of the grounds.[1]

In designing a housing project, therefore, the architect or site planner should choose a building prototype that satisfies the density requirements but minimizes the number of families that have to share the entry to a building. This allows the designer to subdivide the grounds of the development into small parcels which he can then assign to individual buildings or to small groups of residents. Buildings and entries should be positioned so that the grounds around the buildings are easily perceived as having been designated for the use of the families in particular buildings.

If a site planner has the option of providing ten pieces of play equipment for the use of one hundred families, he can either place all ten pieces in one central area to serve all one hundred families, or he can divide up the ten pieces of equipment and assign one piece for the use of ten families. The latter choice is preferable if the designer wishes to ensure residents' use of the equipment and its maintenance over time.

Not all amenities, however, can be allocated with this range of choice. Some large facilities, such as a full-sized basketball court, must serve a larger group of families than ten to justify their inclusion in a site plan. However, rather than group two or three such large facilities together, as is commonly done, it is better to assign each of them to the smallest possible grouping of families.

Assignment of Grounds

To create easily perceived zones of influence, a project site should be subdivided so that *all* the ground areas are related to particular buildings or building clusters. No areas should be unassigned or simply left to be perceived as public. Figures 8.1 and 8.2 compare two planning layouts for the same site developed at the same density; each achieves a different end. In Figure 8.1 most of the ground areas and, by their juxtaposition, the adjacent streets, are assigned to particular buildings. The placement of the buildings themselves serves to break up the grounds and to define their use and their users. The buildings, streets, and grounds are designed as interrelated entities. By contrast, Figure 8.2 illustrates a site plan in which most of the ground area is unassigned and is therefore public in nature. Figure 8.3 is an aerial view of the site plan of Figures 8.1 and 8.2; the grounds around the buildings have been subdivided to serve the needs of the residents of individual buildings, and larger common interior areas serve particular

Fig. 8.1: Grounds areas are all assigned to particular buildings. Streets are encompassed within the zone of influence of the dwellings.

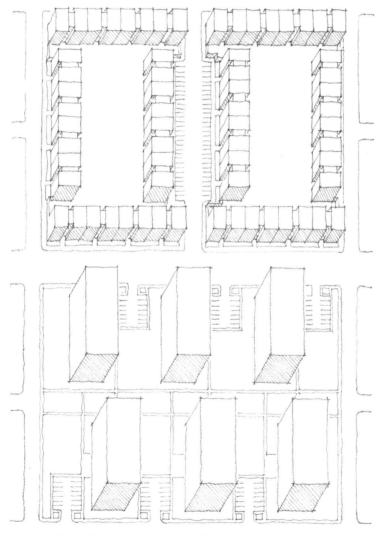

Fig. 8.2: Grounds areas are intentionally left open and unrelated to particular buildings. The streets do not relate either to the buildings or the project grounds.

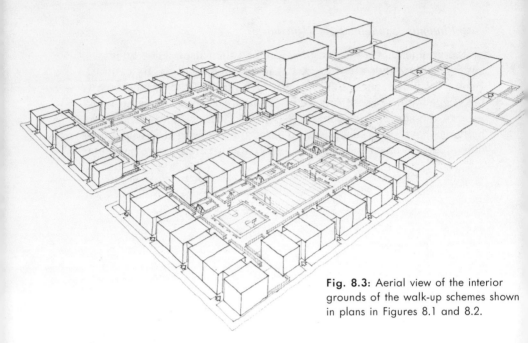

Fig. 8.3: Aerial view of the interior grounds of the walk-up schemes shown in plans in Figures 8.1 and 8.2.

clusters of buildings in the provision of larger amenities, such as ball fields and green areas. These interior grounds are accessible only through the separate rear exits from each building's interior semiprivate space.

Means of Defining Zones of Influence

The physical boundaries necessary to the creation of zones of influence can be defined either by real or symbolic barriers. Real barriers include elements like buildings, high fences, and walls. They have limited portals which require entrants to possess some mechanical opening device to be recognized by a resident to gain entry. Symbolic barriers, on the other hand, define areas, or relate them to particular buildings, without physically preventing intrusion. Symbolic barriers

Fig. 8.4: Examples of symbolic barriers. (a) Change in level; (b) lights and standards used to define transitional space; (c) low walls, posts, and change in paving texture used to define transition.

include elements like low fences, shrubs, steps, changes in paving texture, light standards, open portals, and so on (Figure 8.4).

The success of symbolic barriers, in contrast to real barriers, is dependent on: the ability of intruders to perceive and heed the meaning of the symbols; the evident capacity of the inhabitants of the defined space, or their agents, to maintain control of the space that is being symbolically defined; and the capacity of the space itself to require the intruder to make his intentions obvious—that is, the degree to which the space is defined for a particular activity and has a low tolerance for ambiguous use. Many of these components work in concert; a successful symbolic barrier is one that has all of these conditions operating together.

Transitional Space

In existing housing developments, the subdivision of grounds into distinct clusters defined by real barriers may be difficult to achieve. In such cases, it may be possible to create a series of symbolic boundaries that define a hierarchy of increasingly private zones in transition from public street to private building and apartment. We have called this hierarchy "zones of transition."

As a design tool, symbolic barriers achieve their greatest utility when used to define zones of transition. These boundary definitions act as interruptions in a person's sequence of movement along access paths and create perceptible zones of transition from public spaces to spaces intended for private or semiprivate use. In creating zones of transition, symbolic barriers serve the purpose of informing people that they are passing from a public space, where the range of possible activities is large and not subject to much restriction or control, to more private spaces where activity is limited to what is considered acceptable by *adjacent* residents. Within these defined private spaces, one's presence requires justification. When moving through a sequence of defined areas one can be made to experience these symbolic barriers as a matter of course. Residents have thus been given low-keyed physical supports for their role in defining users' behavior in these areas.

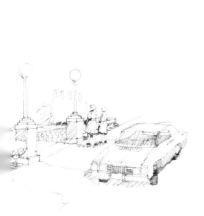

Fig. 8.5: Numerous devices are available to indicate transition areas in existing developments.

Opportunities exist for creating zones of transition through the use of symbolic barriers to define the transition from public street to the semipublic grounds of the project; from outdoors to indoors; and from the semipublic area of a building lobby to the more private corridors of each floor (Figure 8.5). Symbolic barriers are also used by residents as boundaries for defining areas of comparative safety. Parents, for in-

Fig. 8.6: Patio and play area as symbolic barrier defining area of transition.

stance, often use symbolic barriers to delimit the areas in which their young children are allowed to play (Figure 8.6). A parent will say, "Don't play outside the hedge," or "Play on the patio, but don't go down the steps." Similarly, because symbolic barriers make outsiders realize that they are intruding on a semiprivate domain, the barriers can effectively restrict behavior to that which outsiders deem the residents will find acceptable.

The Reinforcement of Zones of Influence
Through the Provision of Amenities

The creation of zones of influence through the assignment of grounds to small numbers of residents is reinforced when amenities directed to the needs of residents are located within these zones. The placement of benches, play facilities, and parking spaces within the defined zones serves to give residents a further sense of identification with these areas. Such identification with particular facilities further reinforces residents' claim to the grounds outside their building. The presence of one's neighbors involved in activities in an adjacent, collectively defined area (whether children at play or adults sitting and talking) serves to reinforce residents' feelings of control. It also brings these areas under surveillance by other family members and neighbors who are within their apartments. If these amenities are juxtaposed with building entrances and windows from adjoining apartments, there is greater likelihood that these defined areas will receive the continual surveillance of residents.

The site plan of a housing project must answer many criteria, some generated by external conditions, such as vehicular access and servicing, and others generated by the needs of the residents for ancillary outdoor activity areas. The juxtaposition of these outdoor areas with particular buildings and the interiors of apartments is critical in determining the degree to which residents will adopt these areas as their own. It may appear obvious, but it should be emphasized that buildings should be grouped together so that they create adjacent open areas which can actually be used by residents for various activities, both individual and collective.

Often architects and landscape designers are content with producing plans in which the configuration of the grounds is simply what is left over after the buildings have been placed in a satisfying composition. It is not uncommon to see site designs for proposed projects in which the architects have labeled the grounds simply as "active" or "passive" space, with no consideration given to the likely activities which might take place in these areas, the needs or ages of the intended users, or the means of access and supervision of these areas from adjacent buildings and dwellings. Recreation areas that have been designed to accommodate specific activities and have been placed within clearly defined zones of influence will not only receive greater use, but they will also improve the security of adjacent buildings by creating outdoor extensions of the dwelling unit that residents identify with and control. Distant and undefined recreation and green areas whose intended users are unclear often go unused and are frequently vandalized. These areas also attract vagrants, spark disputes over rights among potential users, and often create more problems than they solve.

The following suggestions for grounds design relate to the needs of different age groups. First, small children, from one to five years of age, have been found to show a preference for playing in outdoor areas immediately adjacent to their dwellings—preferably just outside the common entry door—in both single-family units and multiple dwellings.[2] As Figures 8.7 and 8.8 illustrate, the careful allocation of such facilities can also serve to create a semiprivate buffer zone separating the private zone of the building interior from the more public zones of the project and surrounding street. These play areas for young children should also be related to the interior circulation areas of a multifamily building and to the windows of the apartments of intended users. This juxtaposition of interior and exterior facilities provides the opportunity for easy, continuous monitoring of outdoor areas by residents within the building. As was mentioned earlier, an additional security benefit accrues from this juxtaposition: the entry to the building now falls under the observation of parents as they watch their children playing outside.

Fig. 8.7: Perspective of play area as buffer.

Fig. 8.8: Play areas as buffers to building entries.

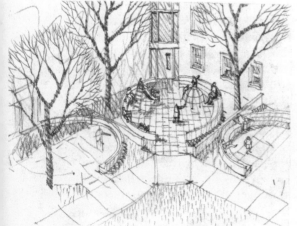

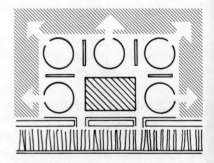

Fig. 8.9: Children's play areas are defined by low walls which are formed by benches. (Clason Point grounds redesign.)

A "tot-lot" should be designed with a clearly demarcated periphery so as to both protect the children and discourage them from wandering off. The provision of rows of benches is one way of satisfying this demarcation requirement while also providing seating for accompanying adults (Figure 8.9).

Because of the noise generated by teen-agers and because of the possible damage a ball can do, play areas for youngsters from thirteen to eighteen year old should not be located immediately adjacent to buildings. However, this does not mean that teen play facilities should be placed in isolated areas of the housing development or totally disassociated from all dwellings. As was said earlier, isolated play facilities often prove to be neglected, vandalized, and underused. In projects where the teen play area appears to be a no man's land, fights for turf rights among competing groups of teen-agers have, in many instances, ended with the decision by managment to remove the play equipment. Ideally, teen play areas should be bordered on two to four sides by dwellings. The windows and entries of at least some of the dwellings in the complex should face onto the play area. In order to minimize the noise problem discussed earlier, these teen play areas should have a thirty- to forty-foot buffer between them and the nearest building.

A teen play area should be large enough to house the play facilities normal to this group: basketball, handball, baseball, and football, when possible. It should be noted, however, that housing developments in dense urban settings can normally only accommodate basketball and handball facilities. Many developers and housing managers make the mistake of providing full-size basketball courts where a single hoop and a 20 foot by 20 foot square will do. Most basketball playing is informal and involves only a few players. It is both preferable and easier to provide a series of individual basketball hoops throughout a development than to provide, at the same cost, only one or two full-sized courts. Large, centrally located basketball courts have still one further disadvantage over small, scattered, individual basketball hoops: the older teen-agers tend to dominate the large courts to the exclusion of younger teen-agers. By contrast, individual basketball hoops located close to home and in defined areas tend to serve all the children living there.

Benches should be placed around teen ball fields to allow other teen-agers to gather and watch. They are also useful in allowing tired players to catch their breath or just as a place for piling extra clothing and equipment (Figure 8.10). In the evening hours when groups are not playing ball, the benches expand the use of these areas for social gath-

Fig. 8.10: A bench, at right, placed adjacent to a single basketball hoop serves to transfer a lone piece of play equipment into a small teen center (Clason Point).

Fig. 8.11: Green areas for adult leisure are screened by shrubbery and further "protected" from youngsters by provision of nearby areas for active play.

erings and serve as a simple device for allowing boys and girls to gather together. A few benches can turn a play court into a small teen-agers' social area.

Large, decorative green areas, edged with flowers, are usually the pride of adult residents and the elderly and are declared "off-limits" to children. Inevitably they prove to be a thorn in the side of every active child looking for somewhere to play. Shrubs and fences, judiciously placed, can help to protect such green areas. However, the only effective means of preserving these decorative green areas for quiet sitting is to provide adequate adjacent play areas for resident youngsters (Figure 8.11).

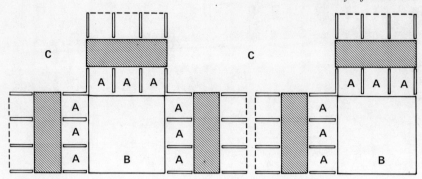

Fig. 8.12: Site plan showing location of amenities for different users. Areas marked A are for preschool children; B, for six- to twelve-year-olds; C, for adults.

Figure 8.12 illustrates a housing project site plan with outdoor areas designed and positioned to meet the needs of a range of particular users. The areas labeled *A* are placed adjacent to the entry of each building and are for the use of one- to five-year-olds, with accompanying seating for adults. The larger areas, *B*, are located in the center of each cluster of three building blocks and are provided with play facilities serving six- to twelve-year-olds. The areas labeled *C* are located away from the main movement arteries and intended as decorative green areas for the quiet use by adult residents. The *C* areas may also be provided with barbecuing facilities and with some seating, but are for the most part simply heavily planted. It is essential that access to these *C* interior areas be limited, preferably *only* from the interior of buildings.

Incorporating the City Streets into Zones of Influence

The zones of influence of residential buildings can be made to encompass adjacent city streets if the buildings and their entries are designed and positioned for this purpose. Residents whose buildings and grounds are closely related to the city streets are more likely to perceive the adjacent sidewalks as an extension of their homes. It is thus possible to encourage residents to extend their concerns and responsibilties to include some of the adjacent street areas.

Inward-facing housing projects—that is to say, developments that have been designed intentionally with building entries placed only off paths that are internal to the project—produce peripheral city streets that are truly public. These city streets are devoid of any association with any buildings and, as a result, receive no surveillance from adjacent homes.

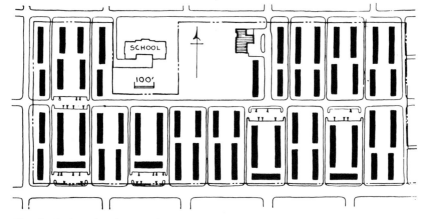

Fig. 8.13: Site plan from early U. S. Government housing manual, showing buildings facing street on end only. (From *Public Housing Design*, National Housing Agency, Washington, D.C.: U. S. Government Printing Office, 1946.)

Following the directives of early planning manuals, many housing projects were intentionally designed to look inward on themselves (Figure 8.13). Buildings usually met adjacent streets only at one end, entrances and windows faced only the project interior, and, as a result, residents had no view of bordering streets. Figures 8.14a and b illustrate both outward and inward facing projects for a six-block residen-

Fig. 8.14: (a) Outward facing project. Arrows designate entries. (b) Inward facing project. Arrows designate entries.

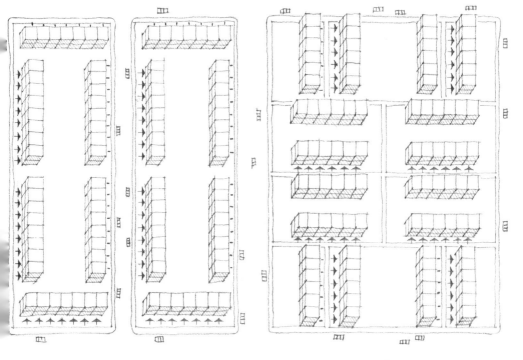

a   b

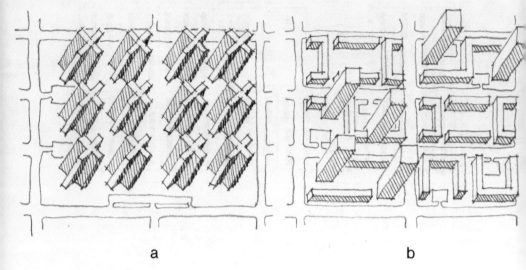

a   b

Fig. 8.15: (a) High-rise superblock formed by closing off public streets. (b) Site plan incorporating public streets and combining various building types.

tial area. Both site plans house the same number of people and provide similar numbers of parking sites. Figure 8.15a illustrates a superblock, created by closing off existing streets. Although the closing of the streets and the use of high-rise buildings were intended to free large areas for recreational use, these areas are not always adopted by residents for these purposes.

By contrast, the site in Figure 8.15b achieves the same density as that in Figure 8.15a through a mixture of walk-ups and high-rises. Each building type is intended to serve that family type which will be comfortably housed within it. The existing streets have been kept intact to provide parking, circulation, open space, and recreation facilities. Although the buildings cover more of the grounds area than those in Figure 8.15a, the grounds that are provided are more clearly related to specific buildings and have been allocated for the recreational use of particular groups of inhabitants. As a consequence, the less extensive grounds of the plan in Figure 8.15b are likely to receive more intensive use than the larger, undefined grounds of the plan in Figure 8.15a.

There are three separate design directives posited in the above comparison. Although they operate in concert, it is important to keep our understanding of them distinct. The first directive is that building types be chosen to suit the need of particular residents. The second directive requires that the buildings be related to specific areas of the site. The third directive requires the positioning of buildings to include the city streets within the zones of influence of residents.

It should be remembered that the lower the building and the fewer the families sharing in its use, the greater will be each family's ties to the grounds and street below.

Figure 8.16 shows two housing projects, one that has and one that has not realized these directives. Both projects are designed at the same density and with similar parking provisions. The high-rise project on the left has all building entries facing the interior grounds of the development. Parking has been designed as a continous strip along the street, further disassociating the buildings from the street. The project on the right is only three stories in height and achieves the same density by covering more of the grounds (37 per cent ground coverage versus 24 per cent). All the buildings and their entries are juxtaposed with the city streets, and each entry has been designed to serve only six families. Small play and sitting areas have been provided near each entry as amenities within the sphere of influence of each of the six families.

The residents in the apartments in the walk-ups are a very short distance from the surrounding streets, and because of the positioning of the entries, play areas, and parking, the neighboring streets are brought within the sphere of influence of inhabitants.

Figures 8.17, 8.18, and 8.19 graphically summarize the major site-planning guidelines that are essential in incorporating the grounds and streets of a housing development into the sphere of influence of inhabitants. All three illustrations show the same four-block area of a city developed in different ways. Figure 8.17 is an illustration of a row-house development with twenty-four units to the acre. The site has been subdivided so that all the grounds, except for the streets and sidewalks, are assigned to individual families. The front lawns, because they are private, need only be symbolically defined. The rear yards are accessible from the interior of the dwelling units only. The close juxtaposition of each dwelling unit and its entry to the street contributes to the incorporation of the sidewalk into the sphere of influence of the inhabitants of the dwelling. This is further reinforced by the fact that the private lawn abuts the sidewalk and the family car is parked at the curb. Residents' attitudes suggest that even this sidewalk and parking area are semiprivate in nature.

Examining the entire four-block area, we find an urban fabric in which most of the outdoor areas and all of the indoor areas are private. In addition, a good portion of what is legally public street is viewed by residents as an extension of their dwellings and under their sphere of influence. Because of its close juxtaposition and its continual use, residents are concerned about ensuring the safety of the street and sidewalk and act to maintain and control it. In actual fact, only the very

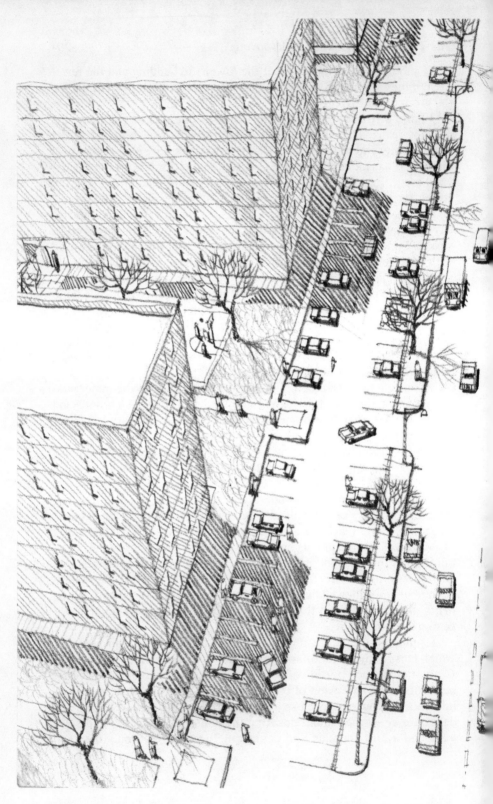

Fig. 8.16: The project on the left is turned in on itself, away from the public street, while that on the right is designed to bring the street within the control of the residents. Both projects are built at exactly the same density.

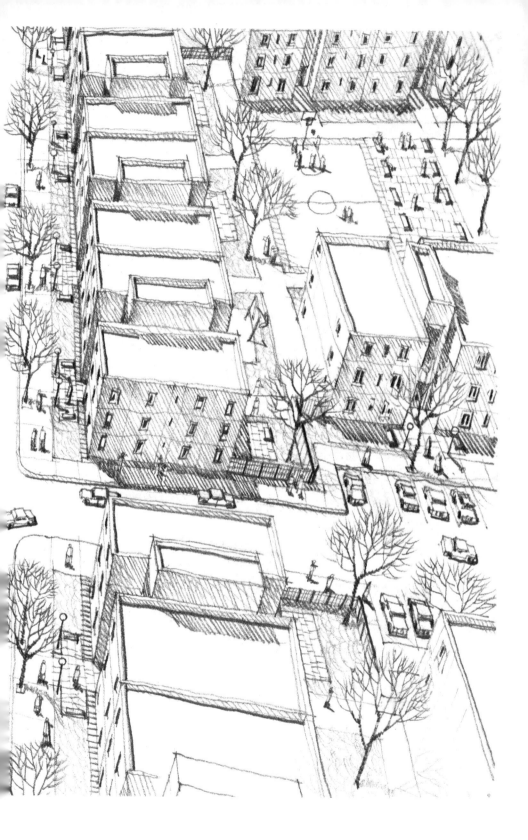

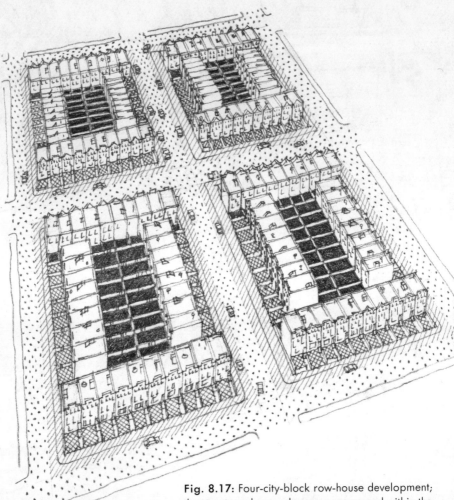

Fig. 8.17: Four-city-block row-house development; the streets and grounds are encompassed within the domain of the dwellings.

central portion of each street is truly public in nature. If the street were narrow, even the activity in this central portion would be considered to some degree accountable to neighboring residents.

Figure 8.18 shows the same four-block area, this time designed to accommodate a three-story garden apartment scheme with thirty-six dwellings to the acre. The grounds have been assigned both to individual families and to small groups of families. The front lawn adjacent to each building entry is the collective area for that entry's inhabitants. The small patios adjacent to each building at the rear are the private

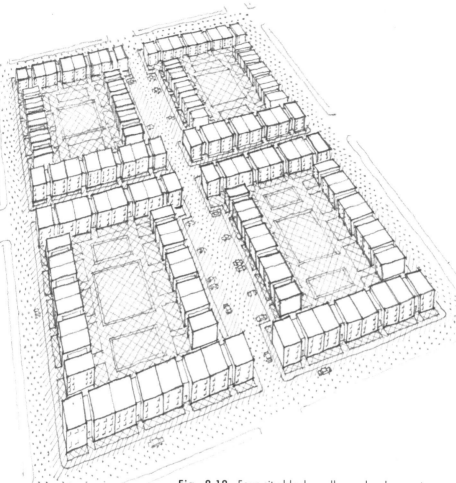

Fig. 8.18: Four-city-block walk-up development; the streets and grounds are encompassed within the domains of the multifamily dwellings.

outdoor areas of the families living at the ground level. The large rear courts enclosed by the four buildings are each the collective recreation area of ninety-six families. These rear courts are only accessible from the semiprivate interior circulation space of each building shared by six families. As in the row house scheme in Figure 8.17, all the entries face the street, but the entries now serve six families rather than one, and are thus semiprivate rather than private. Parking again is on the street immediately in front of each dwelling. Because of the semiprivate nature of the grounds, the sidewalk and streete are not clear extensions of

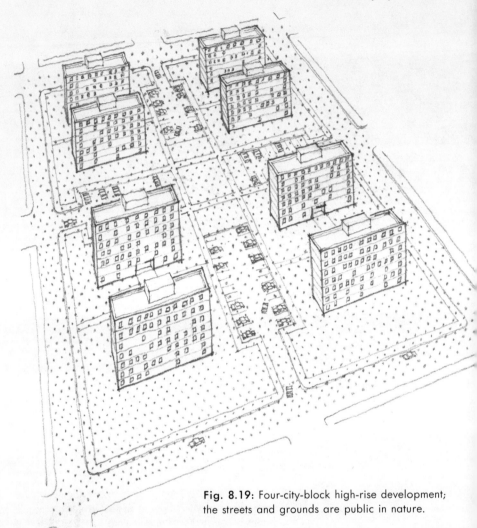

Fig. 8.19: Four-city-block high-rise development; the streets and grounds are public in nature.

the realms of individual dwelling units. But even with all these limitations, the neighboring sidewalk and parking zone on the street are considered by many residents as areas over which they exert some control.

Figure 8.19 is the same four-block area shown on Figure 8.17 and 8.18, but now developed as a high-rise superblock at a density of fifty dwelling units to the acre. Each building entry serves one hundred families by means of an interior circulation system consisting of a public lobby, elevators, and corridors. The grounds around the buildings are accessible to everyone and are not assigned to particular buildings. The residents, as a result, feel little association with or responsibility for the grounds, and even less association with the surrounding public streets. Not only are the streets distant from the units, but no building entries face them. The grounds of the development which abut the sidewalks are also public and, as a consequence, so are the sidewalks and streets. This design succeeds in making the entire ground surface of the four-block area public, and all the grounds of the project must be maintained by management and patrolled by a hired security force. The city streets and sidewalks, in turn, must be maintained by the city sanitation department and patrolled by city police.

The placement of the high-rise towers on the interior grounds of the project in the development shown in Figure 8.19 has produced a system of off-street parking and access paths to the building that involves many turns and blind corners. Residents in such developments complain about the dangers of walking into the grounds to get to their building at night. The proclivity of landscape designers for positioning shrubs exactly at turns in the paths increases the hazards of these access routes. This problem does not arise in traditional row-house or walk-up developments where building entries face the street and are set back from the sidewalk some ten to twenty feet, nor do these fears occur in high-rise buildings whose entries face the streets and are set back slightly from them. In these cases, residents are able to move in a straight line from the relative safety of the public street to what they can observe to be the relative safety of the well-lighted lobby area in the interior of their buildings.

IX

Prototypical Designs for Two New Housing Projects

In this chapter I will endeavor to combine the various principles developed earlier into the programming and design of two new housing developments. My purpose will be to demonstrate which of the principles come into play at different stages in the programming and design process and how they interact with each other to produce an integrated design product. The housing programs and sites being used as prototypes are real and typical of much low- and moderate-income housing being constructed in urban areas today.

The first site, in Newark, New Jersey, is located in an inner-city urban renewal area. It consists of seven and a half acres, made up of portions of four city blocks. The site presently contains the remnants of badly deteriorated nineteenth-century housing, which is being cleared away (Figure 9.1). This new project will house a mix of both low- and moderate-income families and will use both New Jersey State Housing Finance Agency assistance and federal housing subsidies. The developers in Newark are required to achieve an over-all density of at least forty units to the acre to justify the cost of the land. This

Fig. 9.1: Existing housing being demolished in the Newark, New Jersey, site.

means that a total of three hundred units will have to be accommodated on the site.

The local community sponsoring organization, a nonprofit group acting as the developer in Newark, desires to provide housing for a variety of different family sizes and age groups. In a series of community planning sessions, a program was evolved to house one hundred forty elderly families and one hundred sixty families with children. It was felt desirable that half the elderly apartments be efficiency units and half one-bedroom units. The percentage of units of different size to be provided for families with children was worked out as follows: 30 per cent two-bedroom units, 50 per cent three-bedroom units, 17 per cent four-bedroom units, and 3 per cent five-bedroom units.

The Design Process

Following the order of priorities set down in earlier chapters, the first design guideline requires the separation of families of differing age groups and life-styles, each to its own microenvironment—in this case, the separation of the elderly from families with children. A corollary to this design guideline is the proper assignment of the different family types to the building types most suited to their needs. Thus the one hundred forty elderly families will be placed in a single high-rise building and will be given a distinct and separate portion of the site. It will be placed on that portion of the site that abuts the most prominant

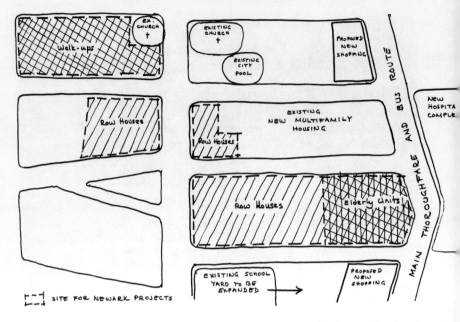

Within the figure the following labels appear:

- EX. CHURCH ✝
- Walk-ups
- EXISTING CHURCH ✝
- EXISTING CITY POOL
- PROPOSED NEW SHOPPING
- NEW HOSPITAL COMPLEX
- Row Houses
- Row Houses
- EXISTING NEW MULTIFAMILY HOUSING
- Row Houses
- Elderly Units
- MAIN THOROUGHFARE AND BUS ROUTE
- EXISTING SCHOOL YARD TO BE EXPANDED →
- PROPOSED NEW SHOPPING
- SITE FOR NEWARK PROJECTS

Fig. 9.2: Rationale for the location of housing types in Newark. The units for the elderly were positioned within walking distance of the hospital, the shopping center, and the bus stop. The large family units (row houses) were positioned adjacent to and near the school.

through street in the area. This area of the site is also directly opposite a new hospital and adjacent to the planned future shopping facilities (Figure 9.2). In this location, the elderly will have direct access to mass transit facilities (buses and taxis on the main street) and will be within easy walking distance of both the shopping and medical facilities.

The placement of elderly residents in their own high-rise building at a comparatively high density in turn allows us to house the families with children at lower densities in either row houses or walk-up buildings.

In the programming of the family units, the second design guideline comes into play: the minimization of the number of persons sharing the entry to a building—particularly the number of children. Thus the families with a large number of children will be housed in the larger dwellings—the row-house units—in which each family has its own entry. The families with few children will be housed in the smaller dwelling units: apartments in three-story walk-up buildings. All the four- and five-bedroom units will therefore be built as row houses and all the two-bedroom units will be placed in walk-up buildings.

Following this guideline further, it is desirable that as many of the three-bedroom units as possible be built as row-house units. However, the density requirements dictate that a significant percentage of the three-bedroom units will have to be accommodated in the walk-ups. The actual percentage was determined from preliminary trial sketch plans which revealed the largest number of row-house units that could be accommodated on the site while still meeting the density and building code requirements. Sixty per cent of the three-bedroom units could be accommodated in row houses, but the remaining 40 per cent would have to be placed in the walk-up units (Table 9.1).

The third design principle requires the assignment of as much of the grounds as possible to specific residential units for each family to maintain and control. Parallel with this, it is desirable to group individual housing units into small clusters. Where, because of density, it is not possible to assign grounds to individual families, our design principles require that small numbers of units be grouped together to share a common entry and its associated, defined grounds. This is true for row houses, walks-ups, *and* high-rise buildings. Recreation facilities directed at the needs of the residents should then be placed within these communal areas.

However, for this clustering to develop into a community of interest, the families that are grouped together should share similar needs for activity areas outside their dwellings. The first design guideline achieves this by advocating the grouping of residents by a similarity in life-style, the second guideline by advocating that these different life-style groups by provided with the types of buildings most suited to their life-style needs.

In the Newark plan, the row-house, walk-up, and high-rise buildings are each grouped into their own clusters. By "cluster" is meant a

Table 9.1: Breakdown of Elderly, Rowhouse, and Walk-up Units, by Apartment Size

144 ELDERLY UNITS	100% of Elderly units High-rise	50% 1 B.R. units
		50% Efficiency units
172 FAMILY UNITS	40% of Family units Row houses	3% 5 B.R. units
		17% 4 B.R. units
		50% 3 B.R. units
	60% of Family units Walk-ups	30% 2 B.R. units

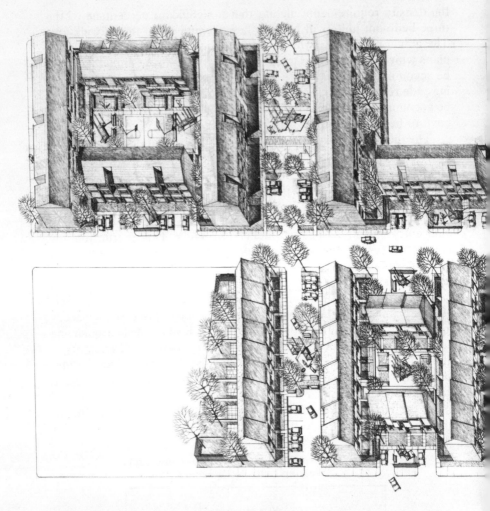

distinctly defined group of buildings that have been positioned together
to share the use of a common grounds area. The clusters of row-house
and the walk-up buildings were designed so that a small number of families share a common court (Figure 9.3).

The amount of six-foot-high fencing needed to define each cluster
was minimized by using the buildings themselves as the defining and
enclosing elements. There are three advantages that come with using
the buildings themselves, rather than fencing, to define collective
ground areas: it is immediately understood which buildings share the
collective area; the amount of fencing is minimized; and, most importantly, the collective grounds and the buildings they serve are automat-

ically placed in close juxtaposition, thus setting up the association between buildings and grounds which facilitates surveillance of the outside areas from within the dwelling units.

The families living in the row houses have each been given their own yards in front and back of their buildings. This is in addition to the collective grounds shared by all the families in a cluster.

In the walk-up buildings, the families on the ground level have been given their own outdoor patios within the enclosed rear clusters. The families on the second and third floors of the walk-ups have been given their own large individual balconies which face on and lead down to the communal rear courts. Small communal play and sitting areas have also been provided in front of the walk-up buildings next to the parking areas.

Fig. 9.3: An aerial view of the entire four-block development being proposed for the city of Newark. The high-rise for the elderly is located in the lower right-hand corner of the drawing. The three-story walk-ups are all located within the block in the upper left-hand corner of the drawing. The remainder of the project consists of row-house units. Only one portion of one existing street is being closed to through traffic. The major through street passes to the right of the high-rise building for the elderly.

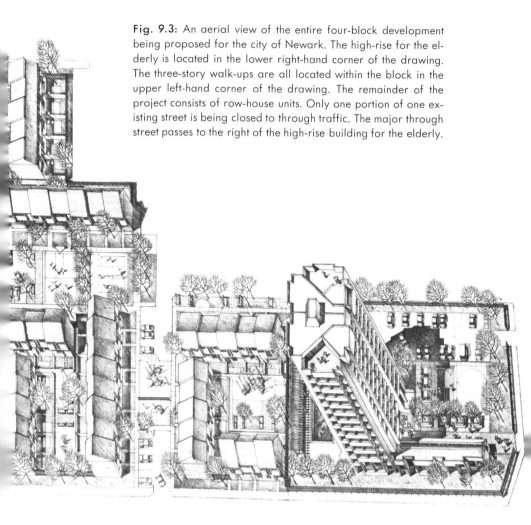

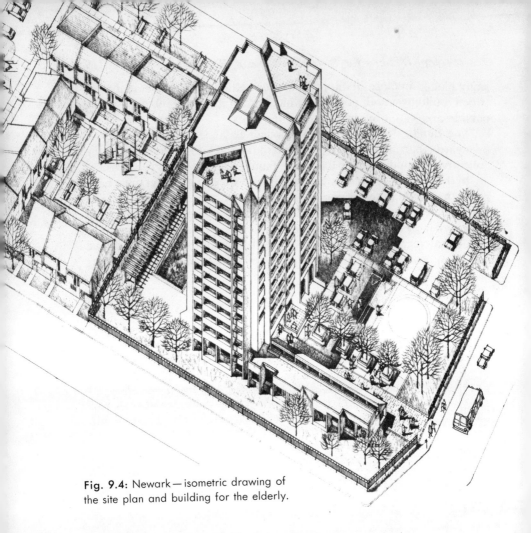

Fig. 9.4: Newark—isometric drawing of the site plan and building for the elderly.

Design of the Building for the Elderly

All the apartment units for the elderly in the Newark development have been placed in a single high-rise building, the ground floor of which will be used for communal activities of all the residents. Because of the large number of people who share in its use, it is difficult to justify the assignment of the grounds around a high-rise building to individual families. The grounds surrounding the high-rise for the elderly have therefore been designed as a single communal area for the collective use of all residents. Even though these communal grounds will serve all of the one hundred forty-four elderly units, this solution is workable because of the way elderly residents use and perceive an environment which is exclusively their own (discussed in Chapter VII).

The grounds area surrounding the building for the elderly will be separated from the rest of the project by a six-foot-high fence so that access is limited to the two designated entry portals of the site (Figure 9.4).

The density of the complex for the elderly, if calculated independent of the rest of the site, is one hundred seven units to the acre. Because the building is intended to function without hired security personnel, the buildings and grounds have been laid out so as to aid the elderly residents in controlling their own environment. The grounds are designed with only one access area (two portals) facing the major public street. These pedestrian and vehicular entries are adjacent to each other and positioned opposite the building entry so as to facilitate natural surveillance by residents sitting in the lobby or on the grounds of their building. The path between the public street and the building entrance follows a short straight line to enable residents and visitors to view the walk, building entry, lobby, and elevator waiting area before leaving the public street. The lobby of the building is provided with seating facilities and card tables to encourage residents to gather informally in and around the entry and elevator waiting area (lower portion of Figure 9.5).

The ground floor of the building has been given over entirely to communal facilities directed to the needs of the elderly residents and to elderly in the surrounding community. The area immediately to the left of the entry door will house the building's adminstration offices and a medical suite.

Opposite the entry is a set of doors providing access to the grounds at the rear of the building. These rear grounds are designed for comparatively passive activity, in contrast with the grounds in front of the building which contain play courts for active games. To the right of the elevators are a kitchen and dining area, designed to seat and serve about a hundred persons at any one time.

Sofas, card tables, and a library are located to the right of the main entry, opposite the elevators. The front of the building opposite the elevators (the side facing the street) is glazed floor to ceiling to allow visual surveillance and the monitoring of outdoor and indoor activities by residents.

The ground floor of the building has been given an additional wing that extends along the entry walk. This wing houses arts and crafts and game rooms. Although this additional wing may be seen as somewhat of a luxury, it is provided here because the ground floor of this building is intended to serve as a "golden age" center for the surrounding community.

The community circulation area of the typical floor of the building was designed as a alternative to the standard long, double-loaded corri-

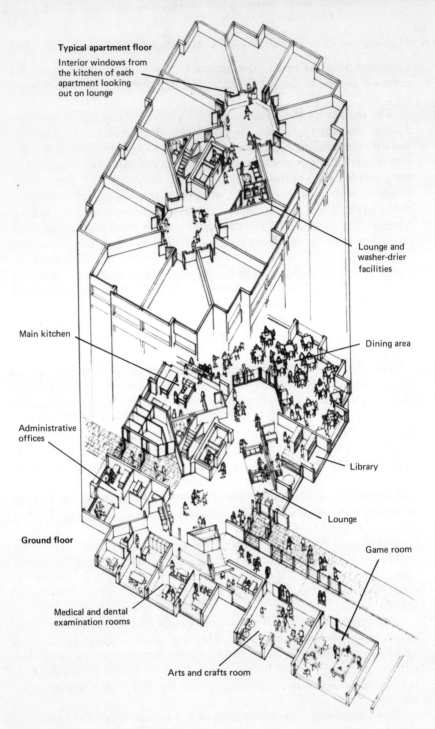

Typical apartment floor

Interior windows from
the kitchen of each
apartment looking
out on lounge

Lounge and
washer-drier
facilities

Main kitchen

Dining area

Administrative
offices

Library

Ground floor

Lounge

Game room

Medical and dental
examination rooms

Arts and crafts room

Fig. 9.5: Newark—isometric drawing of the building for the elderly, showing ground floor (below) and a typical upper floor (above).

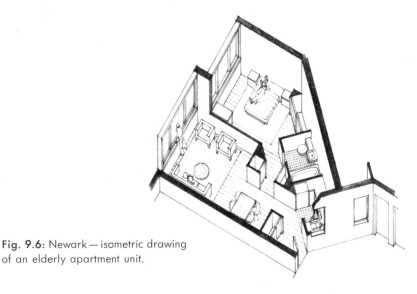

Fig. 9.6: Newark — isometric drawing of an elderly apartment unit.

dor building. In this floor plan, all twelve apartment units have their doors opening onto interior courts (upper portion of Figure 9.5). There are two courts per floor, each court serving six apartment units. Each apartment unit has been provided with a window that faces onto an interior court. The window is located in the kitchen area of each unit, adjacent to the entry door. These windows are made of a nonbreakable fire-resistant glass (Figure 9.6).

On each floor the area opposite the elevator has been provided with a sofa, chair, and table. The common laundry facilities for each floor are also located here, behind glass partitions. From the window of each unit, it is possible to see virtually every door and window in the six-unit interior court. In addition, most residents can, from their interior windows, observe activity in the elevator area, the lounge, and the laundry room of their floor.

The layout of the individual floors and of the entire building is directed at providing opportunities for residents to get together. Many elderly, new to a multifamily building, are shy; although they may desire the companionship of others, they are reluctant, or incapable, of striking up conversations or otherwise initiating contact with unknown residents. On each floor of the building, sofas have been placed opposite the elevators and adjacent to the laundry room to encourage residents to sit in the public area. They provide the opportunity and social pretext for meeting other residents.

Similarly, the interior windows of each apartment allow residents to both see into the corridor and to be seen from it. A resident busying himself or herself in the kitchen can see the comings and goings of other residents and can see other residents sitting in the lounge area near the elevators or going to do their wash. Residents can use the excuse of chance face-to-face encounter through the interior windows of their apartments as an opportunity to join others in their activities. In standard double-loaded corridor buildings residents are hidden behind their locked and blind apartment doors. The opportunity or excuse for chance meetings between residents is limited, thus further reinforcing residents' feelings of being isolated and forgotten—a common complaint among retired elderly.

The wedge-shaped plan of each apartment unit for the elderly was dictated by our desire to group the units to create interior, semiprivate court areas leading to the entry of each unit. The kitchens and interior windows of the units were placed near the entry doors to the apartments to further reinforce the opportunity for chance encounter. On the other hand, when residents desire privacy within their kitchens they can hang a curtain over their window and pull it closed when they please.

The lounging and activity areas provided on the ground floor of the building and on the grounds around the building provide additional opportunities for meeting other residents.

By facilitating surveillance in the public areas of the building, by providing the opportunity for residents to come to recognize their neighbors easily, and by stimulating the use of the common public circulation areas outside the individual apartment units, residents have been provided the opportunity of naturally controlling the use of the public areas of their building and its grounds.

Design of the Row-House Units

The primary intent in the site planning and design of the row-house units in Newark was to assign a large portion of the grounds around each unit for the use, maintenance, and control of individual families. Much of the grounds at the rear of each unit was therefore made private. To ensure further the privacy of this outdoor space and the security of the doors and windows at the rear of the dwelling, the buildings were positioned so that no access was possible between the public streets and the private rear-yard areas. The only access to the private area of the home and its rear yard is through the front door of the unit.

The traditional single-family house is normally designed with at least two doors—a front door and a side or rear door. This allows members of the family to use the side or rear door for everyday access while the front door is used only for occasional formal access by guests or visitors. In this traditional arrangement, the formal part of the house is normally positioned adjacent to the front door of the unit and contains the living room and formal dining area (Figure 9.7). These formal rooms are not intended for everyday use by all members of the family, or, to put it another way, they are used by the family's children only in

Fig. 9.7: Ground-floor plan of the traditional, detached single-family American house.

the company of adults. By contrast, the side or rear door of the traditional single-family house opens onto the kitchen and the informal dining and living areas of the house, which have no restrictions on access for the family's children.

In designing a single-family house with only one entry from the public street it was necessary, therefore, to position the *informal*, heavily trafficked areas of the house adjacent to the entry while at the same time creating a direct means of access to the *formal* area (Figure 9.8a and b). This provides residents with the opportunity to invite visitors into the formal area of the home without having them see the disarray in the informal areas (Figures 9.9 and 9.10).

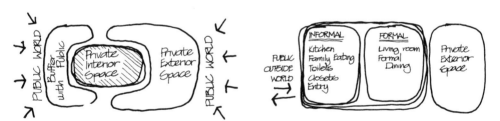

Fig. 9.8a: Home—the private realm of each family.

Fig. 9.8b: The informal and formal zones of home.

Fig. 9.9: Access to fomal and informal zones.

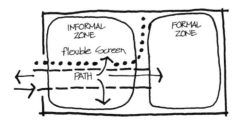

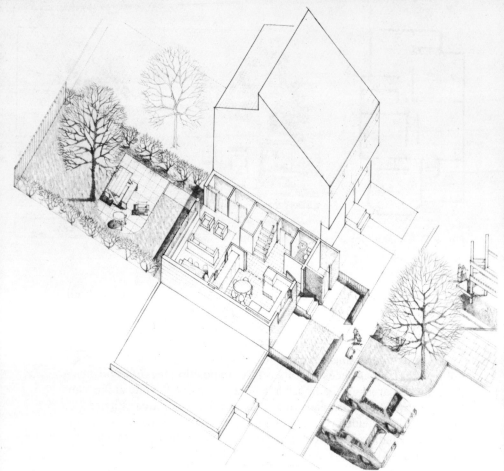

Fig. 9.10: Newark — isometric drawing of the ground floor of the row-house unit.

In the row-house unit design (Figures 9.10 and 9.11a, b, and c), the informal wing of the house (the kitchen and family dining area) are located in the front of the house immediately to the left of the entry to the street. The formal wing of the house, containing the living room and formal dining area, are located at the rear of the house facing the private rear yard of the family. There is a short central corridor that leads directly from the front entry door of the unit to the formal living area at the rear. The informal kitchen and dining area is provided with sliding doors so it can be easily screened from view.

Immediately to the right of the entry door to the unit is a clothes closet and a bathroom containing a toilet and washbasin. Children can clean up (or be scrubbed down) just as they enter the unit and before they are allowed access to the rest of the house. With this positioning of the ground-floor bathroom, children can also dash into the house,

UPPER LEVEL

Fig. 9.11a: Newark—plan of entry and upper levels of typical three-bedroom unit.

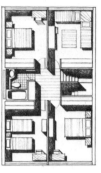

UPPER LEVEL

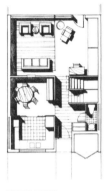

ENTRY LEVEL

Fig. 9.11b: Newark—plan of entry and upper levels of typical four-bedroom unit.

ENTRY LEVEL

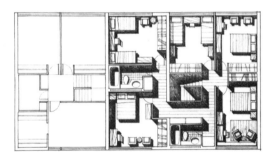

UPPER LEVEL

Fig. 9.11c: Newark—plan of entry and upper levels of typical five-bedroom unit.

ENTRY LEVEL

relieve themselves quickly, and go back out to play without taking off their cold- or wet-weather clothes and without tracking through the rest of the house.

The front portion of the house which contains the kitchen, family dining area, bathroom, and clothes closet is floored with tile so that it can be washed or cleaned easily. The kitchen has been positioned to allow adults working there to easily supervise children at play in front of the unit and to control access to the rest of the house.

It is not uncommon for members of families with children to take meals independently of one another and at varying times of the day. The design and positioning of the informal kitchen and dining area facilitates the preparation and eating of snacks on the run.

Access to the bedrooms on the second floor of the unit is by a stairway off the entry vestibule. The stair has been positioned to allow children and other family members to go to their rooms directly upon entering the unit without having to go through the formal area of the house.

The rear of the house contains a living room and a formal dining area which have been positioned to allow the easy passage of food across a counter from within the kitchen. Sliding panels at counter level are provided to allow the kitchen to be screened off once food has been passed through. The entire rear wall of the living room has been designed with windows looking out to the private yard at the back. This serves both to create a strong association between the dwelling unit interior and the family's private outdoor grounds and to expand the feeling of spaciousness in the living room.

As the row-house units are actually quite small, an endeavor was made to produce as spacious a feeling as possible by creating long sight lines throughout the unit. On entering the house, one can see a relatively long distance in two directions: through to the living room and out into the rear yard, and up the stairs to the second floor. The use of these long sight lines has also made the layout of the row-house comprehensible at a glance.

The private yard at the rear of the row-house unit was conceived as a quiet area somewhat separated from the tumult of children at play. This rear yard is intended to be used for outside family dining in warm weather; as a place where the adults of the family can have a quiet drink at the end of the day, alone or with company; and as a place where a very young child—up to five years of age—can be left outside to play alone without concern that the child will wander off.

Play areas for children five to ten years old are provided in the common interior courts behind the individual rear yards. Access to these play courts is via each family's private yard. Play areas for older

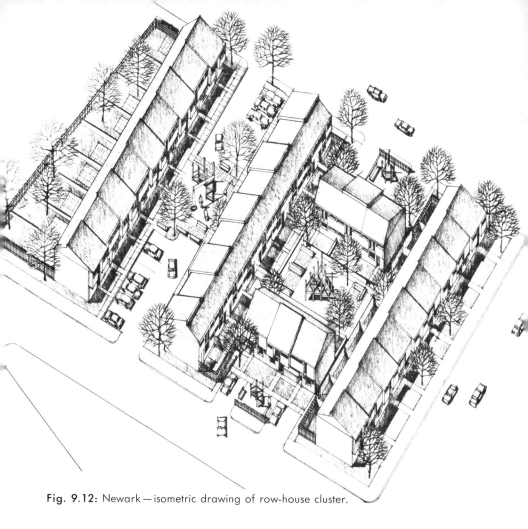

Fig. 9.12: Newark — isometric drawing of row-house cluster.

children are located in the front of the dwelling units, where older children have more ready access to other children and can observe street activities (Figure 9.12).

Parking space for the car for row-house units has been located immediately in front of each house. Both the older children's play areas and the parking spaces are within view of the kitchen window of each unit. This both facilitates surveillance and sets up a direct association between the dwelling unit and these outside areas. This positioning and the surveillance, and associations they are intended to encourage, serve to extend the zone of influence of the dwelling unit to include the street; supervision and control of street activity from within the unit is thus enhanced.

The City of Newark requires that all new housing developments provide on-site parking at the rate of one parking space for every two units. The remaining parking need (considering a typical need of one parking space per unit) is allowed to be provided for with curbside parking. In this scheme, curbside parking is located in front of the entries to each of the units. To accommodate the 50 per cent off-street parking requirement, while still answering our own requirements of locating car parking in front of each unit, we have created cuts in the existing city blocks for vehicular access and parking. These cuts also serve to provide play areas and access to the front doors of the units.

Design of the Walk-Up Buildings

The walk-up buildings were grouped together in a cluster of ten on one city block of the Newark site (Figures 9.13 and 9.14). The configu-

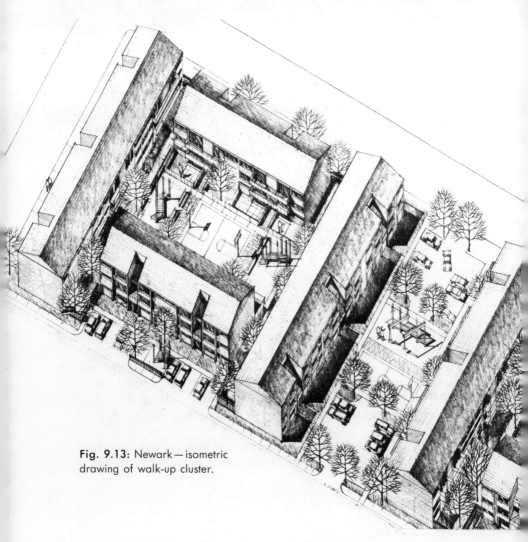

Fig. 9.13: Newark — isometric drawing of walk-up cluster.

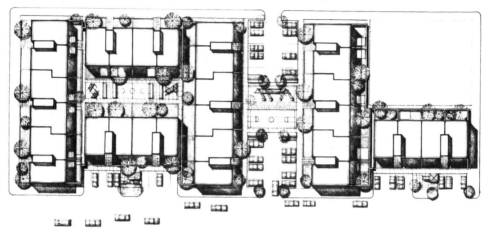

Fig. 9.14: Newark—site plan of the walk-up cluster, including play and parking areas.

ration of the blocks of buildings is similar to the row-house buildings in that buildings are grouped together to create interior courts. As with the row-house blocks, a six-foot-high steel fence between the buildings restricts acess to these rear courts from neighboring streets.

The walk-up buildings have their entries defined by setbacks in the façade of the building. Each entry serves six families, two per floor on each of the three floors. The entry door to each apartment unit immediately abuts the central access stair. This gives residents the benefit of mutual supervision of the common access stair and the apartment door opposite their own. It also helps bring the semiprivate vertical circulation space into the zone of influence of adjacent apartments (Figure 9.15).

The apartment unit itself is laid out so that the entry door is central to the apartment. This allows residents the choice of direct access to either the kitchen and dining area, the living room, or the bedrooms from the one entry door (Figures 9.16a and b). The apartments are designed with the kitchen windows facing the front of the building. These windows are also located adjacent to the building entries to facilitate residents' surveillance and control of the building entrance, their cars, and the older children's play areas.

In each building the living rooms of the apartment units face the common rear court shared by sixty families in the ten-building cluster. The stair leading from the balcony to the grounds below also provides the required second means of egress from the second- and third-floor apartments in the event of fire.

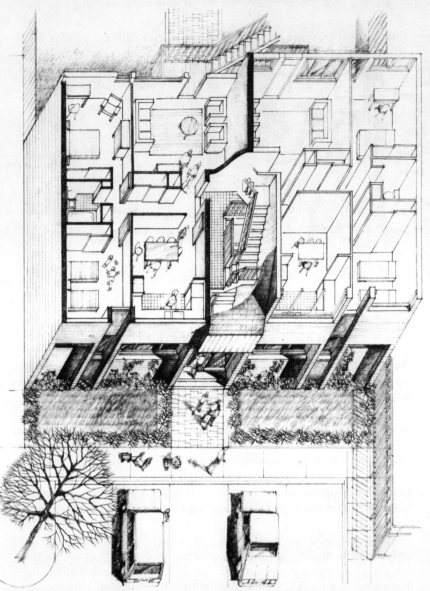

Fig. 9.15: Newark — isometric drawing of walk-up, showing interior of building and apartment.

The families in the ground-floor apartments are provided with patios accessible from a door in the living room. Families living on the second and third floors have equivalent access to balconies that both face on and lead to the communal court at the rear.

Some play areas for teen-agers are provided at the front of the walk-up buildings, but most play facilities and sitting areas are provided in the interior courts at the rear (Figure 9.13).

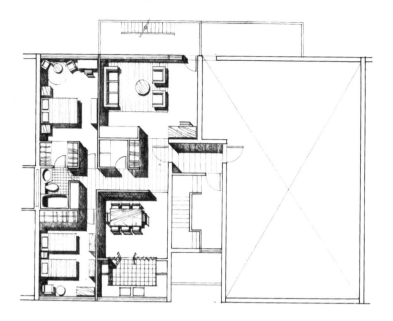

SECOND & THIRD LEVELS

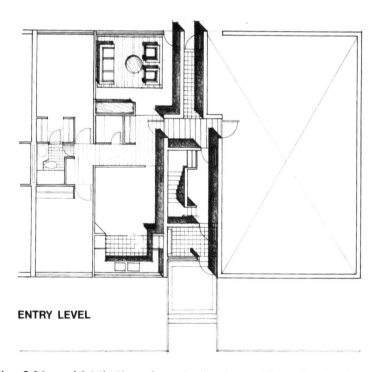

ENTRY LEVEL

Figs. 9.16a and 9.16b: Plans of entry level and typical floor of walk-up building.

Fig. 9.17: View of the one-acre site with the tower for the elderly on the left, above a three-story walk-up for families with children.

Prototype for the Integration of Housing for the Elderly and for Families with Children on a Small Site

The solution provided in the Newark housing development, while typical of urban renewal sites of about five acres in size, does not answer the needs of developers who have to build on small sites of approximately one acre. Because of its comparatively large size, the Newark development allowed the clear separation of elderly from families with children. Also, because the housing for the elderly was built as a high-rise at a density of one hundred forty-four units to the acre, we were able to house the families with children in row houses and walk-ups and still achieve an over-all density for the development of over forty units to the acre. But what options are open to a developer who has only a one-acre site to work with and must build at an even higher density? The following scheme, designed for a New York City site, had the requirements that the developer build at a density of one hundred units to the acre and accommodate elderly and families with children on the same site. This solution endeavors to achieve on a one-acre site in New York City what was achieved on a seven-and-a-half-acre site in Newark.

The site is typical of what most developers can acquire in the heavily built-up areas of large cities. In consists of one third of a city block and is one and one third acres in size. The program provides thirty-six units for families with children in three-story walk-ups and one hundred four units for the elderly in a high-rise, for a total of one hundred forty units to the acre. The one hundred four units for the elderly are located in a nine-story elevator building positioned on top of one of the three-story walk-up buildings (Figure 9.17). The lowest floor of the high rise, which is four stories above the ground, has been designed to serve as the communal indoor floor for the elderly residents of the building. It contains the medical, recreation, and administrative areas that are located in the ground floor of the high-rise at Newark. As an immediate adjunct to this interior floor space, there is a larger exterior area on the roof of the three-story walk-up building which will serve as a communal outdoor sitting and recreation area.

The grounds of the one-acre site, like the buildings, are subdivided into two separate areas: one serving the families with children, the other serving the elderly (Figure 9.18a). These two ground areas do not overlap or touch. They serve to allow both groups to enter their own buildings independently of one another, even where one building sits on top of the other (Figure 9.18b). The grounds and lobby of the building for the elderly face close onto the parking lot and the adjacent city street (Figure 9.19). Some outdoor seating and planting areas are also located here. The outdoor grounds serving the families with children living in the three-story walk-ups are located on the opposite side of the high-rise building and provide parking, recreation, and sitting areas. Individual patios are provided for the families living on the ground floor.

There are thirty-six off-street parking spaces provided for the thirty-six walk-up units and forty-four parking spaces provided for the one hundred four units for the elderly. These ratios are realistic in inner-city areas because, where high-density development is required, mass transit is usually available; where land is cheaper and more plentiful, mass transit facilities are usually less prevalent and reliable and parking ratios must, accordingly, be higher.

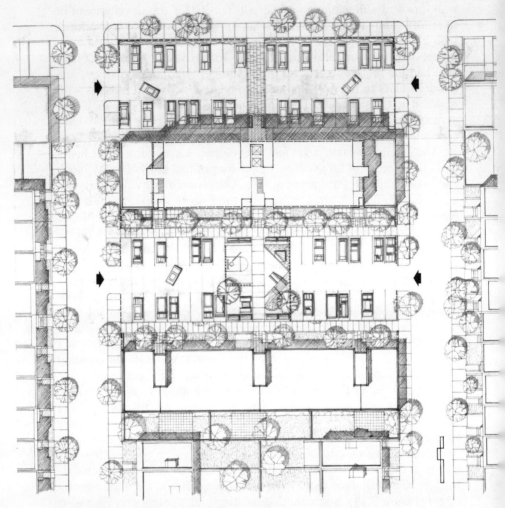

Fig. 9.18a: Plan of the one-acre site serving a total of one hundred forty families: one hundred four elderly and thirty-six families with children.

The walk-up units that do not have a high-rise building above them are identical in design to the walk-up units used in our Newark scheme. The walk-up units that have the high-rise for the elderly set on top of them have had to be designed differently so as to accommodate the structure of the building above with its requirements for secondary fire exits. Three small areas are thus cut out of each three-story walk-up to provide emergency access to the ground for the elderly residents of the building above. Aside from that, the three-story walk-up which sits

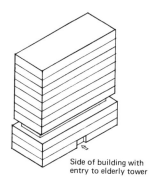

Side of building with
entry to elderly tower

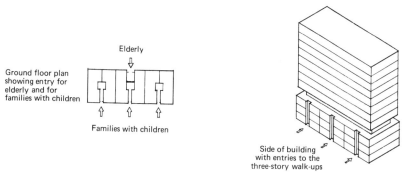

Ground floor plan
showing entry for
elderly and for
families with children

Elderly

Families with children

Side of building
with entries to the
three-story walk-ups

Fig. 9.18b: Schematic of the high-rise building combining three-story walk-ups for families with children and an elevator building for the elderly or families with no children.

Fig. 9.19: Ground floor of the building containing the high-rise for the elderly. The lobby of the latter building is at the top center of the drawing. The other side of the building serves the entries to the walk-up for families with children.

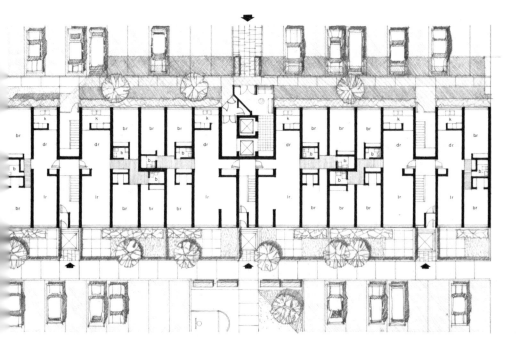

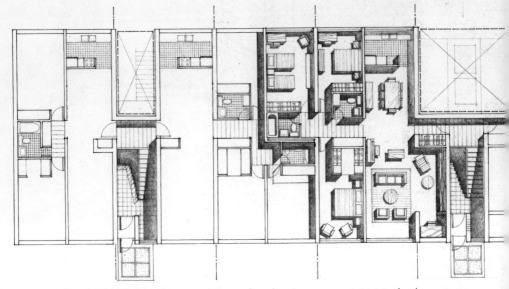

Fig. 9.20: Portion of a typical floor plan showing an apartment in the three-story walk-up located under the high-rise for the elderly.

Fig. 9.21: Portion of a typical floor plan of the high-rise building.

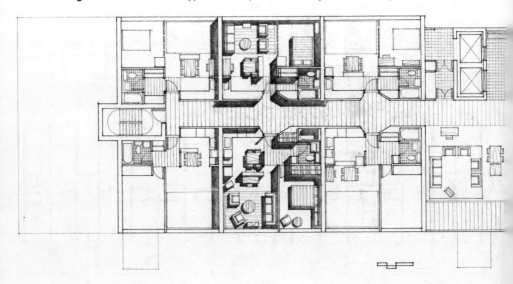

under the high-rise functions much as the three-story walk-up in Newark (Figure 9.20).

The eight floors above the surrogate ground floor of the building for the elderly together provide, as noted above, one hundred four apartment units.The apartments consist of a fifty-fifty mix of one-bedroom units and efficiencies (Figure 9.21). The kitchens have also been placed adjacent to the front door of the units and have been provided with windows to allow residents to look out of their apartments to see the activity in the corridors.

This one-acre design demonstrates that it is possible to apply all the community-of-interest guidelines to a small site and produce a solution which houses different life-style groups at very high densities, but in their own distinct environments. Clearly the solution is not totally satisfactory for either of the life-style groups: the elderly have little outdoor space and the families with children have limited play space and private outdoor grounds. But communal outdoor areas for each group are provided and they are located so as to be of greatest utility and to be under the natural control and surveillance of residents. The solution may not be ideal, but it holds its own rather well when compared with the typical one-building environment which houses elderly and families with children together at one hundred forty-four units to the acre.

X

The Modification of Existing Housing Developments

Chapter IX dealt with the problem of integrating those guidelines addressing the socioeconomic characteristics of residents with those addressing physical design in new housing developments. The Newark and New York City programs and sites were together typical of the problems facing most designers of moderate-income housing developments located in urban settings. The major difficulties presented in both these problems stem, first, from the requirements for high-density development, and, second, from the peculiar conditions of the sites. But in both cases these problems were comparatively simple to resolve because the designer was starting from scratch — with a new program and a fresh site. By comparison, the use of community-of-interest guidelines in the modification of existing housing developments is a far more difficult task.

As it is not probable that this nation will see in the near future a housing boom like that of the 1950s and 1960s the most likely urban housing resource for low- and moderate-income families for the next ten years will continue to be the existing stock of 1.5 million units of federally assisted housing built over the past three decades. The problem, then, is one of developing programs and designs for these existing developments which will make them and their neighborhoods again viable.

Nature of the Problems

If an existing development is composed of a building type which is totally inappropriate to the needs of the family type and income group occupying it, no amount of physical modification is likely to improve conditions for very long. Extensive physical changes coupled with the provision of new superintendents, guards, or doormen may be able to put off the demise of the development for a while, but the cost of these physical changes will be high and the financial burden of the new personnel will be heavy and continuous. The expected life of the development, therefore, even after costly modifications and new personnel, is likely to be short. The best solution in such circumstances is to move the residents out of the inappropriate buildings into those better suited to their life-style and needs. The task of shifting residents is rarely as difficult as it might at first appear since it is probable that the poor fit of resident type to building type has already produced a high vacancy rate.

Then there are cases where the buildings of an existing housing project are appropriate to the needs of the residents but the grounds are poorly laid out. Residents and management may be in accord on how to modify the grounds but actual implementation of the physical changes will produce unexpected surprises. People become accustomed to using their environments in set ways, and changes to the physical environment which prevent access and movement along old paths will be resisted and resented (Figure 10.1).

Fig. 10.1: Openings were made in two newly installed fences by residents who had become accustomed to the convenience of a short cut past their neighbors' backyards to get to the bus stop.

Finally, there are cases where both the buildings and the grounds are appropriate to the needs of existing residents, but the percentage of one-parent welfare families has climbed too high and has sent the development into a spiral of decline and abandonment. Even with a high number of vacancies, it will be impossible to attract two-parent families back into the development because of its past reputation. The strategy that has to be adopted in such cases is far more complex than that involved in the programming and design of a new project from scratch: it may involve the redesign of the project's physical plant: the development of marketing procedures to attract new types of tenants, and a new management and leasing program. In the following pages I present some of the methods we have adopted in the past to address these problems.

The Planning Process: Evaluation

Two summary tables discussed in previous chapters are indispensable tools for the evaluation of existing housing developments. They are reproduced here again for convenience. Table 10.1 speaks to the suitability of various housing types to the needs of different life-style groups, and Table 10.2 speaks to the percentage of one-parent families which can be housed in buildings and developments of different size in order to maintain stability. The first step in the evaluation of a development involves determining whether its buildings are suitable to the needs of the families occupying them.

Table 10.1 provides a qualitative matrix for this purpose in that three degrees of acceptable fit are presented: strongly recommended (**), recommended (*), and barely acceptable (●). In making an assessment of the future of an existing project on the basis of the appropriateness of fit, a planner may have to be content with a classification

Table 10.1: The Assignment of Family Types to Building Types

Family Type	Building Types					
	1. Single-family	2. Walk-ups	3. Medium High-Rise		4. Elevator High-Rise	
			Doorman	Non-doorman	Doorman	Non-doorman
Families with children	**	**	*	●	●	■
Elderly	*	■	**	*	**	*
Working adults	■	●	**	■	**	■

** strongly recommended   ● barely acceptable
* recommended   ■ not recommended

of "barely acceptable" because no option is available which would allow him to consider moving existing residents to another location.

Table 10.2 deals only with families with children. It lists a range of percentages of one-parent families that can be housed in different building types while still maintaining long-term stability. These percentages are in turn adjusted for the size of the development: the larger the development, the lower the percentage of one-parent families that can be housed in different building type. Examination of the percentage of one-parent families in a project in light of this chart will indicate how far along an existing development is in its spiral of decline.

Table 10.2: Percentage of AFDC Families in Stable Mix, as Affected by the Number of Units Sharing a Common Entry and the Size of the Development[a]

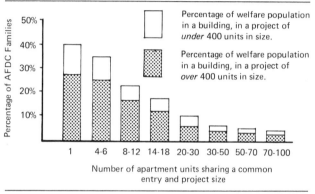

[a]Hypothetical representation based on the experience of housing managers of moderate-income housing containing a percentage of AFDC Families.

The next step in the planning process involves an assessment of the comparative defensibility of the layout of the existing grounds. The principles to be employed in this evaluation were discussed in Chapter VIII. There are physical design factors which define the degree of defensibility of any development, irrespective of building type or the life-style and income of residents. The questions to be asked to determine a project's defensibility are, in order of importance:

1. Do the building entry and exit doors remain locked front, back, and side?
2. Do the main entries to buildings face directly onto a main public-access street?
3. Are the grounds at the rear and sides of buildings physically defined as being for the exclusive use of building residents? Are

the rear and side yards accessible from the interior of buildings only, or can they be reached from the public street?
4. Are the entries to individual dwelling units visible from the grounds, preferably from the main public-access street?
5. Are the grounds surrounding the ground-floor apartment units fenced off with real or symbolic barriers?

Developments which are rated positively in response to the above queries should prove highly defensible. If developments are deficient in those characteristics at the top of the list (1 through 3) a serious security problem is likely present. Those combinations of physical characteristics which satisfy the criteria at the top of the list are better than those which satisfy the criteria at the bottom of the list. Deficiencies in a good many of the above criteria can be remedied through physical modification to the existing grounds and buildings. It should be remembered however that a building's defensibility is also affected by the number of apartment units that share the entry to a building and by the social characteristics discussed earlier in the description of the two charts in this chapter.

Modifications to Row-House Developments

A significant percentage of all public housing in the United States consists of developments made up of row-house buildings. While this is not true for very large cities like New York and Chicago (or for smaller cities like Newark which are located within the metropolitan area of larger cities), it is true even for medium-size cities like Philadelphia, San Francisco, and Washington. In smaller urban areas—the size of Indianapolis and Oklahoma City—public housing for families with children was built primarily as row-house developments. This was a good first step in the programming of these developments. However, many of these developments are today facing serious crime and

Fig. 10.2: Grounds and row-house buildings of a typical public housing project in Indianapolis. The grounds are open and totally unrelated to individual units or their entries.

Fig. 10.3: Grounds of the Raymond Villa housing project in Indianapolis, showing the accumulation of litter and weeds and tracks made by vehicles in the mud.

vacancy problems just as are their high-rise cousins in larger cities. Even row-house buildings, which our guidelines identify as the most desirable form of building for families with children, can be so poorly positioned on their grounds as to make the environment outside the home uncontrollable and dangerous. However, the factor that is usually the first cause of crime and instability in row-house developments is the socioeconomic makeup of the resident population. Row-house developments that have been identified as crisis ridden will usually be found to have an occupancy of 75 per cent or more one-parent families living on AFDC.

The Indianapolis Problem

In Indianapolis, because the housing authority used the same basic plan, all eight row-house developments were built without taking advantage of the possibilities inherent in row-house design. The row-house buildings sit on large open fields — with no attempt made to relate any of the grounds to individual units or to groups of buildings (Figure 10.2). The policy of the Indianapolis Housing Authority has been to discourage residents from adopting the grounds outside their units for their own private use, maintenance, and control: the grounds are intended to be maintained and policed by the housing authority. As a consequence, no fences or shrubs have been used to assign the grounds to individual row houses. Not surprisingly, the grounds between the row-house units now function as continuous public, open space. They are proving too costly for the housing authority to maintain and police, are in dreadful condition, little used, and dangerous (Figures 10.3 and 10.4).

In interviewing the housing authority management to determine why they had adopted this policy, our Institute staff learned that they believe that public housing residents are incapable of maintaining the grounds around their own homes and furthermore, were disinclined to do so. With this as their operating assumption, the management concluded that they had no alternative but to undertake the comprehensive maintenance and policing of the grounds themselves. The grounds maintenance staff also claimed that in order to be able to make use of their large lawn mowers and snow removal equipment, the grounds had to be kept free of any fences, planting, or other individual demarcating elements. As Figures 10.3 and 10.5 attest, however, the large public open areas are not free of litter, and they are hardly cov-

Fig. 10.4: Areas that the residents "consider dangerous and never go to at night" in the Raymond Villa housing project. (Composite based on all interviews.)

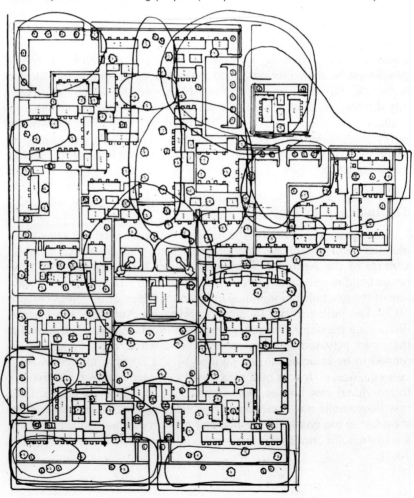

Fig. 10.5 The grounds of the Raymond Villa project. Poor drainage in combination with litter and vehicle ruts have resulted in the creation of permanently embedded garbage mounds.

ered with a carpet of grass. It is obvious that the housing authority grounds maintenance staff cannot keep up with the work load it so jealously insists on guarding for itself.

Our interviews with a random sample of 20 per cent of the residents of the two housing projects in Indianapolis which were most poorly maintained, Raymond Villa and Hawthorne, revealed that 85 per cent of the residents desired to have the public grounds assigned to them on an individual basis and further stated that they were both willing and able to maintain the grounds themselves.

Presented with these findings and with a specific proposal to subdivide the grounds and assign them for the use and control of residents, the housing authority director and staff continued to express their traditional skepticism. The proposal remains unimplemented despite the demonstrated success of past efforts (see the discussion which follows on the experiment involving modifications to the grounds of the Clason Point housing project in New York City).

The Clason Point Experiment

Most public housing residents in the United States now consist of low-income families, a high percentage of them black, many of them supported by welfare. Many of the families come to public housing from single rooms or portions of tenement flats and have had no previous experience with the care or maintenance of a home of their own. Fewer still have, in their past, ever identified a particular parcel of land as their own. This past personal history of public housing residents is known to housing management, and rather than adopt a policy of guiding residents toward the assumption of responsibility and to the care and maintenance of housing, most public housing authorities assume that their residents are inadequate to the task and accept the notion of the residents' full dependency. Our Institute staff became interested in testing this basic assumption on the part of housing authority managements and sought to experiment with breaking up and assigning the public grounds of a row-house housing project to individual residents. We were also interested in determining whether the act of designating ground areas to be under the zone of influence of residents would evoke in residents the notion that they had the right to control activities in those areas outside their dwelling units. We hypothesized that the reassignment of previously public grounds to individual families would stimulate them to adopt these areas as their own and to assume responsibility for maintaining and securing them.

We hoped, too, that residents would begin to perceive the public street which bordered their new grounds in a different way. We reasoned that residents who looked out their windows after the modifications would now see the public street, not as a distant environment, but as an area which abutted their private lawn. We further reasoned that if residents perceived their front yard as a zone which they controlled, then by extension the public sidewalk a step beyond their yard would also come to be seen as being under their influence and scrutiny. In the reassignment of grounds, we were endeavoring to kindle the notion in residents that what takes place in the public street outside their homes is also in their zone of influence.

Our second interest in the row-house experiments was to provide low-income residents, through their successful efforts to improve the grounds around their own homes, with living testament of the success and permanence of their own individual efforts. Essentially, residents' success in improving the grounds would provide both their middle-income neighbors across the street and housing authority management with evidence of the residents' viability in effecting positive change — first, in the physical and, second, it was hoped, in the social and political world around them.

The opportunity to radically redesign the grounds of a row-house project and to reassign it to residents was given us by the New York City Housing Authority. Clason Point Gardens is located adjacent to the South Bronx, a comparatively high-crime area in the city of New York. As these modifications were completed in 1972, we have had the opportunity of measuring the effectiveness of these changes and their viability over time.

The physical modifications at Clason Point had three goals:

1. To assign as much of the public grounds of the project to the control of individual families and small groupings of families through the use of real and symbolic fencing.
2. To reduce the number of pedestrian routes through the project so as to limit access and to intensify the use of the remaining walks. (Only those walks which passed in front of the units

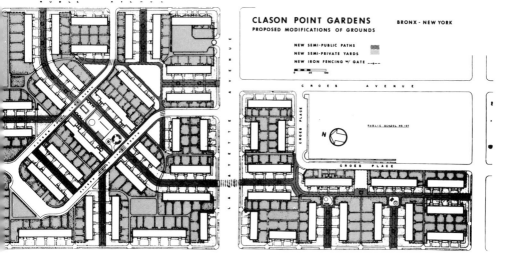

Fig. 10.6: Site plan showing the ground modifications to the Clason Point housing project. The light gray areas show the new semiprivate rear yards, defined by six-foot fences.

would remain in use, and these were widened to allow them to be used for play and sitting areas. New lighting was added to improve visibility and to extend the walks' period of use into the evening.)

3. To improve the image of the project by resurfacing the exterior of the existing cement-block building and by identifying the individual units by varying the color of the resurfacing material.

Six-foot-high iron fencing was used to create real barriers so as to both define and secure the rear-yard areas. The number of families grouped in each cluster was determined not by policy but by the existing disposition of buildings. The clusters ranged from as few as twelve dwellings per cluster to as many as forty (Figure 10.6). This proved unfortunate in that residents in the larger clusters had difficulty keeping the gates to the collective rear-yard area locked. There was also more uniformity in the quality of maintenance of rear-yard areas in the smaller clusters than in the larger. Had we realized how much variation would occur with the size of the cluster, we could have subdivided the larger clusters by running a fence across them to cut them in two.

The six-foot iron fences defined 50 per cent of the previously public grounds located at rear of the units for the private use of individual families. The low concrete curbing placed adjacent to the public walk in front of the units served to redefine an additional 30 per cent of the public grounds as private front lawns (Figure 10.7). It should be noted

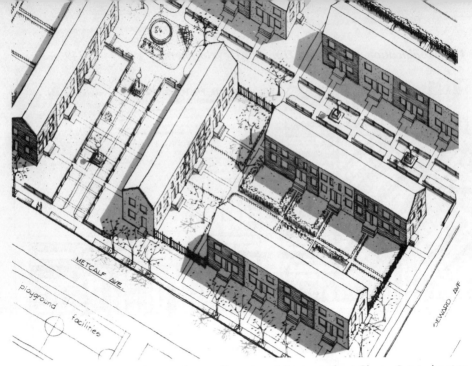

Fig. 10.7: Aerial view of a small portion of the grounds at Clason Point, showing the proposed fencing off of the rear grounds, the defined front walks, the new lighting, benches, and play equipment.

that the fencing and curbing installed only defined collective areas, not individual front or rear yards. If residents desired to define further the boundaries of their own front or rear yards, they had to install their own side fencing. Most of the residents chose to do so after the first year.

Fig. 10.8: The new combination planter, lighting, and seating element and the widening of the walk serve to bring residents out to occupy the areas in front of their homes.

Fig. 10.9: An area of the Clason Point housing project before modification. The original site design provided no grounds in front of the units for individual residents; instead, two central common green areas were provided, one of which was fenced. The photograph reveals how poorly these public grounds were maintained by the housing authority due to insufficient funds.

To improve the usefulness of the major pedestrian walk as a play area, the sidewalk was widened. A combination planter, seating, and lighting element was placed in the center of the public walk at intervals of forty feet (Figure 10.8). The new, decorative lighting served both to highlight the main public walk and to facilitate use of the benches at night. The lighting also increased residents' surveillance potential and feelings of security.

At selected intersections of the primary paths, "play nodes" were created for young children and teen-agers. Seating was placed nearby to allow other children and adults to sit and watch the play activity (Figures 10.9 and 10.10).

Fig. 10.10: View of the identical area, shown in Figure 10.9, after modification and resident response. The central common areas were made into sidewalks, and the grounds adjacent to the units were reassigned as front lawns to be maintained by individual families. The fencing and planting of the front lawns is the work of the residents themselves. A small play area for young children was provided in the foreground.

Fig. 10.11: Clason Point resident at work fencing off and improving the grounds of his rear yard following the installation of the new iron fencing.

We hoped that our first step of assigning 80 per cent of the previously public grounds of the projects to residents, using management-installed fencing and then curbs, would encourage residents to further define what they perceived as their own individual grounds, by installing side fences and then planting grass and shrubs. We saw the residents' assumption of responsibility for their individual yards as the simple action of someone taking care of what he now saw as his own. This proved to be the case (Figure 10.11). It is interesting to note that our creation of collectively held areas requiring joint maintenance by a small group of residents had little or no success. Communal areas were cared for only when one adjacent resident took it upon himself to do so (Figure 10.12).

The reassignment of public grounds was undertaken with the intention of expanding the domain in which individual residents felt they had the right to expect accountability from strangers or other residents. We hoped to be able to extend the private realm of the inside of the apartment to include the outside grounds and, possibly, the adjacent public sidewalk. It was theorized that this reassignment would lead residents to naturally watch the users of the grounds and walks more carefully and to set up in their own minds expectations about the kind of behavior that would be acceptable in these areas. We hoped, through

Fig. 10.12: Planters, located within the central walk, were found to be tended by a single adjacent resident, if at all, but never as the result of a collective assumption of responsibility by a group of adjacent residents.

the reorganization of the grounds, to set up a dependent relationship between spatial organization and social expectations, and that as a consequence of the curbing and fencing, informal expectations on the part of residents would become more exacting and differentiated. The redefined grounds provided clear, well-marked distinctions between public and private zones and eliminated most of the functionless no man's land for which no individual residents felt responsible. We also hoped that crime and fear of crime would be reduced in areas where increased clarity concerning behavioral guidelines was established. Tenants, we hoped, would feel they now had the right to impose social controls and pressures on strangers and neighbors.

Interviews and observations were conducted prior and after the modifications. Changes in residents' conception of the sociospatial order of the project was assessed and an extensive examination made of their change in behavior and attitudes as a consequence of the redesign. A comparison of project crime and vandalism rates as recorded by the New York City Housing Authority police and superintendents was also made before and after the modifications.

Effectiveness of the Modifications

The first year after the modifications took place at Clason Point, the residents raked the topsoil of the grounds in front of their homes and planted the grass seed that was made available to them by the housing authority. To the surprise of many residents, the grass came up in abundance, and the area took on a carpet of green (Figure 10.13). At

Fig. 10.13: Residents' response to the grounds modifications in the spring of the first year.

Fig. 10.14a: View of grounds before modification.

the end of the first summer, residents began to demarcate their own front and rear yards with subfences, in many instances, the better to distinguish their patch of success from their neighbors' inadequate efforts (Figures 10.14a and b). Not to be outdone, unsuccessful residents plowed up the hard ground in their front and rear lawns and reseeded more carefully. In fact, they had acquired the knack of putting in seed, watering, and fertilizing by watching their successful neighbors.

 To the delight of those residents new to gardening, in the spring of

Fig. 10.14b: View of identical area in the summer of the second year.

Fig. 10.15: The installation of the six-foot high fencing to enclose the rear areas of this project has stimulated residents to create their own private patios. Note how barren the project grounds are in the foreground, whereas the grounds within the fenced-off area are planted by residents in grass and flowers, and contain picnic tables and barbecues.

the second year the grass came up by itself and was even more lush than the year before. This prompted residents to invest in small shrubs, trees, flowers, and garden furniture (Figure 10.15). An intense competition began between residents. In the third year the small shrubs had grown a few feet and the perennial flowers had expanded their root system and come up in abundance (Figure 10.16). Now residents began to expand their concern beyond their own front yards to the public sidewalk and the concrete planter in the center of the walk. On a systematic basis, residents began to sweep the public sidewalks in front of their homes, particularly when it appeared as if the authority's maintenance staff were derelict in their duties.

We had anticipated that residents' new assumption of grounds care and maintenance would meet with a positive response from the housing authority grounds personnel since the modifications were intended to decrease the workload of the staff. However, the response of the staff was the exact opposite of the one we anticipated. They complained that the new curbing, fencing, and concrete planters prevented them

Fig. 10.16: The growth of shrubs in the third summer following the modifications.

from using their power equipment. On completion of the modifications, the grounds supervisor at Clason Point put in for additional manpower which he felt was neccessary to handle his new workload. We were informed of his request by an anxious director of housing management who had also hoped that the grounds modifications would have the opposite effect. Following a site visit, however, it was determined by management personnel from the central office that no increase in grounds personnel was required. They concluded that, if anything, the grounds staff could actually be cut back. This decision was not implemented immediately, however, for fear of antagonizing the union to which they belonged. The response of the grounds staff to the negative reply it received to its request for personnel was to slow down their performance of work still further and allow garbage and litter to accumulate in the public walks and garbage disposal areas. Residents responded to this by cleaning up some of the sidewalks and garbage areas themselves for the first time in the history of the project. The slowdown by grounds maintenance personnel continued for over six months and was finally resolved when the Housing Authority replaced the grounds staff supervisor with one who felt comfortable with a policy which allowed residents to care for the grounds themselves. The supervisor in turn, redirected his staff's activity toward the maintenance of the public walks and play facilities. After a few months, the project's grounds maintenance staff was cut in half and the excess men moved to a neighboring project.

The over-all crime rate in the development (including breach of housing authority rules) was reduced by over 50 per cent. The premodification *monthly* average over-all crime rate at Clason Point was 6.91 crimes per 1,000 residents and the postmodification average was 3.16 crimes per 1,000 residents.[1]

The average burglary rate *per year* dropped from 5.15 per 1,000 residents in the premodification period to 3.71 in the postmodification period, a 28 per cent change. The average robbery rate dropped from 1.95 per 1,000 to 0. The average assault rate dropped from .53 per 1,000 to .31, a 42 per cent change.[2] The number of felonies during evening and nighttime hours decreased by more than half.[3] Thus, for the serious crime categories—burglary, robbery, and assault—the average crime rate was reduced by 61.5 per cent.[4]

The percentage of people who felt they had a right to question strangers on the project grounds increased from 27 to 50 per cent. Residents' fear of crime was reduced even more dramatically than the actual crime rates and, for the first time in years, most residents said they had little fear of walking on the project grounds at night.

Fig. 10.17: View of the Hamilton Courts public housing project in Oklahoma City.

Creation of a More Stable Tenant Body:
Oklahoma City Row Housing

Many of the problems at the Clason Point Gardens row-house project in New York City lent themselves to remedy by physical modification to the grounds. The project was 90 per cent occupied; the existing tenant body was 30 per cent one-parent families; 37 per cent of all families listed welfare as their major source of income; and the racial and ethnic composition was 40 per cent black, 30 per cent Puerto Rican, and 30 per cent white. This mix makes for a stable community by current public housing standards. On the other hand, the tenant profile in Oklahoma City's four large row-house developments reveals that 90 per cent of the households consist of one-parent families, of which 80 per cent receive AFDC assistance.

In 1971 the Oklahoma City Housing Authority constructed the four new housing projects in three different areas of the city, away from the low-income black ghetto. By 1976 all but one project were half vacant and boarded up, and the Authority found itself on the receiving end of a lot of bad publicity generated by crime and other deleterious effects the projects were having on surrounding communities.

In 1977 the largest and most notorious of the four projects, Hamilton Courts, contained three hundred ninety-two units, only ninety of which were occupied. This project, like the three others, consists of handsome, single-family detached and row-house units (Figure 10.17). It is located in a white moderate- to middle-income community in the southeast quadrant of the city, some five miles from the central business district and Oklahoma's largest black community.

Fig. 10.18: View of the Robert S. Kerr Village housing project showing the extent of the boarded-up units.

Robert S. Kerr Village, the second largest of the two projects, contains two hundred eighty-eight units, one hundred thirteen of which were occupied in 1977 (Figure 10.18). The project is located in the southwest quadrant of the city, in a white middle-income community of newly constructed, single-family detached homes. The project is the most distant of all four from the central city: six miles away. In the five years from 1971 to 1976, the community immediately surrounding the project turned from white to predominantly black. Housing values fell and mortgages went into default. Many of the lower-costing homes were purchased by black working-class families. HUD, in turn, found itself in receivership of those homes whose mortgages it had guaranteed. Unable to sell them on the open market, HUD gave them to the Oklahoma City Housing Authority. The authority rented them to the Kerr project tenants, many of whom could not maintain them. The pattern of vacancy and deterioration thus spread into the surrounding community (Figure 10.19).

Fig. 10.19: View of abandoned and boarded-up, newly built single-family houses adjacent to the Kerr Village housing project.

"Southeast Fifteenth and High" is both the name and location of the third largest Oklahoma City project. It consists of two hundred row-house units, one hundred ten of which are occupied (Figure 10.20). The project is also located in the southwest quadrant of the city, some two and a half miles from downtown. The community surrounding Southeast Fifteenth and High streets is of moderate income and racially mixed.

The smallest of the four Oklahoma City projects is Sooner Haven. It consists of one hundred fifty units, one hundred thirty-eight of which where occupied in 1977. The project is located in a black middle-income community composed of older single-family homes. It is located three and a half miles from the center of town.

The high vacancy rates and crime problems being suffered by these projects are the result of poorly defined policy at both the local and federal levels. The projects were built away from the downtown area and the existing black comunity because court orders prevented the construction of public housing in low-income communities. The new housing was therefore located in moderate- and middle-income residential communities—only one of which, the area where Sooner Haven was constructed, was black. The three projects located in predominantly white communities were away from the new residents' relatives and friends and from job and recreation opportunities. Too many of the public housing residents did not have cars, and the distances were too great, the public transportation too infrequent, to enable them to main-

Fig. 10.20: View of the housing project at Southeast Fifteenth and High streets.

tain contacts. The residents who remained living in these projects the longest were those resigned to isolation and chronic unemployment.

The four projects were completed in 1971 and fully leased in a few months. No criteria were used in tenant selection other than that families displaced by urban renewal had first priority. No attempt was made to have a certain percentage of residents employed and paying the maximum allowed rental; no attempt was made to attract and keep a minimum percentage of two-parent families or to attract working-class or white families, even though the number of white families who qualify for public housing in Oklahoma City, both by their income and the condition of their homes, exceeds that of black families three to one. The housing projects were viewed by the authority and the city as temporary shelter for dislocated low-income families, predominantly black. The authority's tenants' records reveal that those families who stayed for the shortest period of time were two-parent and working. The few white families who were attracted to the projects stayed a shorter time than the black families. It is apparent that those who could exercise greater choice in the housing market place (the white families) moved out; those who remained were either those who could not afford to leave or who had nowhere else to go. As the reputation of the project deteriorated, the remaining low-income, one-parent families were joined by others like themselves. The 1971 rental for welfare-dependent families was $42.00 a month, barely enough to cover maintenance and utility costs. But worse was still to come.

In 1972 the Brooke Amendment provisions were applied to welfare recipients in the Oklahoma City public housing projects. The amendment set a maximum rent for these families at 25 per cent of their adjusted income. The effect of the amendment was to reduce the average rent paid by welfare families in Oklahoma City from $42.00 to about $17.00. Since the minimum required by the city's housing authority to operate a unit was $22.00 per month, the tenant body, which consisted of a majority of welfare families, became an economic liability. The projects began to experience a gradual rise in vacancy rates as the authority implemented three new policies: (1) The authority refused to re-lease vacated units that required more than minimal reconditioning because there was no hope of recouping this cost. (2) In 1974 the board decided to begin to evict tenants for nonpayment of rent; this reversed the previous, more permissive, practice of allowing residents up to a year in rent-payment arrears if they offered sound excuses. (3) Vacancy rates took a significant jump as residents chose to move out rather than settle old accounts.

As part of its policy to reduce the crippling effects of the Brooke Amendment, HUD allowed local housing authorities to introduce a "rent range" program to ensure that the average rent they received was sufficient to enable them to maintain both their projects and their solvency. The purpose of the rent-range program was to attain a more balanced population in public housing, which, on the average at least, would produce a higher rental income. The new program effectively allowed housing authorities to limit the percentage of low-income and welfare residents to whom they could lease units.

In Oklahoma City the new policies were implemented too late to be much use. Those lower-income families who could afford to pay something toward their rent moved out when the Oklahoma City Housing Authority demanded payment of rent arrears. It was simply a better deal for these residents to apply their back rent toward the lease of a new apartment in the private sector (or in HUD-subsidized, moderate-income housing) than to pay their rent arrears in order to be able to go on living in their public housing apartments. The newly vacant and boarded-up units gave the projects a look of insolvency and abandonment. Vacant units were broken into by criminals and the plumbing fixtures, stoves, and refrigerators stolen. The concentration of one-parent welfare families with a large number of resident teen-age children produced a high crime rate. As conditions deteriorated further, it became impossible for the housing authority even to contemplate attracting higher-income two-parent families. The projects would now have to be completely overhauled if the authority desired to change their image. But the cost of rehabilitating the vandalized units was too high for the housing authority to consider undertaking at its own expense. It is interesting that the only project in which residents chose to pay up their back rents was Sooner Haven, the one hundred ten-unit project located in a black, middle-income community. That project was also small enough not to have created, of its very self, a critical mass of low-income welfare families. In our survey, the project was found to be the most attractive of all to both existing and prospective residents.

In 1976 HUD made funds available from its Public Housing Modernization Program to allow the Oklahoma City Housing Authority to rehabilitate half of two of its projects on an experimental basis. The purpose was to see whether an upgrading of the physical plant of the projects would provide the mechanism for attracting higher-income, more stable residents. Before such a rehabilitation effort could be embarked upon, however, the authority felt it was mandatory for it to demonstrate to itself and HUD that there was a market for Oklahoma City public housing by this type of proposed new resident. The authority desired to determine why two-parent, low-income working families had in the past not considered public housing and under what conditions they might consider it in the future.

Market Survey

In the first step of our market analysis, various sources were examined to determine the number and location of households in Oklahoma City with incomes, family make-up, and housing conditions which qualified them for admission to public housing. It was determined that thirteen thousand households composed of families with children qualified for, and had need of, public housing in Oklahoma City.

Of these thirteen thousand households, 25 per cent were black, 2 per cent American Indian, 2 per cent Spanish, and 71 per cent white. But in all of the housing authority's developments, only 9 per cent of the residents were white. It was clear that the city's low-income white families with children, living in dilapidated housing, were not considering public housing as one of their options. In order to determine why, a random sample of four hundred families from low-income neighborhoods located within a mile or two of one of the four large projects were interviewed.

Each interview was designed to determine how knowledgeable people were about the housing authority, what their perceptions about the image and location of the developments were, what they felt about current living conditions in the projects, and, finally, under what conditions they would consider moving in. The random sample of residents was stratified to reflect the percentage of qualifying black, white, and Indian families in the city. While 60 per cent of the black respondents knew of the housing authority, only 35 per cent of the white population and 29 per cent of the Indians had heard of it. Most of the families in the survey, different from current project residents, had access to automobiles which were in working order. Seventy-nine per cent of the white families, 74 per cent of the black families, and 81 per cent of the Indian families owned or used automobiles and therefore had some degree of mobility for maintaining employment and friendships.

All of the respondents were asked if, in their opinion, it was the *image* or the *location* which contributed most to the lack of desirability of public housing. The responses of the three groups, shown in Table 10.3, differed significantly.

Pursuing the question further, the interviewers asked the respondents which factors contributed most to their perception either of the project's negative image or of its poor location. Tables 10.4 and 10.5 give the proportion each factor was mentioned in relation to other factors. An asterisk is used to denote the factor which was mentioned most frequently as being most important.

Too much crime proved to be the overriding factor associated with the bad image of public housing among all three groups interviewed.

Table 10.3: Factors Contributing to the Vacancy of Projects

QUESTION: Which of the following two factors do you think contributes most to the vacancies in public housing: (1) image — what people think about the projects; or (2) location — where the projects are located in the city?

Response	White respondents	Black respondents	Indian respondents
Image	74%	33%	84%
Location	26%	67%	16%
Number of respondents	85	78	31

Table 10.4: Factors Contributing to Bad Location

QUESTION: In order of importance, which factors do you think make the location bad?

Responses	White respondents	Black respondents	Indian respondents
Away from job	22%*	29%*	33%
Not close to good schools	24%	22%	13%
Not close to shopping	24%	22%	7%
Away from friends	21%	13%	34%
Not close to recreation	9%	15%	13%
Number of respondents	85	78	31

Table 10.5: Factors Contributing to Bad Image

QUESTION: In order of importance, which factors do you think contribute most to the bad image?

Responses	White respondents	Black respondents	Indian respondents
Too much crime	27%*	25%*	31%*
Badly kept up	18%	22%	11%
Badly managed	14%	19%	2%
Too many black families	19%	4%	30%
Too many children	6%	12%	10%
Too many welfare families	4%	10%	15%
Badly designed housing	2%	7%	0%
Other	10%	1%	1%
Number of Respodents	85	78	31

Our further analysis revealed that it was mentioned first most often. Among whites and Indians the factor mentioned second most frequently was too many black families. The present racial composition of the projects is, apparently, a deterrent to those groups currently underrepresented among tenants.

The dominance of black families is a characteristic common to many public housing developoments, and this is generally known in Oklahoma City. The following question explored what, in the respondents' opinions, was an acceptable mix of racial groups. The results indicate that racial integration was acceptable to most of the respondents, but that no group considered a minority status for themselves as acceptable. It is important to note that the American Indian respondents categorized themselves as white in this interview (Table 10.6).

Table 10.6: Perception of Acceptable Racial Mix

QUESTION: What do you think would be an acceptable mix for those of your neighbors who would consider moving in?

Response	White respondents	Black respondents	Indian respondents
20% white and 80% black	2%	17%	0%
40% white and 60% black	1%	17%	0%
50% white and 50% black	70%	51%	0%
60% white and 40% black	6%	10%	26%
80% white and 20% black	21%	5%	74%
Number of respondents	85	78	31

Where most black and white respondents indicated an acceptable racial mix of 50 per cent white and 50 per cent black, the Indian respondents made a greater demand for a white majority. A parallel survey of a random sample of residents currently living in public housing revealed a similar desire for a fifty-fifty mix of black and white residents in the projects. The Oklahoma City Housing Authority felt that this level of compatibility in opinions was essential to their adoption of a strategy that would result in a change in the present racial composition of the developments.

Those respondents who indicated that they would not be willing to move into public housing were asked for their reasons. More than 50 per cent of this group expressed a preference for the environment provided by single-family detached homes as opposed to row-house apartments. Their preference for single-family housing was further defined as a desire for privacy, ownership, and lower density.

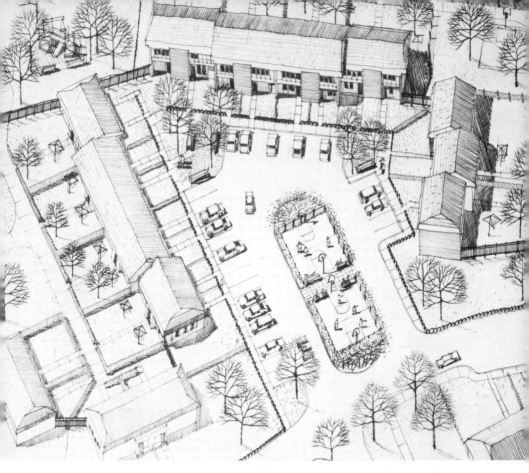

Fig. 10.21: Aerial view of the proposed modifications to a portion of the grounds at Kerr Village. Six-foot-high iron fences seal off the rear grounds from access from the street. Front lawns are defined by low, iron picket fences. Teen play areas are located on the street in front of the units and play areas for young children are located within the newly defined rear courts.

The respondents were then shown photographs of the public housing developments and it was explained that the row-house units were single-family homes although not detached. The respondents were then asked whether in their minds the addition of fencing would improve the desirability of the units and why. In all three groups of respondents, a large majority of them responded affirmatively, citing increased privacy and security as their reasons for desiring fencing.

The photographs that were shown to the respondents were taken shortly after the initial occupancy of the developments in 1971. We suspect that these photographs helped precondition some of the respondents and resulted in the majority of affirmative responses to the question "Would you move in?" It is quite probable that if, instead of

Fig. 10.22: View of the proposed rear grounds at Southeast Fifteenth and High streets for the area shown in Figure 10.20.

these old photographs, respondents were shown photographs of the development with the boarded-up windows, most of those interviewed would not then have viewed the housing as either livable or desirable.

With the market for the public housing units established and the social and physical conditions under which two-parent white, black, and Indian families would consider moving in defined, it now became a problem of finding the best strategy that would turn the largely vacant, uneconomical projects into viable housing for the working poor as well as for welfare families. The first step was clearly the rehabilitation of the units and the grounds so as to alter both the condition and image of projects. Otherwise it would by very difficult to attract working-class families to them. Plans were prepared to rehabilitate the inside of the units and to radically redesign the grounds of the development (Figure 10.21). Following the principles our Institute developed at Clason Point, 80 per cent of the grounds of the Oklahoma City projects were redefined and assigned to individual units (Figure 10.22). Some 50 per cent of the grounds were also enclosed within collective, rear-yard areas, accessible only from within the units themselves. The rear-yard clusters were also intentionally designed to be small to avoid the problems with large clusters experienced at Clason Point. This redefinition of the rear yards also succeeded in fencing off the grounds from their surrounding neighborhoods—which were, on some sides, of questionable physical quality. New trees were planted and located within the newly defined front yards. Play equipment for youngsters was provided in rear-yard clusters, and equipment for teen-agers was placed in front of the units adjacent to the parking areas.

Strategy for Leasing the Units

Following the experience of other housing authorities, and the findings of the survey, the Oklahoma City Housing Authority decided to embark on a strategy of leasing the units to working families and to make a concerted effort to attract a high percentage of white and Indian families. The projected benefits of the working-family strategy would be neighborhood stability, the reduction of vandalism and crime, the achievement of full occupancy, the longer term use of the city's low-income housing assests, and the city's recognition of the potential viability of public housing.

This strategy required a radical change in the marketing and tenant selection procedures engaged in by the authority. In our study we also found that the white low-income population of Oklahoma City was not using public housing as a resource. A higher percentage of white households in public housing was deemed desirable by everyone. To achieve this goal, it was essential that the housing authority embark on an aggressive program to attract and keep white and Indian families.

A majority of the white households interviewed said that they had not considered public housing in the past because of its poor image. Crime was the factor most frequently identified (by all races) with poor image. Any action that would result in the the reduction of project crime, therefore, would likely enhance the authority's ability to attract white families. Three programs were therefore adopted to reduce crime: (1) physical modifications to improve the projects' defensibility; (2) the introduction of a higher percentage of working-class families to achieve a higher ratio of parents to children; and (3) the use of security personnel during the transition period.

Our study of the Oklahoma City Housing Authority's records on the length of tenure of residents showed that a family was likely to leave after only a short stay if they were part of a racial minority, either white or black. A fifty-fifty mix of white and black families was therefore thought to be essential to retaining white families. It was thought that the institution of a new rent-range policy for selecting families could contribute to the maintenance of a racially balanced community. The authority agreed to adopt a program of increasing the required proportion of families who pay in excess of $50.00 per month.

Media coverage of the Oklahoma City Housing Authority, its projects, and its activities contributed much to the negative image held of it by the larger Oklahoma City community. A posture of less visibility was recommended to the authority and its board members. During the period of transition, even good or interesting news would, from the authority's point of view, prove to be bad news in helping it to attract new applicants. If the authority was serious about making its public housing more like housing in the private sector, it would have to adopt a different public relations style. Tenants of housing in the private sector do not expect themselves or their housing management firm to be constantly appearing in the media. To further these goals, it was also suggested that the public housing projects be renamed or, better still, have their names removed completely.

Our survey indicated that there was a limited knowledge about the programs of the Oklahoma City Housing Authority, particularly among the working-class, white population. Direct promotion would therefore be required in the neighborhoods surveyed and others of a similar composition. Examples of promotional activities include: the use of neighborhood newspapers; door-to-door distribution of printed flyers; talks to religious groups and union organization; and the placement of signs in neighborhood laundromats, clinics, and shops. The promotional literature emphasized that it was good housing at a very good value for the families who qualified; it minimized the fact that it was government-owned or -subsidized housing. The units were described as "individual town houses with their own gardens and yards," never as "multifamily units." The use of television or radio promotion was avoided.

Other policies adopted by the authority to help in both the recruitment and retention of white families were: the hiring of white as well as black management staff; the use of live-in managers and superintendents; and the provision of six-month to two-year leases as an alternative to the current month-by-month leasing policy. The previous leasing format left applicants with the unmistakable impression that public housing was for temporary use only. To further simulate the practices of housing management in the private sector the authority set up leasing offices within the projects themselves and staffed them in the evenings and on weekends. Previously, potential residents could only apply for housing at the authority's cental office between 8:30 A.M. and 4:30 P.M., Monday through Friday. Applicants could now tour their prospective homes at a time convenient to working adults, without first having to go through the process of filling out a formal application form in the hectic atmosphere of the housing authority offices.

The authority correctly anticipated that some groups within the Oklahoma City community would see its proposed new lease-up program as discriminatory. In fact, it was the old racial composition of the developments that had resulted in segregation. The new policy was a positive effort to redress this condition and the authority staff met with minority group leaders to explain its new policies. It was the long-term interest of the authority to provide more housing for white as well as black low-income families in Oklahoma City. The previous status and reputation of the housing authority projects came close to seeing them abandoned and sold; the new program of attracting a higher percentage of two-parent and white families would, it was reasoned, actually provide more occupied housing for low-income, one parent black families than before. A repetition of the original leasing program would only result in the projects being, once again, totally occupied by one-parent black welfare families. This, in turn, would only result in the recurrence of the crime and vandalism problems and the consequent high vacancy rate. The new strategy also offered the possibility of improved relations with the residents of the communities which immediately surround public housing projects. It was hoped that it would also change the image of public housing in Oklahoma City. Broad community acceptance was thought to be essential to the continuing vitality of the authority and its growth.

The HUD Area Office approved funds for the modification of a little less than 50 per cent of the Kerr Village project, on an experimental basis. When the modifications were completed, the authority set about attracting two-parent, working black and white families, in accordance with the strategy outlined. Within six months the authority was able to claim that it had reduced the vacancy rate in the test portion of the project from 65 per cent to 29 per cent, whereas the vacancies in the unmodified half remained unchanged at 45 per cent. But the most promising turn of events involved changes in the percentages of one-parent and working families. At the end of the first six-month period, 39 per cent of the families in the experimental half of the project consisted of two-parent households, whereas before the modifications there were only 8 per cent two-parent households in the entire project. The percentage of working families in the experimental portion of the site more than trebled, climbing from 6 per cent to 19 per cent. Finally, of the forty-six new families, the authority was able to attract to the modified site, one third were white.

Modification to Three-Story Walk-Ups:
Marion Gardens in Jersey City

Marion Gardens is a four hundred sixty-unit public housing project in Jersey City composed of three-story walk-up buildings. Not much remains of the garden image that originally evoked its name. Over the years, the grounds were increasingly paved over; the surface is now virtually wall-to-wall asphalt. The designated parking areas of the project are ignored by the residents, who prefer instead to park their

Fig. 10.23: The residents of Marion Gardens park their cars near the entry doors to their buildings.

cars adjacent to the front door of their building (Figure 10.23). The children's play facilities, located in the large central open areas of the project, were reduced to twisted skeletons and are now virtually nonexistent (Figure 10.24). The frequency of boarded-up windows is an indication of the extent of the current vacancies. The development is more than 40 per cent vacant and has recently only been considered for occupancy by the most desperate of low-income families. The current, population consists primarily of AFDC families.

Although the project looks grim and uninviting, this visual effect is

Fig. 10.24: The play equipment at Marion Gardens was unrelated to the building entries and quickly vandalized.

more the result of the boarded-up windows and the deteriorated grounds than of any decay to the buildings' structure, interior, or façades. The buildings were initially soundly constructed, and the mechanical equipment and the interior of apartments show little of the signs of wear and neglect of the outside.

Most residents at Marion Gardens are house-proud and spend much effort in creating a cozy living environment within their apartments, warm in feeling and mood and groomed with care. This not only suggests that residents aspire to a clean well-kept environment, but that they can and do provide it for themselves within areas they control. However, once one leaves the interior of the private apartments and steps out to the areas which are no longer the private domain of residents, one encounters a radically different world. It is like stepping out of *House Beautiful* magazine into war-devastated Europe. The public interior hallways in the three-story walk-up buildings, which, like the grounds, are supposed to be maintained by the housing authority, suffer the same neglect and abandonment. The lack of adequate funds, the misappropriation of monies, the inadequacies of both management and maintenance staff, the concentration of poor, one-parent families, and the rapid turnover of residents have all combined to produce the present malaise.

Our Institute was asked by the authority to prepare plans to modify the project in a way which would extend the concern and commitment of residents to include the public hallways and stairs of the buildings and the grounds below. The authority reasoned that because it had limited funds available for maintenance staff, much of the cleaning of the areas outside apartments would have to be adopted by the residents themselves.

Fig. 10.25: Aerial view of Marion Gardens.

Design Principles Used in the Modification of Grounds

Different from Clason Point and the Oklahoma City projects Marion Gardens is not a row-house development, in that six families, rather than one, share the entry to a building. The grounds outside therefore cannot be allocated for the use of individual families. At best, it would only be possible to subdivide and assign the grounds to small groupings of from thiry to thirty-six families. The grounds are now unassigned to any families. Vehicles can and do drive onto the project grounds from virtually any direction (Figure 10.25). The first step in redesigning Marion Gardens was to define all of the projects grounds as belonging to the residents only. A mixture of decorative fencing and shrubbery was proposed as the elements to be used in defining the periphery of the project and limiting access to it (Figure 10.26). The six-foot fencing will be made of steel, with the look of quality wrought iron — typical of the fencing which surrounds libraries and expensive housing estates. A single access street entering off the only major street bordering the project would then be run through the center of the development. The other streets bordering the project would continue to serve as roads for neighboring industrial sites. There would now be only one entry into the development available for both pedestrians and vehicles. Parking areas would be placed off this main access artery as close as possible to building entries.

The second step in applying our design principles requires the subdivision of the interior grounds of the project to create small areas for the use of the residents of particular buildings. This will be accomplished by creating cul-de-sacs at the entries of the parallel buildings (Figure 10.27). The cul-de-sacs will form courts which are related to building entry groupings. Play facilities for the very young children will be placed within the cul-de-sac courts just outside the entry to each building. Play areas for teen-age youngsters will also be placed within the courts but located adjacent to each of the parking areas rather than in juxtaposition with building entries. The teen-age play facilities will be intentionally designed to serve small groups of families in particular buildings.

The rear walls of the buildings were not designed with an access door to the grounds below. It was therefore decided to fence these rear areas off and turn them into planted green areas. Access to these green areas will be through a keyed gate only. The keys will be held by adult residents in neighboring buildings. The green zones will serve as a park preserve at the rear of the buildings and counterbalance the active, paved play and parking areas at the front. To further discourage their use for ball playing, the green preserves will be heavily planted with

Fig. 10.26: Site plan for the modification of Marion Gardens.

trees. The fenced-off green areas are not intended to be used for active children's play—they would be worn down in a month if they were. Rather, these areas are intended for quiet sitting and picnicking—oases away from the bustle and noise of the project. They will be accessible to children only in the company of adults. They will border each building and will be visible from every dwelling unit and so will provide a real feeling of green to the entire project which, as the picture illustrates, now looks like a factory yard. It is expected that teen-agers will use these green zones for occasional evening activities, but they will only have access to them as a consequence of their ability to climb over the fence.

Further Defining Provisions

Each building entry, which serves six families, two per floor, will be provided with an intercom. Our past studies have shown that this is a small enough number of families to ensure that the intercom will operate for a good many years. If the residents choose to limit access to the grounds of the development to only those who have a legitimate presence, they will be able to request that the housing authority place a guard adjacent to the single entry to the projects grounds. With a six-foot fence surrounding the entire project, a guard booth located next to the only entry gate will prove very effective not only in controlling access but in controlling egress—an equally important deterrent to intruders intent on burglary.

Our past experiments have taught us that not all public housing residents view fencing benignly. We were concerned that residents might see the fencing as a device to keep them in rather than one for keeping unwanted strangers out. We were equally uncertain as to whether residents would understand our purpose in creating subdivided areas within the project for limited numbers of families to use, control, and maintain. However, in our presentations to them, residents quickly perceived that the proposed fencing would give them an opportunity to extend the control they now had over their own apartments out to encompass the buildings and grounds surrounding it. They also understood and welcomed the concept of subdivision of the grounds into small clusters. It was not the residents but the new management of the authority that perceived the fencing negatively.

Anticipated Problems with the Proposed Modifications

We anticipate that the proposed modifications, when implemented, will produce a radical change in the way residents perceive the grounds of their project. As inadequate as the grounds are now, they provide

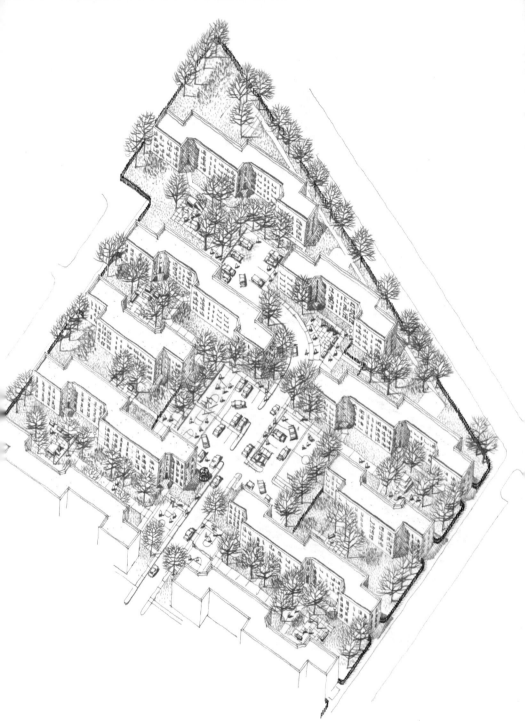

Fig. 10.27: Isometric view of a portion of the proposed grounds modifications for Marion Gardens showing the new cul-du-sacs, parking areas, play facilities and guard booth.

many short cuts, parking areas, and a freedom of access to every area.
With the modification of the grounds, this freedom will no longer be
availabe. It will take a while before residents are able to weigh the
benefits from the redesign against these deprivations. From our past
experience in modifying other housing developments, we know that
this transition period will be a difficult one for many. It will also take a
while before residents are able to learn to make full use of the new opportunities made available to them. It is even more likely that a good
many outsiders, whether welcome visitors or not, will perceive these
changes as undesirable. Equally, a good many residents may not prefer
to have their visitors screened. Female heads-of-household receiving
AFDC assistance are theoretically living without a man in the household. In fact, they may have boy friends or husbands who are frequent,
it not permanent, guests. Such residents may see the presence of the
guard at the entry to the project grounds as an agent of the housing authority or the welfare department, monitoring their activity to determine whether they continue to qualify for either housing or welfare.
Under such circumstances, it is likely to be difficult to persuade the
residents that the guard is there primarily to provide them with security. It may also be difficult to prevent housing authority management
from abusing this opportunity created for monitoring residents.

In implementing physical modifications like those at Marion Gardens, we should not deceive ourselves into thinking that because we
have been successful in changing the physical image of the project, we

Fig. 10.28: A partial view of the Greenwood Gardens (right) and Martha Manor
(left) housing developments.

have also changed its socioeconomic milieu. Under the authority's current leasing policy, Marion Gardens will likely remain a low-income development, occupied predominantly by AFDC families. This is a social environment which is not the most desirable for raising new generations of low-income children we wish to provide with opportunities for upward mobility. However, as Marion Gardens looks today, the housing authority cannot even begin to contemplate attracting anyone to it but AFDC families. The physical transition of Marion Gardens from a bombed-out slum to a "garden community" is a necessary first step in making the development attractive to the working-class intact families who might qualify for public housing. With such families forming half the residents the social environment will change as well.

Had much of what we proposed in terms of physical modifications and socioeconomic makeup been initiated by the housing authority years ago, the present state of deterioration and abandonment would never have come to pass.

Rehabilitation of a Two- and Three-story Moderate-income Complex: Greenwood Gardens/Martha Manor in Seattle

The Greenwood Gardens/Martha Manor complex in Seattle was built to house middle- and moderate-income families. The two adjacent developments were built in 1971 with funds provided by HUD through Section 236 of the 1968 National Housing Act. Together they provided a total of three hundred seventy-eight additional units of housing to the southeast section of Seattle, an older, working-class community undergoing renewal and transition. Some six years after their initial occupancy the Greenwood Gardens/Martha Manor complex was 88 per cent vacant. Those units that were still occupied were located in the two-story buildings and inhabited by retired, elderly families.

The "GG/MM complex," as it is referred to locally, became an example of the total failure of a middle-income rather than a low-income housing development. It was a failure which was, for the most part, the result of a combination of poor initial housing design and bad location.

The Greenwood Gardens/Martha Manor complex demonstrates that it is possible to design a three-story walk-up with all the disadvantages of a twelve-story high-rise (Figure 10.28). It also serves to illustrate why the physical mechanism of "number of units sharing a common entry" is more important than "building height" in predicting the dissolution of community, high crime and vandalism rates, and, finally, abandonment. This complex is also interesting because its failure was influenced by the community immediately surrounding it—a large, public housing project. Once built, this complex and the neighboring public housing project together formed a critical mass of low- and moderate-income housing that could not remain stable.

It is interesting that of the two neighboring projects—the public housing and the moderate-income complex—it was the poorly designed moderate-income complex which failed. The public housing project, Holly Park, was fortunately built as row-house units. There are no interior public areas within the buildings at Holly Park because each family has its own entry and controls the grounds around its dwelling unit. But at the Greenwood Gardens/Martha Manor complex, the three-story walk-up buildings had as many as seventy families sharing a building's multiple entries and interior circulation areas (Figure 10.29). The Greenwood Garden stairs and corridors form a maze. Martha Manor is a slightly better design in that it is mostly a single-loaded corridor building (Figure 10.30). But then the peculiar form of apartment groupings at Martha Manor result in a good many of the corridors being hidden both from outside view and from the view of the residents within their apartments. Thus the three-story buildings at both Greenwood Gardens and Martha Manor achieve the dubious distinction of creating an anonymous, public environment equivalent to what is normally found only in high-rise buildings.

One of the two-story buildings at Greenwood Gardens was oc-

Fig. 10.29: Existing site plan of the Greenwood Gardens/Martha Manor complex, showing the disposition of interior corridors and apartments.

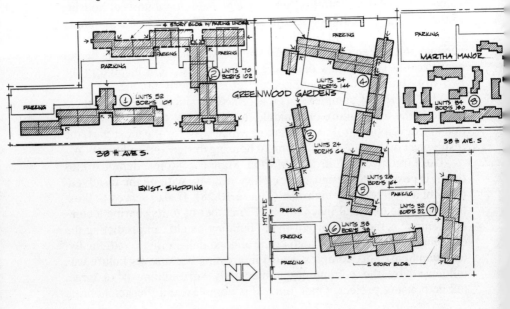

Fig. 10.30: View of the interior court at Martha Manor.

cupied by a majority of elderly families. And even though it was designed as a double-loaded corridor building with thirty-six apartments sharing three common entries, it proved both stable and crime free. This was because the elderly residents were retired and sat together in groups in the entrance foyers of the building or just outside the door on sunny days. All the doors to the building were kept locked and the elderly residents were very conscientious about keeping them that way. The building was so secure that, once inside the interior corridor, one found many of the doors to individual apartments left open while residents visited one another or went down the corridor to the laundry room to do their wash.

Unfortunately, all the other buildings at Greenwood Gardens and Martha Manor were occupied by families with children. Because of the way the buildings were designed, residents' vulnerability within their buildings was very high. And because the complex was, in turn, surrounded by a large, low-income public housing project with a high percentage of low-income teen-age residents, this vulnerability proved critical.

As the moderate- and middle-income families with two heads-of-household moved out of the Greenwood Gardens/Martha Manor complex, they were replaced by the only families management could attract: low-income, public-housing-eligible families receiving rent supplements or on welfare. Most of these new families had only a female head. The crime and vandalism problems at the complex then began to be generated from within and not just from the project surrounding it. Its final demise was just a question of time.

The larger community bordering the public and moderate-income developments began to suffer the spillover effects of the increasing crime and social malaise in the complex. Burglaries increased in the modest, single-family privately owned homes, robberies on the public streets, and vandalism and assault in the public schools and parks. Many residents from southeast Seattle, particularly those immediately bordering the complex, felt that the nature and character of their community was being seriously threatened by the new, large concentration of low-income families.

The sudden influx of a large number of low-income children into the public schools serving the complex radically altered their racial mix; so much so that the white working- and middle-class parents in the area began to send their children to private schools or to seek other neighborhoods to live in.

Alternative Plans for Rehabilitation

In 1976 the Seattle Housing Authority was asked to enter into a preliminary loan contract with HUD to explore either the sale, rehabilitation, or demolition of the Greenwood Gardens/Martha Manor complex. Any rehabilitation alternative involving HUD monies would require the complex to come under the ownership and management of the Seattle Housing Authority—in which case, applicants would have to qualify as public housing residents.

Because of the past history of the complex and its negative impact on the surrounding community, the fundamental issue in any form of rehabilitation was the impact of the new complex on the surrounding community.

In contemplating alternatives for the rehabilitation of the Greenwood Gardens/Martha Manor complex, consideration had to be given to the fact that the existing Holly Park public housing project already consisted of a large concentration of low-income families. Any proposal which would add to this concentration would be viewed skeptically by the neighboring community.

Examination of the structural condition of the two developments revealed that Martha Manor, though better designed, was far less well constructed than Greenwood Gardens and had aged accordingly. The outside circulation stairs and balconies were seriously rotted, cracked, and decayed. The exterior shingle wall had weathered poorly and been assisted in its deterioration by resident children who had torn away the rotting shingles. Rehabilitation of Martha Manor would require the complete replacement of the outside circulation balconies and stairs and much of the shingles. A cost analysis showed that this would not be a sound investment.

Alternative 1: Redevelopment of the GG Complex for Families with Children and Some Elderly

This solution proposed to house elderly residents in the complex in the two existing two-story, double-loaded corridor buildings which would be marginally modified, and the families with children in the three- and four-story buildings at Greenwood Gardens that would be completely modified. Some of the buildings at Greenwood Gardens would be torn down to free the grounds, lower the density, and reduce the Chinese Wall image of the development (Figure 10.31).

The two existing two-story buildings would be exclusively for the use of elderly families. These buildings would be grouped together with their own clearly demarcated grounds. Six-foot-high fences and shrubs would be used to define the elderly portion of the Greenwood site (Fig-

Fig. 10.31: The endless rambling buildings of Greenwood Gardens produce the effect of the Chinese Wall. (Note the extent of boarded-up units.)

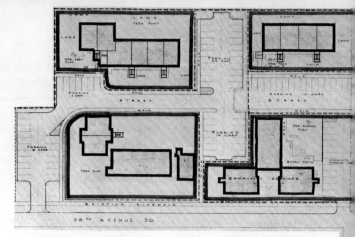

Fig. 10.32: Alternative 1 provides one hundred two units for families with children in buildings redesigned so that only six families share a common outside stair and two families share a landing. It also provides sixty-five units for the elderly in two buildings which are clearly separated from the rest of the complex.

ure 10.32). Access to the grounds of the elderly housing would be via its own road and through a single portal.

Community facilities directed at serving the needs of the elderly residents would be located within the two elderly buildings and on adjacent grounds. These facilities would include medical examination rooms, a dining room and kitchen for the meals-on-wheels program, and a community room—all to be located within the buildings. Sitting areas, shuffleboard courts, and individual gardens would be located on the adjoining grounds outside the buildings.

As these two buildings would be occupied exclusively by elderly families and as the units are small, there would be no need to modify their interior circulation system or the layout of apartments. By enlarging one of the windows in each apartment into a door, the ground floor

Fig. 10.33a: View of the two existing buildings currently occupied by the elderly.

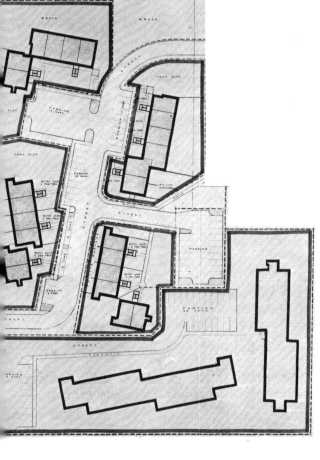

units would be given access to their adjoining grounds. This door would connect the living room of the unit to its outside garden which would now be fenced off (Figures 10.33a and b).

By comparison, the existing three- and four-story buildings would require extensive modifications to the interiors to make them usable for

Fig. 10.33b: View of the same area shown in Figure 10.33a after modification.

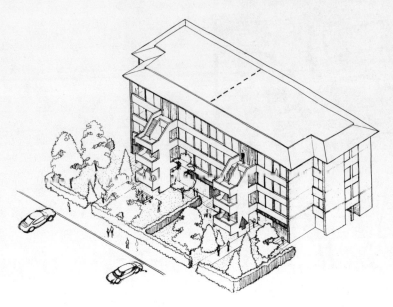

Fig. 10.34: View of converted buildings to be occupied by two groupings of six families.

families with children. The interior stair and double-loaded corridor circulation system would have to be removed and the building redesigned to use a series of outdoor stairs. In the new scheme, only six families would share a common stair. The isometric view shows how the buildings would be reorganized (Figure 10.34). The interior corridor will be removed and each family unit will be converted into a "floor through" apartment — that is, each unit would have windows on both sides of the building rather than on just one, and would be entered by the new outside stair. The balcony of each floor would serve only two families. The stair would open to both view and air will be provided with a roof overhead as a rain cover. The entry door to all apartments would be visible from the grounds below. A second set of stairs — for emergency fire exit — would be provided at the rear of each apartment. The grounds surrounding each building would be subdivided to form distinct areas around each stair serving six families.

About 25 per cent of all the buildings at Greenwood Gardens would be removed and the image of the complex modified to produce the effect of a grouping of small buildings. Each of the new buildings in the proposed solution would be assigned its own particular portion of the site. Parking would be designed to relate directly to each building. Play facilities for teen-age children would be located on the grounds of each building, and play areas for preteens located adjacent to each stair within the further subdivided grounds serving only six families.

Wherever the existing site permits, the grounds would be sub-divided to give small individual yards to the families living on the ground floors. Access to the individual yards would be provided at the rear of each unit through a newly positioned door.

A centrally located building would be allocated for use as a new community center and to house various social service institutions that would serve the new residents of Greenwood Gardens and the sur-rounding community.

This solution would provide a total of sixty-five units for the elderly and one hundred two units for families with children. The community center would provide fifteen thousand square feet of institutional space.

As this would be close to the maximum number of units that the surrounding community, HUD, and the Seattle Housing Authority felt should be redeveloped for this site, it lent further support to the recom-mendation that the Martha Manor project be torn down.

Alternative 2: Redevelopment of the GG Complex Exclusively for Elderly Families

Because of the strong resistance of the surrounding community to the redevelopment of the Greenwood Gardens/Martha Manor com-plex for families with children, we also developed a second solution which we felt would prove easier to implement in the face of commu-nity resistance. This solution proposed to use the existing buildings in Greenwood Gardens solely for housing the elderly. As in Alternative 1, it was recommended that some 25 per cent of the existing buildings be torn down so as to lower the density and to change the Chinese Wall-like image of the complex.

The grounds of the entire elderly complex would be surrounded by a six-foot-high fence enclosed within a thick hedge and broken only by the vehicular and pedestrian access portals (Figure 10.35). The suc-cess of an all-elderly complex in this location is dependent on the grounds being clearly defined for the exclusive use of its residents and their guests. Elderly developments in similar settings have not proven workable when their grounds and buildings were left open to free public access. Once the grounds are understood as being for the exclusive use of the elderly residents, control of access should prove simple. The elderly themselves do not normally commit crimes and it would be difficult for teen-agers, who make up most of the criminal population in public housing, to enter the grounds of the elderly complex without making themselves evident. As teen-agers would not be living within the complex, their presence would mean that they were

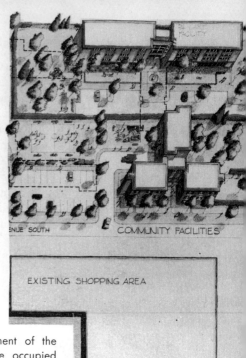

EXISTING SHOPPING AREA

Fig. 10.35: Alternative 2, the redevelopment of the Greenwood Gardens as a complex to be occupied exclusively by the elderly. The plan calls for the removal of portions of the existing buildings (shown with dashed lines). The entire complex would be surrounded by a fence and shrubs. Alternative 2 would provide for a total of one hundred fifty-seven elderly units and forty-eight units to be used as a three-quarter care congregate facility.

Fig. 10.36: Reuse of the ground floor of the existing four-story buildings for a recreation area.

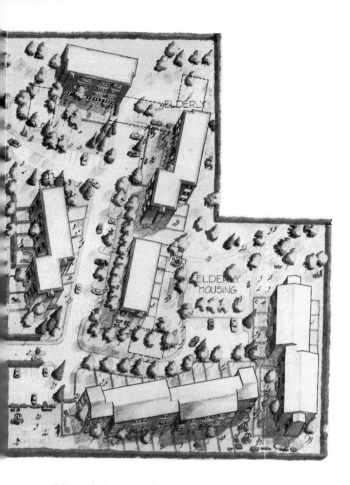

either visting relatives or that they were intruders. Thus it would not be socially awkward for residents to monitor the activity of intruding teenagers to determine their purpose.

The entrance to the grounds of the elderly complex would be positioned to facilitate access to the shopping mall and the surrounding major arterial streets. As the site of the Greenwood Gardens complex is a flat plateau which surrounds the shopping center, the elderly would have easy access to shopping and the bus routes.

The two existing two-story buildings would remain intact as in Alternative 1 and the ground floor units would be provided with doors leading out onto individual patios. The remaining three- and four-story buildings would each be provided with an elevator. The existing double-loaded corridors would remain intact, as they have proven to be workable in an all-elderly building. The two-story duplex apartments would be converted to one story apartments with access to the top floor units provided through a new corridor connecting to the new elevators. The ground floor units would, where the site allows, be provided with their own patios, accessible from the interior of each unit.

The existing, covered parking areas in the four-story buildings would be removed and the area enclosed and converted to recreation rooms, medical offices, dining areas, and other community rooms. These rooms would be designed to open up to adjacent grounds and gardens in good weather (Figure 10.36).

The community service building provided in Alternative 1 would also be provided in Alternative 2. However, in this alternative it would serve more of the community outside the development, as the elderly would have their own facilities located within their buildings.

An essential requirement for community acceptance of any rehabilitation proposal for Greenwood Gardens is the radical alteration of its physical and social image. Conversion of the development to all-elderly use would change its social image. It is equally important that the visual image of the rehabilitated project endeavor to capture the residential scale and quality of the surrounding community. The complete removal of Martha Manor and some 25 per cent of the buildings at Greenwood Gardens would be the first step in this direction. A revamping of the façades of the buildings and landscaping would be a further requirement. (Figures 10.34a and 10.36 illustrate our suggestions for achieving this image change. Many architects will probably choke at our suggestions, because the new imagery is pure kitsch. Our purpose is to remove the strong institutional image the project now has. New brightly colored wood siding, shutters, and simulated brick surfacing in stucco would be added to change both scale and character of the buildings. New trees, paving, lighting, grass, shrubs, seating, and recreation areas—directed to the needs of residents—would also be located throughout the site. These changes should make the old Greenwood Gardens development unrecognizable.

XI

Whose Failure Is Modern Architecture?

In response to growing public disaffection with contemporary buildings, the modern movement in architecture has been singled out for attack by architectural critics and the practicing profession. Philip Johnson, the 1978 recipient of the highest award bestowed by the profession, the Gold Medal of the American Institute of Architects, lamented the inadequacies of the modern style in his acceptance speech. This is the very same man whose seminal work on Mies van der Rohe in 1947 brought modern architectural style into prominence among American cognoscenti. To express the full measure of his conversion Johnson will, in his forthcoming American Telephone & Telegraph Building, subject his otherwise modern building to the symbolic appendages of the Roman Empire (Figure 11.1). Another example, if one is needed, is provided by Peter Blake, for twelve years editor of the prestigious *Architectural Forum* and author of *The Master Builders*, a series from the 1960s which deified Frank Lloyd Wright, Le Corbusier, and Mies van der Rohe. He, too, has joined the ranks of defilers in his new book *Form Follows Fiasco: Why Modern Architecture Hasn't Worked.*

Fig. 11.1: The American Telephone & Telegraph Building, by Philip Johnson, proposed in 1978. In the chaos that has resulted from the current disenchantment with modern architecture, Johnson has been able to return to his first love and give free vent to monumental classicism. (*Photo by Louis Checkman*)

But from what is being said and written, the current stoning of modern architecture does not appear to be a reappraisal of the modern design philosophy but is simply a voguish abandonment of the style which dominated architectural design in America for half a century. There were three facets to the modern architectural revolution in the twenties and thirties: the concern with social issues; the functional planning philosophy; and the spare style. Unfortunately, the social values and planning methods of the modern movement, which were its most important contributions and are still its saving grace, are also being abandoned. The failures of modern architecture in the postwar period are not the consequence of flat roofs or spare façades as Philip Johnson would have us believe, but are rather attributable to poorly conceived and laid out buildings. It is these unusable building interiors and their poor relationships to outside grounds, rather than their façades, which has resulted in their rejection. Most of these inadequate interior layouts were produced by a specific group of contemporary practitioners in service of what they have labeled modern architecture, but which careful examination reveals instead to be little more than a Beaux-Arts spin-off of the modern movement. There are some European critics who claim that the only facet of modern architecture that was ever transferred to America was its style.[1] In that light, it isn't modern architecture that has failed but the straw man that was made of it.

It is also possible that the failure of modern architecture runs much more deeply; that it is in fact the architectural profession that has been unable to define and adopt a useful role for itself in twentieth-century society. The modern architectural movement provided the vehicle to allow such an evolution, but this aspect of modernism was shunted. The general practitioner, because he persisted in viewing himself in the traditional role of Renaissance Man, failed to appreciate the new tasks required of architectural form in the twentieth century. Modernism was reduced to the status of a new style and functional planning became maidservant to form. To understand the current malaise one must look to the origins of the modern movement in Europe, examine the buildings of the 1920s and 1930s that were its best achievements and then follow its descent and usurpation by those practitioners who could not relinquish their cherished historical roles even at the expense of facing obsolescence.

The search for a modern style was not born simply of the pursuit of new fashion. It was initiated as a result of architects' having become consciously aware of four things: (1) that in the new industrial society the mass of people attracted to the large industrial centers replaced the rich and the established institutions as the architects' new client; (2) that the buildings their new clients needed were not palaces, temples, or mausoleums but housing, schools, factories, and office buildings; (3) that if architects were to provide the quantity of these buildings needed to satisfy the new, urban mass society, they would have to do it expeditiously: the new industrial technology would have to be both the source of the materials and the means for putting materials together into buildings. The fourth new area of consciousness that one detects in the first modern architects is their growing discomfort with the use of traditional styles. They perceived that the draping of schools, office buildings, and factories in steel and concrete replicas of Roman temples would be a disservice both to the activities to be housed and to the materials and technology employed.

One of the more important attributes of the modern architectural style was the freedom it gave architects to plan the interior areas of buildings without regard to the conventions which had previously required them to house activities within contemporary duplicates of building forms of the past, whether Classical, Gothic, or Romanesque. The modern style also gave architects license to expose the materials used rather than to cover them with plaster appliqué columns. With the new style, architects could open whole wall surfaces to light and air. They were freed to assemble their new materials within the framework of a new form language that owed more to modern art and the form of ships, airplanes, and warehouses than to the rule systems for applying the old architectural orders.

The pity is that few architects were able to rise to the occasion— they were unable to cope with the formal liberty that modern architecture gave them. The old architectural styles may have been a hindrance, but they were also a crutch. In the absence of these aids many of the "lost generation" of architects sought out a new order. The restrictions of the old were soon to be replaced by the restrictions of a new, codified style. The activities of the new society were to be regimented into a new formal order; the satisfaction of the spatial needs of the buildings' users were again to be relegated to secondary importance. Much of the form language of Mies van der Rohe, for instance, was as restrictive as it would have been had he housed such activities within a Greek temple. The minutia of a Mies steel detail is also as taxing as the form ordering systems of the Baroque, and, I must add, as unrelated to the inherent capacities of the materials used (Figure 11.2).

Philip Johnson's recent dismissal of the modern idiom and his adoption of a Neoclassical style has surprised and shocked the practicing profession and its critics. But from his writing and work, it is clear that Johnson was always disdainful of both the social concerns and planning methods of modern architecture. His selection of Mies van der Rohe as his master and as the architect with whom he would introduce modern architecture to America is consistent with his stylistic predilections. For of all the identified pioneers of the modern movement, Mies's language of forms and planning method is the most classical and

Fig. 11.2: Photo and detail drawing of a corner of Mies van der Rohe's Alumni Memorial Hall at the Illinois Institute of Technology in Chicago. The external column and its complex connections to the brick wall are unnecessary artifacts. The detail reveals the internal structural steel column buried in concrete to meet the local fire codes. The external steel column and brick walls are decorative, nonload-bearing elements.

Fig. 11.3: Crown Hall on the IIT campus, by Mies van der Rohe. *(Photo by Hedrich-Blessing)*

geometrically constrictive. His architecture is less concerned with the activities that are to be housed than with maintaining the purity of his forms. Some of Mies's buildings at the Illinois Institute of Technology in Chicago are little more than monumental sculptures which incidentally and almost *post facto* also house things like administrative offices and classrooms (Figure 11.3).

Most of Philip Johnson's buildings also fall into this category. It is clear that his primary interest was with the visual imagery of his buildings and not with satisfying the spatial needs of the buildings' eventual users. Johnson's major architectural successes have, as a consequence, been buildings in which the programmatic needs were simple and could be satisfied with virtually any kind of large open space — his churches and exhibition galleries (Fig. 11.4). How, then, do Johnson's obsessions

Fig. 11.4: Philip Johnson's Amon Carter Museum of Western Art, Fort Worth, Texas, 1961. *(Photo by Ezra Stoller)*

and predilections differ from those of the architects of Classical times? Very little. How are his buildings "modern"? Only in that they appear to be done in what, in America, has been loosely termed the "modern style." The buildings of Mies van der Rohe and Philip Johnson, evaluated in terms of their planning freedom, their ability to serve their clients' needs, and their use of contemporary technology, are not really modern. Johnson's decision to place an open Greek pediment atop his new American Telephone & Telegraph building in New York City does not make this building fundamentally different from any of his previous, so-called modern, buildings; it may be that the demise of Modernism has allowed him to come out from being a closet classicist.

In the four or so generations of architects that have been produced by American schools since World War II, following the adoption of modern architecture as the vogue, it is hard to find very many American practitioners who are aware of the sociopolitical roots of the modern movement or of the planning and technical disciplines that were its foundations. Modern architecture in America has simply been "the modern style." The prevailing ignorance of these roots in America is not surprising. The European practitioners who fled the Nazi holocaust to introduce modern architecture to America were not willing to live through another witch hunt. McCarthyism was running rampant in this country just at the time when modern architecture was beginning to come into its own. It would not have been wise at that time to have referred to its social concerns. Hitler had already labeled modern architecture *Kulturbolschewismus;* who knows what McCarthy would have called it had he been made aware of its origins.

But, in fairness, it must be admitted that the very birth of modern architecture in Europe was itself steeped in philosophical conflict. From its earliest discernible signs, at the turn of the century, there was already evidence of two distinct schools of modernism. While one school was determined to use the new technology and materials to address the needs of the new urban populace, the other became enamored with the forms of the new machines and engineering structures — that is, the form language of transportation machines and factories became the inspiration for the creation of a new style. Both schools talked of the "liberating qualities" of the new architecture — but their work suggests that each meant very different things by it.

I have labeled one group the "social methodologists" — both for making their central concern the definition of the building needs of the mass of society and for their evolution of a design methodology which strove for an unrestrictive development of a building layout and straightforward use of the new industrial techniques. The other group I have

Fig. 11.5: The Zonnestraal Sanatorium in Hilversum, The Netherlands, by Bijvoet and Duiker, 1928. The reinforced concrete construction allowed large sections of the building's peripheral skin to be clad in glass, where sunlight, view, and association with outside areas were deemed desirable. The form of the building grew from the assembly of the building's internal volumes which the architects were nevertheless able to reconcile into an acceptable formal composition. (*Photo by J. G. van Agtmaal*)

labeled the "style metaphysicists" — first, for making/their prime interest the creation of a new architectural style and, second, for their belief in the deterministic qualities inherent in the intangible symbolism of spatial and formal configurations. Assigning particular architects or groups of architects to one or the other of these two schools is a more difficult task than the identification of the values of each school. Many practitioners and theorists managed to keep a foot in each camp — often to their own continuing imbalance and dismay. Walter Gropius certainly managed to do so, while Le Corbusier — the greatest achiever of the style-metaphysicist camp — at times produced exemplary buildings in the social-methodologist tradition.

The social methodologists recognized the potential benefits of mass production and the availability of products at a mass scale as the means of providing for the needs of a mass society. They were committed to the use of the new technology to provide the new working- and middle-classes with decent housing, schools, hospitals, factories, and recreation areas. This group can be recognized as early as the turn of the cen-

Fig. 11.6: The Van Nelle tobacco factory, in Rotterdam, The Netherlands, 1928, by Brinkmann and Van der Flugt. The factory provides natural light and ventilated work areas for both office and factory workers. It also includes recreation rooms, lounges, and dining facilities. It compares well with the best of contemporary, humane working environments. (*Photo by E. M. van Ojen*)

tury in the arts and crafts movement in England, the Chicago school in America, and the German rationalists of Hendrik Berlage, Peter Behrens, and Adolf Loos. The practitioners of the 1920s and 1930s who followed in their footsteps were the Germans Hugo Haring, Mart Stamm, Ernst May, and Hannes Meyer; the Dutchmen B. Bijvoet, J. Duiker, and L. C. van der Flugt; and the Finn Alvar Aalto. Their buildings are noted for the freedom with which the various facilities to be housed are positioned on the site and placed adjacent to each other so as to be of greatest utility to the buildings' users. The internal uses dictate the shaping and assembly of spaces and the final building mass. Yet in spite of the fact that a formal mishmash might easily have resulted from such a method of shaping and grouping areas, these architects succeeded in creating a form language which gave their buildings a satisfactory unity. In addition, these buildings are noted for their direct use and expression of contemporary materials. The new building technologies (the ability to span large distances and to free walls of their load-bearing function) are also employed to produce internal spaces which have more natural light and greater flexibility of organization. The Zonnestraal Sanatorium in Hilversum, The Netherlands, designed in 1928 by Bijvoet and Duiker (Figure 11.5), the workers' housing in Germany, designed in 1926 by May, and the 1928 Van Nelle factory in Rotterdam of Brinkmann and Van der Flugt (Figure 11.6) are all excellent examples of the social methodologists school of modern architecture.

The style metaphysicists, on the other hand, chose to see in the new technology, the new materials, and the rapid growth of cities a liberation from the traditional stylistic and technical restrictions of the past. They saw in the forms of factories, trains, ships, and planes a new aesthetic, a new style that could be applied to the three-dimensional art of architecture. Instead of seeing these forms as direct expressions of their own particular utilitarian functions (the equivalent of which would have to be found for schools, housing, etc.), they saw in the stylistic language of these machines forms which could be cut out and applied to buildings independently of any consideration of their function (Figure 11.7). The fact that many of the "new" buildings, such as houses, also had to fulfill rather traditional functions was obviously somewhat bothersome. Those architects who were troubled by these

Fig. 11.7: Illustration from Le Corbusier's *Towards a New Architecture,* first published in English in 1927. The forms of the new airplanes were used by architects as direct source material in devising a new form language for modern architecture. The style metaphysicists did not study the forms of the new machines in light of the jobs they had to perform and then try to find an equivalent for buildings; they simply "stole" the machine forms and applied them to buildings directly and, often, inappropriately.

Fig. 11.8: Le Corbusier's city plan for Algiers. The project was entitled "Shrapnel" by the architect, "with the intention of breaking through, for once, all the administrative red-tape and to establish in city-planning the new scales of dimensions required by contemporary realities."

contradictions reconciled them by turning a group of houses into a massive tower, and conceived of homes as "machines for living." For the style metaphysicists, the stylistic purity of their new form language became their dominant concern; the activity to be housed within their buildings was relegated to secondary importance—it was either strait-jacketed into the new form or only minimally provided for (Figures 11.8 and 11.9). Having justified the revolution in architecture with claims that the old revivalist schools put impossible constraints on the planning of contemporary buildings, they, in turn, fell into exactly the same trap: the stylistic demands of their brand of modern architecture soon made it difficult to address their design problems in a straight-forward manner.

In their search for a way to use modern technology to meet the building needs of the new concentration of urban populations, architects had sought a form language that would not require costly hand labor and ornamentation. The richness and pleasure in form was to come instead from the geometric play of proportions, color, and materials. The spareness of means evoked the search for and the heralding of the spare style. But the new style soon became mistaken for its purpose; the medium had become the message.

In the planning of housing developments the style metaphysicists saw only the opportunity to design on the grand scale, to wipe out the relics of the past—the traditional buildings and endless rows of single-family workers' houses—and to replace them with an architecture that reached up to assume in height its relative proportion to the horizontal spread of the city. They designed buildings that could be seen for miles, that moved along highways the length of a city, that housed the new masses in a mass architecture (Figures 11.10, 11.11, 11.12, and 11.13).

Fig. 11.9: The Schröder House in Utrecht, The Netherlands, by Gerrit Rietveld, 1924. For all the planning freedom this formal geometry allowed the architect, a rationale he employed to justify its style, it is disappointing to find the house poorly laid out, its various functional requirements seriously compromised to serve the formal idioms. (*Photo from Doeser-Fotos*)

Fig. 11.10: Le Corbusier's plan for a new town on the left bank of the Schelde River, Antwerp (1933). The plan uses the basic building blocks of his Ville Radieuse, or Radiant City. Le Corbusier expressed the concern that contemporary society did not possess architectural forms for housing which were large enough to keep pace with the incredible spread of urbanization. Thus the building blocks of Ville Radieuse are made to read, from the air, as sculptural elements in a three-mile-long new town. This concern for the visual became the most important criterion answered in his concept for a new town, and it is a devastating example of how the basic values satisfied by the architectural profession are often unrelated to the needs and values of those they serve.

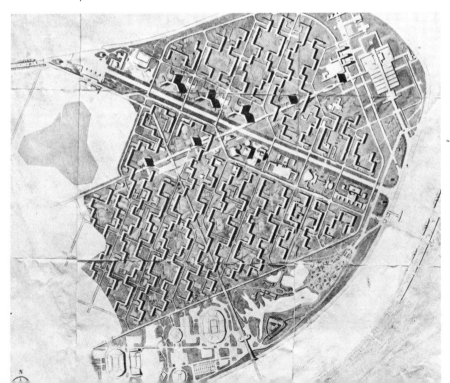

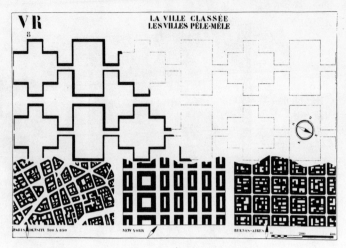

Fig 11.11: Le Corbusier's comparison between the scale of traditional cities like Paris, New York, and Buenos Aires and the scale of his proposed building blocks for Ville Radieuse (1930): "The drawing shows the astonishing contrast between the size of the open space provided in Ville Radieuse and the atrocious narrowness of our present cities."

Fig. 11.12: Model of the Bijlermeer New Town, outside Amsterdam, as it was realized. Forty years after Le Corbusier prepared his plan for the Antwerp New Town (Fig. 11.10) the government of The Netherlands actually was able to implement an equivalent outside Amsterdam. The only body both able and prepared to commit such vast resources to an untried concept was a government with total control of the residential construction industry, not the "captains of industry."

Fig. 11.13: The thirteen-thousand-unit Bijlermeer New Town is the largest housing disaster yet built anywhere. The photograph illustrates what a scale that is conceived from the air produces at ground level. As many as twelve hundred families share the entry to a single building. The vandalism and litter in the foreground is typical of conditions everywhere in the project including the interior lobbies, elevators, and hallways. The 88 per cent of the ground area which is free of building (Le Corbusier's proudly claimed achievement) goes unused and unattended. Residents are terrified to move through the grounds and the interiors of their buildings. Nowhere else in Holland are the problems of crime, vandalism, and vacancies so consuming of the energies of the Dutch police and housing ministries. (Photo courtesy of Gem. Dienst Volkschulsvesting Amsterdam.)

The architects advocating this philosophy labeled themselves Neoplasticists, Purists, and *de Stijl,* and included the practitioners Gerrit Rietveld, Theo van Doesburg, Mies van der Rohe, and Le Corbusier.

In the early 1930s there appeared to be little conflict between the two philosophies. To each of their proponents they seemed united by a common goal. Their dispute was with a common enemy: the traditional practitioner still caught up in the endless application of Neo-Gothic, Neoclassical, and Neorenaissance styles. But as one traces the association between the members of the two groups, their differences become more clear and their conflict and parting becomes inevitable.

The International Congress of Modern Architecture (CIAM) was, from the late 1920s to the mid-1950s, the organization which was both the arena for and spokesman of the modern movement. Walter Gropius, Sigfried Giedion, Mies van der Rohe, Le Corbusier, and many others were among its founding and active members. From its inception it managed to serve the interests of both the stylists and the methodologists. But after their initial meeting in 1928, in La Sarraz, Switzerland, one can trace the increasing rivalry, misunderstanding, and dominance of first one group, then the other, to the final dissolution of CIAM at the Dubrovnik, Yugoslavia, conference in 1956.

The purpose of the first CIAM conference was to frame the association's aims and statutes and to enunciate some general working principles:

> It is the destiny of architecture to exhibit the preoccupations of its time; works of architecture cannot help but be reflective of their current circumstance. Modern architecture therefore can only move into a direction determined in concert with economic factors.
>
> The ratios between housing areas, areas set aside for parks (including play areas), and areas required for circulation are determined as a consequence of the current social and economic milieu. The very act of establishing a housing density effectively predetermines the social class of the user.
>
> — *From the CIAM La Sarraz Declaration*

The theme at the 1929 meeting at Frankfurt am Main, in Germany, was "Dwellings for the Lower Income Groups," and the work presented at that occasion can be considered as nothing less than a revolutionary approach to the problems of contemporary housing. The Frankfurt meeting laid a foundation for modern architecture much beyond the limits of the immediate problem tackled. The same theme was taken up again in 1930 at Brussels and extended to the town-planning scale. Walter Gropius' speech, summarizing the most recent experiences of German rationalism, raised for the first time the question of the relationship between flats, buildings, neighborhood units, and the town and offered a precise set of formulations for discussion.

In 1933 CIAM met in Athens on the theme "The Functional City" and issued the so-called Charter of Athens. This document represents the conclusive outcome of a period of issue related and fruitful work — the results of what must now be viewed as a golden age in modern architecture. For the first time in the history of architecture, a group of architects from every industrialized country in the world devoted themselves to a survey of the problems of human settlements and recognized the shortcomings of architectural action which did not proceed from an understanding of the urban phenomenon which it found itself confronting. The ninety-five articles of the charter examine

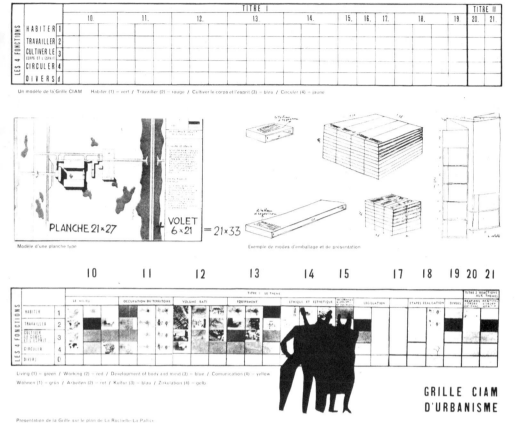

Fig. 11.14: Le Corbusier's "La Grille CIAM," a system devised to co-ordinate graphic presentation of projects by CIAM members. It also succeeded in systematizing how members perceived and addressed the problems they were commissioned to study.

these many questions as specific planning issues. The problem of style is not raised, only that of method. Style and the metaphysics of space appear as issues several years later at the Paris CIAM meeting in 1937, when CIAM began to rest in the shade of Le Corbusier's prestige.

In 1947, at Bridgwater, England, the CIAM meeting was devoted to reestablishing contacts severed by World War II and to reviewing the past ten years. From now on the style metaphysicists would dominate the Congress. The theme of the Bergamo, Italy, meeting in 1949 was "The Architecture of Settlement," but the main interest was in Le Corbusier's "La Grille CIAM," a graphic system devised by Le Corbusier and his disciples by which all presentations of projects would be made to conform to a uniform style (Figure 11.14). While a war-devastated Europe grappled with the enormous task of reconstruction,

Fig. 11.15: Low-income housing scheme in Frankfurt-am-Main, on Bruchfeldstrasse, by the city architect, Ernst May, 1926–28. The housing is grouped around a court which leads to the community center.

CIAM discussed the usefulness of the Le Corbusier grid, how to employ the grid, the best way to pack the grid. The credibility of the architectural profession in lending knowledge and method to problems of reconstruction was at stake.

The theme of the 1951 CIAM meeting in Hoddesdon, near London, was "The Core of the City." The report that was drafted at the meeting contains such a collection of inaccurate statements and idle speculation on the relationship between urban problems and built form that one wonders how so many of those who also participated in drafting the Charter of Athens ever put up with it.

Looking back at the workers' housing of the German architects Mart Stamm and Ernst May presented at the CIAM conference in Frankfurt in 1929, it is so clear, by contrast, what a solidly grounded theory of architecture could accomplish. The workers' housing in Frankfurt is a model that is relevant to the needs of low-income groups even today. Stamm and May labeled their projects "existence minimum," by which they meant to define the minimum home and environment that should be provided each family, regardless of income. Theirs was an architecture which employed contemporary materials and technology to produce, at very low cost, a decent house in a well-planned community for even the poorest family (Figure 11.15). When at the Otterlo, The Netherlands, meeting of Team 10 in 1959, following the dissolution of CIAM, the philosopher-architect Aldo van Eyck stated, "Existence minimum' be damned; we are not interested in minimums, we are interested in maximums," he was speaking as a middle-class Dutchman in postwar Holland — a country that had managed to rebuild its bombed cities, eradicated its slums, and provide a very desirable minimum of housing for all its population. The Netherlands, like Van Eyck, was ready to consider the next step, but most of the rest of the world, including the United States, was not anywhere near ready.

The major weakness of the social methodologists was that the form of their architecture was not poetic enough; it was prosaic by definition and subservient to the building program, the materials used, and cost. Their form language was not allowed to run off and pursue an inner lyricism. As a consequence, it could not easily inspire or win over the new generation of young architects. In its bid for their loyalties the social methodologists lost. That problem is still with us today, even as we have become aware of the bankruptcy, not of modern architecture, but of the methods, ideas, and form language of the style metaphysicists. For example, in the design of housing, young architects are now trained to acquire a visual perception which makes them appalled by the endless sprawl of suburban development. They are not taught to be inquisitive enough to learn whether most families living in single-family houses in a suburban tract find their homes the closest image of their affordable ideal — whether their homes satisfy their aspirations and represent, in tangible form, what they have worked all their lives to attain. Architects and urban designers may be outraged by the endless visual monotony of suburban tract development, but the families that occupy them do not see the over-all tract — they see only the glory of their own individual homes. For them, their single-family house is symbolic of arrival. For the architect or urban designer driving by or flying over these tracts, they form a boring, endless, uninspiring landscape. Architects and architectural historians have been damning the suburban tract development since the 1930s, but social scientists and realtors will tell you that tract houses continue to be the most sought after and the most successful form of moderate- and middle-income housing ever built. The hardest lesson for architects to learn is that for the consumer, the least important of requirements to be satisfied in housing is the visual composition created by the total assembly of a hundred or more units. And yet the satisfaction of this very requirement — the production of an over-all inspiring urban view — is the primary, self-imposed criterion

Fig. 11.16: Habitat 67, by the Israeli architect Moshe Safdie, built for the Montreal Worlds Fair, Expo '67. The primary criterion that this housing was made to satisfy by its architect was visual excitement. Built at a density of twenty units to the acre, the equivalent of row housing, it cost over ten times as much to build. The units are stacked up into the air, depriving families of easy access to the grounds. It is true that it provides some of its residents with an interesting view, but at that cost per unit residents could have purchased a mansion on half an acre of land in an exclusive community on the top of Mount Royal. This option was not open to them, however, as nine tenths of the cost of the project was in the form of a hidden subsidy provided by the Canadian Government as its contribution to Expo '67.

for the architect involved in the design of mass housing. For the architect knows that it will be the first criterion that will be used by his peers and critics in evaluating his design (Figure 11.16).

By the late 1940s the modern movement in architecture had become dominated by the style metaphysicists and their desire to institutionalize a new architectural form language. The incomparable creator and master of the new architectural style, Le Corbusier, so captivated and mesmerized the architects attracted to the modern movement that he succeeded in becoming at once creator, impresario, and finite master of the entire movement. Toward the end of his career the social methodologists could only see him as the man most responsible for leading the modern movement off its main track and down the siding of stylistic showmanship. On the other hand, his followers saw him then, as they do now, as the supreme being who codified the modern movement and gave it its final form and international recognition and acceptance.

A further weakness resulting from the stylists' preoccupation with image is that it kept them from giving thought to the institutional and financial framework necessary to the implementation of their plans. Le Corbusier's obsession with design on the grand scale also required him to advocate a centralized bureaucracy of businessmen in order to achieve it. His grand designs, which relegated the home of the individual man to insignificance, would take a bureaucracy of a size comparable to his plans (and with an equal lack of concern for the needs and aspirations of individuals) to implement them. This was a fundamental weakness in Le Corbusier's thinking and in the thinking of contemporary architects intrigued by the practice of urban design. Socially conscious disciples of Le Corbusier have difficulty reconciling the fact that he looked to what he called the "captains of industry" ultimately to build his vision of the future city.

The French Communists termed Le Corbusier's futurist city, Ville Contemporaire, "fascistic" because it implied a strong, centralized government and an elite corps of businessmen to run it. This was a rare group of Communists indeed who could perceive the dangers of large, centralized government and appeared committed to the rights of individual men and their separate actions. Or perhaps it was only the ogre of a centralized government by "capitalist" businessmen that they were objecting to so strongly.

It is interesting that today's newly emerging schools of self-identified "Marxist" planners and environmental psychologists in the United States and Europe are strongly advocating that the ownership of *all* urban land be assumed by the state, as they feel this will greatly facilitate large-scale planning and development. They argue that the problems currently attending the assemblage of endless tracts of small, individually owned parcels of land could thus be avoided. Whether from the extreme right or from the extreme left, the average citizen must take heed of those who would deprive him of his quarter acre of land — for the plans that are being made for the physical counterparts of these brave new societies will make his place in the sun as insignificant as the social role that is being planned for him. There will be little to the new form of the physical representation of his place on earth that will satisfy his need for individual rights and recognition. His identity will be obliterated in the grand scheme. The form and character of the large redevelopment schemes we have been witnessing these past thirty years suggest that we could do much worse as planners than enable the average citizen to prevent the proliferation of such developments by means of his individual ownership of a small parcel of land in the middle of them.

The implementation of a grand physical plan always necessitates the establishment of a large autocracy – whether the autocracy is a centralized revolutionary government, a state housing agency with powers of eminent domain, or a consortium of large industrial companies. Le Corbusier was politically astute enough to realize that only a large, autocratic, centralized authority – whether of the left or the right – could marshal the resources and maintain the singularity of purpose over time to implement one of his urban megastructures. Only such a centralized institution would be able to suppress the personal preferences and actions of thousands of individuals in order to force compliance with the grand plan. Perhaps the most difficult pill today's socially concerned urban architects and planner's have to swallow is the knowledge that, at the urban scale, what they perceive as visual *disorder* is the ultimate expression of a pluralistic society in which each individual is free to implement his own plan because he controls enough of society's resources and land to be able to satisfy his own needs.

The team of young architects – known as "Team 10" – who planned the tenth CIAM conference in Dubrovnik in 1959 strove to redirect CIAM to its original goals, but it was clearly too late. CIAM had become a large, institutionalized bureaucracy that no single group could change or redirect. Team 10 opted for the bold alternative of declaring CIAM dead – although it took another meeting to put it properly to rest. The 1959 meeting in Otterlo finally saw the burial of CIAM.

Team 10 called itself the "Group for the Research of Social and Visual Interrelationships." But having failed to learn the historic lesson of CIAM, they were forced to repeat it. Like CIAM, Team 10 could not reconcile the conflict between its social commitments and the need to produce stylistically captivating architecture. The stylistic commitments and metaphysics of Le Corbusier persisted in those of his followers who were present at Otterlo, as witnessed in the statements of André Wogenscky, an architect who was Le Corbusier's second in command for many years. Wogenscky criticized a low-income housing project by one of the other participants, the Italian architect Giancarlo De Carlo. (The project was designed as three-story walk-ups with four to six families sharing an entry [Figure 11.17]. Although unmistakingly modern through the use of exposed concrete and brick, the buildings are small in scale and have sloped tile roofs. De Carlo intentionally

Fig. 11.17: The low-income housing development in Matera, Italy, by Giancarlo De Carlo, criticized by Andre Wogencsky, the architect who ran Le Corbusier's office. (*Photo by Italo Zannier*)

used a form language which would relate the form of the buildings to the houses of the well-to-do-citizenry in the area.) Unable to accept both the concerns and accomplishments of De Carlo, Wogenscky proved, as illustrated by his statement below, that the self-delusion of the style metaphysicists lived on even more strongly in the followers of Le Corbusier:

> It is the responsibility of the architect . . . to give to the people a conception of the space of our time. Perhaps I am using rather severe terms, but I think that you [De Carlo], through your plastic conception, are betraying your clients. There is no doubt that you have a difficult task here. For these people have not received an education into the new plastic relationships of our epoch and do not understand the poetry of modern space and movement. But you must talk to them about these concepts which are a real result of the "plastique" of our time. You must, if you hope to lead them to the future, introduce this new plastic expression and fight to make it clear and understandable to them.
>
> The plastic (three dimensional) conception of architectural space cannot be independent of the culture of our day, with its advances in scientific and artistic thinking. I do not think it is possible today to conceive of an architecture which is not based on a relative conception of space—a space which is non-

Euclidian. This building is conceived in a totally Euclidian spirit, in which all the elements are fixed and of the same value. You, as an architect, have returned architecture to the level of conception which is purely aesthetic. This building does not open these people's eyes to the whole of the actual situation in the world of today, either artistically or technologically, but rather turns them back to the past and, if anything, hinders them from this realization.[2]

Wogenscky could not reconcile the obvious success of this form of housing (in meeting the needs of the client) with De Carlo's intentional rejection of the imagery of Le Corbusier.

It was the belief of the style metaphysicists that the modern style itself could be liberating and that a modern, collective society could be achieved by housing people in new, communal environments. It was almost as if the poor could be at once both liberated and politicized by being introduced into mass housing designed within a Mondrian or Corbusierian format. But these were also physically complex environments which required sophisticated communal social structures to survive in and operate. In contemporary American society, when the poor are housed in such environments, the projects are run paternalistically by large housing bureaucracies. There is little liberation, no autonomy, and no separate identity for the individual family.

The British architects Peter and Alison Smithson, the sustaining theorists of Team 10, also appeared, in the design of their own buildings, unable to provide the bridge between their social commitment and an architectural style in which to express it. Like almost every other member of Team 10, they did not seem able to escape the magnetism of the purist's style of Le Corbusier. The Smithsons advocated a form of housing environment which would produce "the feeling that you are somebody living somewhere." To this end they evolved, in 1960, a set of social criteria for mass housing, many of which remain valid today:

1. Can the dwelling adapt itself to various ways of living? Does it liberate the occupants from old restrictions or straitjacket them into new ones?
2. Are the spaces moulded exactly to fit their purpose, or are they by-products of structural tidiness or plastic whim? Is the means of construction of the same order as the standard of living envisaged?
3. Is there a decently large open-air sunlit space opening directly from the living area of the house? Is there a place in the open air where a small baby (1–3 years old) can be left safely?
4. Can the weather be enjoyed? Is the house insulated against cold weather, yet made to easily open up in good weather?

5. Are the extensions of the dwelling (garden, patio, etc.) appreciated from inside?
6. Does it take account of the 3–5-year-olds' play?
7. Is it easy to maintain (keep fresh-looking with just a cleaning down)?
8. Is there a place for the belongings or special tasks peculiar to the class of the occupants — skis, camping gear, mending motorbikes, etc.?
9. Is there enough storage? (There is never enough storage.)
10. Can the dwellings be put together in such a way as to contribute something to each other?
11. Is the house as comfortable as a car of the same year?
12. Where do the 5–12-year-olds go? And what do they do?
13. Is there something worth looking at out of every dwelling or does one merely stare out at another dwelling opposite?
14. Does the public vertical circulation system (elevators, stairs, etc.) really work? Is there any indication that where people have been put up into the air it is really getting them somewhere?[3]

But the Smithsons in fact built their London housing project, Robin Hood Gardens, in the idiom of the grand style (Figure 11.18). Their own criteria were addressed only secondarily, and sometimes ignored entirely, by the compromises they had to make in their adoption of the

Fig. 11.18: The Robin Hood Gardens housing development in London's East End, by Alison and Peter Smithson, 1962–73. The Smithsons were seldom able to reconcile their excellent planning criteria with the built environment which they, in the end, produced. One must conclude, sadly, that they lacked the courage to stand up to the style metaphysicists. Their architecture gives in to the taste demands of the elitist designers who surrounded Le Corbusier.

form language of Le Corbusier. When asked to discuss the vandalism and residents' active dislike of the housing project they designed (Figure 11.19) Peter Smithson came up with the response one hears all too often from contemporary architects: "The residents are just not ready for the form of living we have provided them."[4]

The unanswered challenge being posed to the architectural profession today was formulated at the first CIAM conference in 1928: Can we harness the new technology and our social awareness to provide the majority of people with a living environment which answers both their needs and their image of themselves? Modern architects seem to have thrust that challenge aside. Is it because the task is too difficult or simply that the solutions are too obvious and, therefore, uninteresting?

In their search for a new form language, the pioneers of the modern movement sought to symbolize the values and aspirations of the new industrial society in building forms. But little thought was given to the question of variation in the values and aspirations among different segments of the population. Given these variations, whose values were to be embodied in the forms of the new architecture? As the only values and aspirations that the architects were familiar or sympathetic with were their own, these were the only ones they addressed. It should come as no surprise, then, that the form language of modern architecture symbolizes little of the values of most of society—and least of all those of low- and moderate-income groups. Little of the form language

Fig. 11.19: Vandalism by residents became pervasive in the public circulation areas at Robin Hood Gardens within months of its occupancy.

and scale of modern buildings has been adopted as symbols by the working and middle classes. Architects get around these questions by saying that they are advocates of a classless society, but this does not explain why architects so often design homes for the working class and the poor that are so peculiar in form — the high-rise, superblocks of subsidized housing. Inadvertently, architects may have committed the final outrage against lower-income groups: representing them to the rest of society — through their housing — in ways they do not want to be represented; providing them with necessarily communal environments when they do not want to live communally; and giving their homes a form language of peculiarity when they do not want to be singled out as peculiar. It is one thing for rich patrons of contemporary arts to choose the forms of modern architecture to live in themselves — and quite another for low-income groups to be given them without their consent. In their advocacy of the symbolic importance of the modern style as a visual representation of the new liberty, the style metaphysicians have insisted on trying to do with form what cannot in fact be done with it; at the same time, they have neglected to do with form what can be done with it.

The modern movement in architecture, while succeeding in establishing a new style, neglected its most revolutionary attainment: an open system for planning areas and a freedom to assemble them into building forms which reflected contemporary technology and which did not have to pay lip service to past styles. The most successful modern buildings are those in which internal areas and their assembly are determined by the form of activities that are to take place within them. The genius of the modern architect is then revealed not by his ability to refashion or squeeze this assemblage of volumes into a single geometrical image, but rather by his ability, using contemporary materials and technology, to find a form language which provides unity to the totality.

The failure of modern architecture is twofold: first, the style, with its emphasis on the use of steel, glass, and concrete, has proved harsh and monotonous and does not reflect the social aspirations of most of its users; and, second, once the modern style had become established, the tradition for functional planning gave way to the old tradition of squeezing internal areas together to fit into predetermined three-dimensional forms. Thus we find ourselves living with the ultimate irony: modern-looking, and therefore supposely functional, buildings which are impossible to live in and to use. The most dramatic failure of modern architecture in this regard is in the production of mass housing for low-, moderate-, and middle-income groups.

However, a critical question arises implicitly here but remains unanswered. If, as I have maintained, the most important three tradi-

Fig. 11.20: The Cedar-Riverside housing development, by Ralph Rapson. The scheme is based on the utopian notion that one can create community by crowding together old and young, rich and poor, in high-density apartment houses by providing wide corridors every few floors which would function as pedestrian streets in the air. The project is proving very costly to secure and to maintain and is undesirable as a living environment, particularly for families with children. Much of the development's current problems were predicted well before construction began, but the architect was not to be dissuaded. The community which surrounds the development has prevented the construction of the final phase, at great cost to HUD.

tions of the modern movement were the commitment to social purpose, open planning, and the straightforward use of contemporary technology, can one have a modern architecture without the fourth tradition, the modern style? It is this last tradition, the modern style, which in itself is proving objectionable to many users of modern buildings, particularly those of low and middle incomes who find the raw concrete and exposed steel unrelated to their image of desirable housing. The question then becomes: Can we have a modern style which, through its symbolism, also succeeds in addressing the aspirations of the common man?

The lesson architects have failed to learn is that the symbol of modern housing for the contemporary liberated man is not the mass buildings of Le Corbusier's Unité d'Habitation in Marseilles, Minoru Yamasaki's Pruitt-Igoe in St. Louis, Rapson's Cedar-Riverside in Minneapolis (Figure 11.20), the Smithson's Robin Hood Gardens in

London, or Moshe Safdie's Habitat 67 in Montreal (Figure 11.16), but the privately owned single-family house which, in form and tenure, allows the occupants the maximum ability to pursue independent action and decision making.

The Functions of Form in Modern Architecture

In my advocacy of functionalism, I hope I am not misunderstood as suggesting that the form of buildings should be little more than an expression of their interior functions. The demands on modern architects are far greater than that, for most residents desire that the form of their housing be symbolic not only of their current attainments but also of their social aspirations. The form of their houses must not only satisfy their current life-style needs but also relate to houses occupied by higher income groups. The housing must be a stage set for the enactment of dreams and the realization of aspirations.

John Johanson's Municipal Theater, in Oklahoma city (Figure 11.21), although unpopular with the community there, is a very important contribution to the evolution of architectural thought. The building demonstrates that the architectural theory of functional expressionism, applied with conscious and intentional disregard of both the intuitive and acquired notions of visual order, will have little public appeal and prove nonsensical to all but the architect and his fellow theoreticians, who are sufficiently steeped in intellectual theory to structure their aes-

Fig. 11.21: Main entry to the Oklahoma City Municipal Theater, by John Johanson.

thetic judgments. Johanson's building may function well as a place to create theater (although there is some debate on this score, too), but the decision to make the form of the building no more than an expression of its functional areas and utilities was not, as he has claimed, the result of merely allowing various areas, facilities, and utility lines to find their own shape—it was a conscious decision on his part to give each of these elements a formal expression in the exterior of the building. The theater's form expresses the various internal areas and utility lines not because the architect simply allowed them to do so nor because he thought it more *honest* not to hide them, but rather because he *consciously chose to express them* as a formal decision. That is to say, the architect had to manipulate the form of the building and its internal areas (and probably increased his costs accordingly) in order to be able to expose the piping—just as he would have to had to manipulate these elements in order to hide them, whether behind a classical or a modern façade.

A rational theory for the design and layout of buildings should not be construed as an excuse for accepting the functional dictates of the program as the final arbiters of building form. Architects can manipulate areas and link them together in a variety of different ways, each of which will produce equally satisfactory spaces and interrelationships but very different building forms. The architect who claims that a building's function alone has determined its external form is a sham. That may be the theory to which he is committed, but the resulting form owes as much to conscious choice and deliberation as any Georgian façade.

It is impossible to design a building without addressing the aesthetic expectations of a particular audience. The only question is: Which audience will the architect choose to address—the taste and status needs of his client or those of his professional peers? There is little doubt that the tastes of these two groups often conflict, particularly where there is a big difference between the income of the architect and that of his client. To date, the avant-garde of the profession has not found a way of allowing the practitioner to address the taste needs of his client while at the same time basking in the approval of his fellow architects. The problem is that by the nature of his servitude to the current taste hierarchy, the architect cannot cater to the taste of low-, moderate-, or middle-income groups. The architect is slave to the rules of the game; his education, his peers, his critics, and his own revulsion prevent him from even considering the possibility of designing for any taste but that currently accepted by his professional peers.

The demands on the architect are actually even more stressful in that success in the profession is also contingent upon being recognized as an innovative designer. Therefore, not only must an architect keep up with the styles in vogue, he must also work at giving them a sufficiently new twist that will bring him to the attention of his contemporaries.

The hierarchy of architectural taste is much like a ladder paralleling the hierarchy of class in society. The lowest rung of the taste ladder is occupied by the lowest-income group and the highest rung by the highest-income group. The artifacts that each class chooses to surround itself with — and by which to symbolize its social status — are the objects they perceive as representative of the class immediately above them, that is, of the class to which they aspire. People therefore select and choose objects (and housing) which they see in use by the people in that class. Ironically, those very objects are not likely to be in current vogue among members of the class above, because that class also has its sights raised to the class above it. Inevitably, what each class is able to afford for itself is a less expensive reproduction of the artifacts of the class to which they aspire. The point, though, is that no class but the wealthiest aspires to the tastes of the architect.

The architect, as taste maker, by definition occupies the very top rung of the taste ladder. Unfortunately, the only segment of society that shares his elitist tastes are some of the very rich on the rung of the taste ladder immediately below his. The predilections of the architect-taste maker are therefore important to this group alone — that is, they are important to the very wealthy who are trying to keep up with the current vogues in architectural taste.

Many of the successful architects practicing today were educated in a tradition which relied heavily on the use of three-dimensional, gray, cardboard models during the design process. These models intentionally refrain from any representation of real materials, colors, or textures. As simulations of actual environments, the models are more severe than anything that could actually be built. The literal translation of the color and texture of these models into buildings would require the production of raw concrete surfaces both inside and out. Raw concrete, although highly satisfying to the Purist and *de Stijl* aesthetics, is a material which is alien to the tastes of most users.

Most people enjoy variations in the color and texture of natural materials in the environments they inhabit, particularly in their homes. Richly textured and colored environments not only provide gratification to the senses, in that they are rewarding to the touch and sight, but are also perceived as expressions of affluence — a form of conspicuous consumption.

The capacity to enjoy the purity and severity of raw concrete is a predilection of only the most sophisticated in our society. Low- and

Fig. 11.22: The Clason Point row-house project, in New York City, built of exposed cement block, prior to modification.

middle-income people usually associate the austerity of raw concrete with military bunkers and prisons. A very wealthy client by contrast may have learned to acquire the tastes and values of the architect and may find status rewards in living in buildings which represent the most avant-garde of current architectural idioms. If an architect's clients have had money for a few generations, they may be sufficiently self-assured to be able to perceive raw concrete as representative of high style and the most current of fashions. Most of the middle and upper-middle-class nouveaux riches are not that self-assured.

The sociologist Lee Rainwater, in his study of residents of low- and moderate-income housing, recognized that with increased income there is an accumulation in the clients' articulated needs of what criteria must be satisfied in their housing.[5] All groups are concerned about the urban location of their housing, but, that aside, the poorest in our society can only afford to frame criteria which are concerned with basic shelter from weather, rodents, insects, and other people. The working class is able to add to these basic requirements a need for separate bedrooms for parents and one bedroom for each sex of the children. There is also a demand for a certain "coziness." The middle class has a greater need for expanded living area and expresses a desire for varied materials, textures, and color. The upper middle class requires that all this be assembled into an individual single family house with a recognized style: Tudor, Colonial, etc. Finally, the very rich require that the assembly be in a style which is current or "chic."

Fig. 11.23: Moderate-income homeowners' efforts at individualizing and enriching their small, uniform houses.

My own research experience has led me to conclude that although the requirements of shelter and control may dominate the concerns of the lowest income groups, those groups are nevertheless very conscious of color, texture, and "appearances" in housing. The limits of their concerns, as expressed by what they live in, are determined not by what they think they need but by what they can afford.

I was made very conscious of the tastes and values of low-income clients while modifying the grounds and buildings of existing public housing to improve residents' control and involvement with their housing environment. This was at Clason Point in New York City in 1970. One of the projects had been built during World War II as temporary housing for munitions workers. It was constructed of gray concrete block (Figure 11.22). The weather penetration and heat loss through the porous concrete block was so great that the New York City Housing Authority concluded that it would be a worthwhile investment to cover the block with three coats of cement. We used this as an opportunity to go beyond this basic functional requirement and add both color and texture to the surface of the buildings and the grounds of the project.

Our ideas for upgrading the projects were derived from observations of what neighboring moderate-income residents, living in a row of small, uniform single-family houses, had done to enrich and individualize their homes (Figure 11.23) by adding surface colors, shutters, and awnings.

We persuaded the contractor carrying out the resurfacing work to consider varying the colors in his final cost of cement and had the contractor prepare a sample wall on site to demonstrate to the residents the system of application and the range of colors available (Figure 11.24). We also produced a color chart which illustrated possible color combinations. Our goal was to replicate, through the addition of color and texture and the visual "definition" of each unit, the tone of the surrounding middle-income community: that is, to make the public housing blocks indistinguishable from the neighboring row houses. Although each unit would have its own color, we suggested that only two colors be used for each row-house building. Residents had to get together with their neighbors and agree on their selections. We had to relax the restrictions on color combinations somewhat when residents reacted negatively to some of our more conservative suggestions.

The contractor estimated that the additional colors and the scoring of joints to simulate brick course work would add 25 per cent to the cost of the cement refinishing. I suggested to the board of the New York City Housing Authority that the cost would be worth it, that it would result in an environment which would be radically different in feeling—one in which residents could take pride and which would stimulate them to undertake their own decorating, maintenance, and care of grounds. The initial building which we had the contractor prepare on an experimental basis did, in fact, produce such an incredibly different mood and atmosphere. Following a site visit, the housing authority board members agreed to provide the additional funds.

These project modifications were, in part, experiments aimed at determining the extent to which residents responded to external changes made to their environment. The interviews and observations conducted by our Institute over the next few years proved quite telling. Not only did the residents respond by painting their own doors and windows in the first year, but in subsequent years they made extensive improvements to their gardens and to the interiors of their houses. Rich variations in color and materials began to appear on the grounds and insides of apartment units as well.

Our contractor also told us that at the beginning of construction his equipment was being so vandalized he found it necessary to remove it each evening. However, once the project had come along far enough so that the effect of the modifications became apparent to the residents, the abuse of his equipment ceased.

Subsequent interviews with residents showed that they were very conscious of the change in the "look" of their housing development brought about by the addition of color and texture. They actually valued the changes to the building façades more highly than either the

Fig. 11.24: Sample wall at Clason Point, showing a variety of brick colors and door and window treatments that residents could choose from.

new lighting, benching, or fencing provided. The low-income residents were found to be very articulate and finicky about color and texture and knew exactly what effect they wanted. They were very clear about their likes and dislikes, and their tastes were very much at variance with the tastes and values acquired by architects in school.

In our further survey of residents in other public and moderate-income housing, we were made very aware of the antagonistic differences between architects' tastes and those of their clients. This was evidenced by the incredible contrast in the colors, materials, and textures used by residents in decorating the inside of their own apartments as compared with the architect's treatment of the buildings' surfaces outside. Within the realms under their control, residents produced colorfully decorated environments—not necessarily at great cost—while outside their apartments was the gray world the architects had designed. Raw concrete was the prevalent material of the building, gray and off-white the dominant colors. Only the large glass areas occasionally broke up the drabness by reflecting a blue sky. Our interviews at Clason Point had revealed how strongly the residents appreciated and responded to the rich, varied, and individualized colors of their new environment. If architects need insight and direction into peoples' preferences, let them get their inspiration from how people decorate and color the inside of their own houses and apartments.

Although the layman might conclude that the absence of varied materials and colors on the surfaces of residential buildings is the result of an inadequate budget given the architect, it is more likely the result of the architect's personal tastes and preferences.

Much of contemporary architectural education is actually a form of brainwashing. I recall the self-satisfaction with which one of my architectural students at Columbia University, returning from a summer's recess, recounted proudly how he had not realized before just how bad his parents' tastes were. In the pursuit of our own aesthetic as tastemakers and educators, we have succeeded in estranging ourselves from the tastes, values, and aspirations of much of the society we claim to be serving.

When the results of our experiments in modifying housing projects were published in 1972, they were ridiculed by the architectural profession who saw our efforts as little more than window dressing—and kitsch at that. They said that we were pandering to the lowest levels of taste and that, as an architect, I had the responsibility to elevate the tastes of my clients. Therein lies the quandary: there must be a way that we can satisfy the tastes and symbolic aspirations of our client groups while still satisfying our own professional values and the aesthetic predilections of our peers.

The architectural education process produces severely disoriented practitioners. Not only are young architects kept ignorant of the tastes, values, and perception of the client groups they will be serving, but they are also intentionally trained to develop values which are antagonistic to them. I recently attended a community meeting in which a young black architect was presenting a preliminary design for a housing project to be built in the neighborhood in which he grew up. He was representing a large firm, and to make his link with the community evident he brought to everyone's attention the fact that his mother was in the audience. He then went on to present a very contemporary, exposed concrete, high-rise scheme. The community rejected his plan. His mother's astonishment at her son's design was only exceeded by her public embarrassment.

Most of our architectural schools are geared to turning out the occasional genius—the future master of the new style—and the next generation of tastemakers. Their competence in addressing their clients' needs is given secondary importance. Architectural students are not familiarized with the principles governing the layout of various building types, whether houses, schools, or office buildings. Their studio masters delude them into thinking that in the design of any building they must themselves rediscover the "essence" of that building type from scratch. Little effort is made to have students first familiarize themselves with the work of other architects and developers who have built such buildings before. There is no discipline or method that says that the development of a few new changes to perfect existing models further is a worthwhile pursuit. For most architects commencing to design a new building, the work of all other architects is studiously avoided so as not to taint themselves with the sin of plagiarism. As a consequence, we turn out professionals who design housing projects, dormitories, schools, and office buildings which may be handsome and which will win design awards, but which will also likely prove impossible to live or work in. The full extent of this tragedy is best appreciated when we realize that the most recognized of architects are often those who turn out the most dramatic failures. Architectural genius such as theirs works best in designing buildings which are predominantly non-utilitarian. Society should not reduce the esteem in which it holds its most prominent architects by requiring them to concern themselves with the building chores of domesticity.

I have identified three functions required of the new form language of modern architecture: (1) that it be open enough to allow freedom in the planning and laying out of areas, but still sufficiently uniform to result in a recognizable totality; (2) that it allow the *expressive* use of contemporary materials — not only in enabling the new building materials to be revealed (exposed) but also in allowing an expression of the work the new materials were capable of (spanning large distances, opening walls to light and air); and (3) that the form language symbolize the aspirations of a building's user, both in linking the present building to those of the past he desires to identify with and in the employment of materials and colors that are evocative of well-being.

It is clear that in asking the new form language to answer the third function, the designer often comes into conflict with some of the requirements of the second function. How does the designer reconcile this apparent conflict? With skill and good humor. It must be possible to have a recognizably modern architectural form which, in addition to answering the first two requirements, can occasionally make use of traditional formal elements and materials to enrich it and address the needs of the client. Examples of architecture which are unmistakably modern even though they make important use of traditional formal elements do not come to mind easily, but they do in other art forms such as music, dance, and painting. It cannot be that difficult to create the equivalent in architectural form of what the Beatles and Leonard Bernstein, for example, have produced in music.

The revolution in architecture in the 1920s and 1930s was a revolution in planning methods and in the adoption of social concerns. The challenge posed then is yet to be understood or assumed. Modern architecture in America is not dead, as our critics claim — it has yet to see life.

NOTES

Introduction

1. U.S. Department of Housing and Urban Development, Office of Policy Development and Research, *A Survey of Citizen Views and Concerns about Urban Life, Final Report, Part I,* conducted by Louis Harris and Associates, Washington, D.C., 1978, p. 17.

2. Ibid.: "Americans are almost unanimous (82%) in rating large cities as the 'worst place to raise children.' Also, 62% rate large city public schools 'worst'; 62% attribute the worst housing to the large city; 54% say the highest taxes are in the large city. Further undermining the image of family life in the city is the widespread perception, voiced by 57%, that divorce rates are highest there. A near-unanimous 91% point to large cities as having the highest crime rates."

3. Ibid.: "Crime is most frequently ranked by city residents as a severe problem (72%), followed by drug addiction (60%), and unemployment (58%)."

Chapter I

1. T. K. Hareven, "Family Time and Historical Time," in A. Rossi, J. Kagan, and T. R. Hareven (eds.) *The Family* (New York: Norton, 1978).

2. U. S. Bureau of the Census, *Statistical Abstract of the United States: 1972* (Washington, D.C.: U.S. Government Printing Office, 1972), pp. 26, 27, 36.

3. M. Messer, "Engagement with Disengagement," paper presented at the 1966 Annual Meeting of the American Sociological Association, Miami Beach, Florida.

4. From data collected by the New York City Housing Authority on the increase in the victimization of white elderly in predominantly black developments, conveyed in a conversation with Harry Fialkin, Chief of Statistics, 1971.

5. B. L. Ackerman, "Integration for Subsidized Housing and the Question of Racial Occupancy Controls." pp. 267–68.

Chapter II

1. U. S. Bureau of the Census, *Demographic, Economic, and Revenue Trends for Major Central Cities* (Washington, D.C.: U. S. Government Printing Office, 1971).

2. U. S. Bureau of the Census, *1970 Census of Population and Housing* (Washington, D.C.: U. S. Government Printing Office, 1971).

3. E. Grier and G. Grier, *Privately Developed Interracial Housing: An Analysis of Experience.*

4. B. L. Ackerman, "Integration for Subsidized Housing and the Question of Racial Occupancy Controls."

5. M. Jahoda and P. West, "Race Relations in Public Housing."

6. U.S. Department of Housing and Urban Development, Office of Policy Development and Research, *A Summary Report of Current Findings from the Experimental Housing Program*, Washington, D.C., 1978.

7. Housing Affairs Letter, "Can You Grow to Love $710,300 for a 40-Year Subsidy on One Unit?," Community Development Services, Washington, D.C., March 23, 1979.

8. H. J. Aaron, *Shelter and Subsidies* (Washington, D.C.: The Brookings Institution, 1972). p. 163.

9. E. P. Wolf, "The Tipping Point in Racially Changing Neighborhoods."

10. W. Ryan et al., *All Together: An Evaluation of Mixed Income Multi-Family Housing*, p. 10.

11. G. Grier and E. Grier, *Equality and Beyond: Housing Segregation in the Great Society*, p. 20.

12. A. Downs, *Opening Up the Suburbs*, p. 61.

13. B. L. Ackerman, "Integration for Subsidized Housing and the Question of Racial Occupancy Controls," p. 308.

Chapter III

1. O. Newman, *Architectural Design for Crime Prevention*, Ch. 4, "The Pattern of Fear in Housing, pp. 88–95. See also report to the National Institute of Law Enforcement and Criminal Justice, the study by O. Newman and K. Franck, *Factors Affecting Crime and Instability in Federally-Assisted Housing*, 1979, unpublished.

2. A. F. C. Wallace, *Housing and Social Structure: A Preliminary Survey with Particular Reference to Multistory, Low Rent Public Housing Projects*, Philadelphia: Philadelphia Housing Authority, 1952.

3. O. Newman and K. Franck, *Factors Affecting Crime and Instability in Federally-Assisted Housing,* Report to the National Institute of Law Enforcement and Criminal Justice, Washington, D.C., 1979, Grant No. 79NI-99-0036-S-2, unpublished.

Chapter IV

1. *FBI Uniform Crime Reports, 1973* (Washington, D.C.: U. S. Government Printing Office, 1974).

2. Ibid. Table 22, p. 120. Table 1, p. 58 of the FBI 1973 report lists 382,683 robberies and 2,540,907 burglaries nationwide.

3. Robbery totals presented here exclude the classifications of "Highway" and "Miscellaneous Robberies," which together total 203,663. The "Miscellaneous" category includes crimes in other buildings not listed or unclassified by location; the Highway category includes street crimes, which also could have occurred in streets within or bordering residential areas.

4. *FBI Uniform Crime Reports, 1972* (Washington, D.C.: U. S. Government Printing Office, 1973), pp. 17, 20.

5. *FBI Uniform Crime Reports, 1973* (Washington, D.C.: U. S. Government Printing Office, 1974).

6. G. L. Kelling et al., *Kansas City Preventive Patrol Experiment* (Washington, D.C.: The Police Foundation, 1974).

7. T. R. Repetto, *Residential Crime,* p. 50.

8. P. A. Morrison, *San Jose and St. Louis in the 1960's: A Case Study of Changing Urban Populations,* prepared for the National Science Foundation (Santa Monica, Calif.: RAND, 1973), pp. 21–22.

9. St. Louis City Plan Commission, *St. Louis Redevelopment Program* (St. Louis, Mo., June, 1973), pp. 34–43.

10. Ibid., p. 52.

11. Ibid., p. 53.

12. O. Newman, final report to the National Institute of Law Enforcement and Criminal Justice on the project entitled "Security Design in Urban Residential Areas" (Institute of Planning and Housing, New York University, New York, 1973, Unpublished). Regression results, pp. 8–11.

13. Adapted from O. Newman, *Defensible Space,* p. 33.

14. Results from on-going research at the Institute for Community Design Analysis. Grant entitled: Factors Influencing Crime and Instability in Urban Housing Developments, – sponsored by the Law Enforcement Assistance Administration, Grant No. 76-NI-99-0036-S-I, 1978.

Chapter V

1. E. Dickinson, "Lefrak City, Crucible of Racial Change," New York *Times,* Feb. 1, 1976.

2. E. Eaves, *How the Many Costs of Housing Fit Together,* Research Report No. 16, prepared for the consideration of the National Commission on Urban Problems (Washington, D.C.: U.S. Government Printing Office, 1969).

3. Mayor's Policy Committee, *Housing Development and Rehabilitation in New York City* (City of New York, N.Y., 1974).

4. G. Sternlieb et al., "Housing Abandonment in the Urban Core."

5. R. Sadacca, M. Drury, and M. Isler, *Ownership Form and Management Success in Private, Publicly Assisted Housing,* Working Paper No. 209-3, The Urban Institute, Washington, D.C., 1972, p. 3.

Chapter VI

1. Excerpts from an interview by Institute staff with the president of the Westminster Place Corporation in St. Louis, on March 27, 1974.

2. Excerpts from an interview by Institute staff with a resident of Cabanne Place in St. Louis, on March 28, 1974.

3. Excerpts from an interview by Institute staff with a resident of Cabanne Place in St. Louis, on April 24, 1974.

4. Bureau of Labor Statistics, "Homeownership, Series C-7, St. Louis, Mo.-Ill." (Washington, D.C.: U.S. Government Printing Office.)

Chapter VII

1. In our study "Factors Affecting Crime and Instability in Federally Assisted Housing" (footnoted in Chapter III, above), residents in forty-four sites, consisting of high-rises, walk-ups and row houses, were asked: *Is there a problems with residents not controlling their children?* Their response, by building type, is shown in the table below:

Respondents in	*Uncontrolled children*	
	A VERY BIG PROBLEM	NO PROBLEM AT ALL
High-rises	22%	7%
Walk-ups	5%	60%
Row houses	3%	50%

2. Our Institute's study of the effectiveness of intercom installations in New York City public housing showed that the number of resident teen-age children sharing the entry to a building was a significant factor in predicting the ability of the intercom installations to reduce crime (*Final Report of Project for Residential Security Design,* prepared for the National Institute of Law Enforcement and Criminal Justice, Washington, D.C. 1973, Addendum B, Intercom Effectiveness Study).

3. In our Institute's current study *Factors Affecting Crime and Instability in Federally Assisted Housing,* the parents of 1,627 moderate-income households (located in high-rises, walk-ups, and row houses) were asked what type of residential environment they preferred for raising children: 49 per cent of all respondents chose row houses; 37 per cent chose two-story garden apartments (with entries provided directly to the ground from each unit); 9 per cent

chose subdivided walk-ups (designed with only six families sharing an entry); 2 per cent chose walk-up gallerias; 1 per cent chose walk-ups with long interior corridors; and 1 per cent chose high-rises. Of the respondents living in high-rises, only 3 per cent chose high-rises as the preferred environment for raising children; 37 per cent chose row houses; and the remaining 60 per cent chose either garden apartments or walk-ups. Less than 1 per cent of the respondents living in row houses and walk-ups chose high-rises as their preferred environment for raising children.

Chapter VII

4. These findings from informal interviews conducted in 1973–74 with residents of all-elderly buildings in public housing projects in New York and Jersey City, by staff of the Institute for Community Design Analysis, supported Richard Lamanna's study, "Value Consensus Among Urban Residents," in which he found that older people were significantly *more* likely to rate the opportunity for socializing as a factor in their choice of a living environment than were families with children (*Journal of the American Institute of Planners*, Vol. 36 [1964], pp. 317–26).

5. In a June 1971 interview with the author, the Chief of Statistics of the New York City Housing Authority, Harry Fialkin, revealed that whereas the crime rate experienced by the elderly was normally about three and a half times that experienced by other housing authority residents, when white elderly were a minority living among black families with teen-age children, crime against the elderly climbed to five times the average.

6. M. Messer, "Engagement with Disengagement," paper presented at the 1966 Annual Meeting of the American Sociological Association, Miami Beach Florida.

7. S. R. Sherman, "The Choice of Retirement Housing Among the Well-Elderly," in *Aging and Human Development*, Vol. 2 (1971), pp. 118–138.

8. T. Caplow and R. Forman, "Neighborhood Interaction in a Homogenous Community." I. R. Kohn, K. A. Franck, and A. S. Fox, "Defensible Space Modifications in Row-House Communities."

9. U.S. Department of Housing and Urban Development, *Minimum Property Standards*, Vol. 4910.1 (Washington, D.C.: U. S. Government Printing Office, 1973). Building Officials & Code Administrators International, Inc., *Basic Building Code/1970* (Chicago, Ill., 1970) *New York City Building Laws*, Vol. 1 (New York: New York Society of Architects, 1972).

10. N. Foote et al., *Housing Choices and Constraints* (New York: McGraw-Hill, 1960).

Chapter VIII

1. In a comparison of tenant identification with and use of grounds in three New York City housing projects—a walk-up, a medium high-rise, and tall high-rise (Brownsville, Bronxdale and Van Dyke)—residents in the Brownsville walk-ups were found to participate in grounds cleaning and in planting flowers. In interviews it was learned that they also found the grounds they maintained

safer than did residents of elevator buildings. Residents at Bronxdale, a seven-story medium high-rise with many moderate-income residents, did not view the grounds below as safe or feel they could control activity there, nor did they participate in any ground maintenance or planting. Lower-income residents at Van Dyke, a twelve-story high-rise, rated the grounds as even more unsafe than did residents at Bronxdale and felt even more disassociated and lacking in the ability to control activity there. Parents there said that their young children were not allowed down to the ground without an adult. (From an unpublished final report to the National Institute of Law Enforcement and Criminal Justice on research activity conducted at the Institute of Planning and Housing, New York University, between June 1, 1970, and June 24, 1971.)

2. Department of the Environment, *Children at Play,* Design Bulletin 27 (London: Her Majesty's Stationery Office, 1973).

Chapter X

1. "Crimes" is defined here as *all* categories of crime and breach of housing authority rules. The premodification period under study was January 1967 to September 1970. The postmodification period was June 1972 to November 1974 (I. R. Kohn, K. A. Franck, and A. S. Fox, "Defensible Space Modifications in Row-House Communities," a final report submitted to the National Science Foundation, Grant No. Apr 74-04012 A01, 1975, p. 111).

2. Ibid., Table 4.2 p. 111.

3. Ibid., Summary Report, p. 14.

4. Ibid., pp. 117–18.

Chapter XI

1. C. St. J. Wilson, "A Letter to an American Student," *Program,* No. 3 (Spring 1964), pp. 72–74.

2. André Wogenscky commenting on the work of Giancarlo De Carlo, in O. Newman (ed.), *New Frontiers in Architecture: CIAM '59 in Otterlo,* p. 90.

3. A. and P. Smithson, "Criteria for Mass Housing," in O. Newman (ed.), op. cit., p. 79.

4. Peter Smithson's comment to the author at the Institute for Contemporary Arts, in London, Fall, 1973.

5. L. Rainwater, "Fear and the House as Haven in the Lower Class."

BIBLIOGRAPHY

ACKERMAN, B. L. "Integration for Subsidized Housing and the Question of Racial Occupancy Controls." *Stanford Law Review* (January 1974), 245–309.

ALLPORT, G. W. *The Nature of Prejudice.* Reading, Mass.: Addison-Wesley, 1954.

AXELROD, M. "Urban Structure and Social Participation." *American Sociological Review,* 1956, *21,* 13–18.

BAUM, A., and S. VALINS. *Architecture and Social Behavior.* Hillsdale, N.J.: Lawrence Erlbau, 1977.

BECKER, F. D. "Design for Living: The Residents' View of Multi-family Housing." Unpublished final report to the New York State Urban Development Corporation. Center for Urban Development Research, Cornell University, Ithaca, N.Y., 1974.

BELL, W., and M. T. FORCE. "Urban Neighborhood Types and Participation in Informal Relations." American Sociological Review, 1956, *21,* 25–34.

BELL, W. "The City, the Suburb, and a Theory of Social Choice." In S. Greer et al., eds., *The New Urbanization.* New York: St. Martin's Press, 1968.

BLAKE, P. *Form Follows Fiasco: Why Modern Architecture Hasn't Worked.* Boston: Little, Brown, 1977.

———. *The Master Builders: Frank Lloyd Wright, Le Corbusier, Mies van der Rohe.* New York: Knopf, 1960.

BLALOCK, H. M., JR. *Toward a Theory of Minority-group Relations.* New York: Wiley, 1967.

BRADBURN, N. M., S. SUDMAN, and G. L. GOCKEL. *Racial Integration in American Neighborhoods.* Chicago: National Opinion Research Center, 1970.

BROADY, M. "Social Theory in Architectural Design." In R. Gutman, ed., *People and Buildings.* New York: Basic Books, 1972.

BROLIN, B. C. *The Failure of Modern Architecture.* New York: Van Nostrand, 1976.

BROWER, S. N., and P. WILLIAMSON. "Outdoor Recreation as a Function of the Urban Housing Environment." *Environment and Behavior,* 1974, *6,* 295–346.

CAPLOW, T., and R. FORMAN. "Neighborhood Interaction in a Homogenous Community." *American Sociological Review,* 1950, *15,* 357–66.

CENTER FOR COMMUNITY CHANGE AND NATIONAL URBAN LEAGUE. *National Survey of Housing Abandonment,* 1971.

CHERMAYEFF, S., and C. ALEXANDER. *Community and Privacy.* Garden City, N.Y.: Doubleday, 1963.

CHICAGO CITY PLANNING COMMISSION. *Cabrini-Green Proposal.* Chicago: Internal Report, 1973.

COLEMAN, J. S. *Community Conflict.* Glencoe, Ill.: Free Press, 1957.

COOPER, C. "Residents' Attitudes Toward the Environment at St. Francis Square, San Francisco." Working Paper No. 126. Berkeley, Cal.: Institute of Urban and Regional Development, 1972.

––––––. *Easter Hill Village.* New York: Free Press, 1975.

––––––. and P. HACKETT. "Analysis of the Design Process at Two Moderate-income Housing Developments." Working Paper No. 80. Berkeley, Cal., Institute of Urban and Regional Development, 1968.

––––––, N. DAY, and B. LEVINE. "Resident Dissatisfaction in Multi-family Housing. Working Paper No. 160. Berkeley, Cal.: Institute of Urban and Regional Development, 1972.

DEUTSCH, M., and M. E. COLLINS. *Interracial Housing: A Psychological Evaluation of a Social Experiment.* Minneapolis: University of Minnesota Press, 1951.

DOWNS, A. *Opening Up the Suburbs.* New Haven: Yale University Press, 1973.

EFFRAT, M. P. "Approaches to Community: Conflicts and Complimentaries." In M. P. Effrat, ed., *The Community: Approaches and Applications.* New York: Free Press, 1974.

EMPEY, L. T., and R. L. LUBECK. *Explaining Delinquency.* Lexington, Mass.: Heath Lexington Books, 1971.

FEAGIN, J. R. "Community Disorganization: Some Critical Notes." In M. P. Effrat, ed., *The Community: Approaches and Applications.* New York: Free Press, 1974.

FESTINGER, L. "Architecture and Group Membership." *Journal of Social Issues,* 1951, *7,* 152–63.

––––––, S. SCHACTER, and K. BACK. *Social Pressure in Informal Groups.* New York: Harper, 1950.

FRANCK, K. A. "Environmental Psychology: A Call for Discipline and Imagination." Paper presented at the New England Psychological Association, Clark University, Worcester, Mass., November 13, 1976.

FREEMAN, L. C., and M. N. SUNSHINE. *Patterns of Residential Segregation.* Cambridge, Mass.: Schenkman, 1970.

FRIED, M. "Grieving for a Lost Home." In L. J. Duhl, ed., *The Urban Condition.* New York: Basic Books, 1963.

————, and P. GLEICHER. "Sources of Residential Satisfaction in an Urban Slum." *Journal of the American Institute of Planners,* 1961, *27,* 305–15.

FRIEDEN, B. J. "Housing and National Urban Goals: Old Policies and New Facilities." In J. Q. Wilson, ed., *The Metropolitan Enigma.* Cambridge, Mass.: Harvard University Press, 1968.

GANS, H. J. *The Urban Villagers.* New York: Free Press, 1959.

————. *The Levittowners.* New York: Pantheon Press, 1967.

————. *People and Plans.* New York: Basic Books, 1968.

GIEDION, S. *Space, Time and Architecture.* Cambridge, Mass.: Harvard University Press, 1941.

GILLIS, A. R. "High-rise Housing and Psychological Strain." *Journal of Health and Social Behavior,* 1977, *18,* 418–31.

GINSBERG, Y. *Jews in a Changing Neighborhood.* New York: Free Press, 1975.

GLAZER, N. "Housing Problems and Housing Policies." *The Public Interest* (Spring 1967), 21–51.

GREER, S. "Urbanism Reconsidered: A Comparative Study of Local Areas in a Metropolis." *American Sociological Review,* 1956, *21,* 19–25.

————. "Neighborhood." In D. L. Sills, ed., *International Encyclopedia of the Social Sciences,* Vol. 2. New York: Macmillan, 1968.

GRIER, E., and G. GRIER. *Privately Developed Interracial Housing: An Analysis of Experience.* Berkeley: University of California Press, 1960.

————. "Equality and Beyond: Housing Segregation in the Great Society." In T. Parsons and K. Clark, eds., *The Negro American.* Boston: Houghton Mifflin, 1966.

GRIER, G., and E. GRIER. *Equality and Beyond: Housing Segregation and the Goals of the Great Society.* Chicago: Quadrangle Books, 1966.

GROPIUS, W. *The Scope of Total Architecture.* New York: Crowell-Collier, 1962.

————. *The New Architecture and the Bauhaus.* Trans. P. Morton Shand. London: Faber & Faber, 1935.

GUTMAN, R. "Site Planning and Social Behavior." *Journal of Social Issues,* 1966, *22,* 103–15.

HILLERY, G. A. "Definitions of Community: Areas of Agreement." *Rural Sociology,* 1955, *20,* 111–23.

HITCHCOCK, H. R., and P. JOHNSON. *The International Style.* New York: Norton, 1932.

HOMANS, G. C. *The Human Group.* New York: Harcourt, Brace, 1950.

HUNTER, A. *Symbolic Communities.* Chicago: University of Chicago Press, 1974.

————. "The Loss of Community: An Empirical Test Through Replication." *American Sociological Review,* 1975, *40,* 537–52.

————. "Reply to Luloff and Wilkinson." *American Sociological Review,* 1977, *42,* 828–29.

ITTELSON, W. H., et al. *An Introduction to Environmental Psychology.* New York: Holt, Rinehart and Winston, 1974.

JACOBS, J. *Death and Life of Great American Cities.* New York: Random House, 1961.

JAHODA, M., and P. WEST. "Race Relations in Public Housing." *Journal of Social Issues,* 1951, 132–39.

JANOWITZ, M. J. *The Community Press in an Urban Setting.* Chicago: University of Chicago Press, 1952.

JENCKS, C. *Modern Movements in Architecture.* Garden City, N.Y.: Doubleday, 1973.

————. *The Language of Post-modern Architecture.* New York: Rizzoli, 1977.

JOHNSON, P. C. *Mies van der Rohe.* New York: Museum of Modern Art, 1947.

KAIN, J. F., and J. J. PERSKY. "Alternatives to the Gilded Ghetto." *The Public Interest,* (Spring, 1969), 74–87.

KANTER, R. *Commitment and Community: Communes and Utopias in Sociological Perspective.* Cambridge, Mass: Harvard University Press, 1972.

KASARDA, J., and M. JANOWITZ. "Community Attachment in Mass Society." *American Sociological Review,* 1974, *39,* 328–39.

KELLER, S. "Social Class in Physical Planning." *International Social Science Journal,* 1966, *18,* 494–512.

KOHN, I. R., K. A. FRANCK, and A. S. FOX. "Defensible Space Modifications in Row-House Communities." Unpublished report to the National Science Foundation (RANN). Institute for Community Design Analysis, New York, 1975.

KORNHAUSER, W. "Mass Society." In D. L. Sills, ed., *International Encyclopedia of the Social Sciences.* Vol. 10. New York: Macmillan, 1968.

LAND, K. C. "Principles of Path Analysis." In E. F. Borgatta, ed., *Sociological Methodology, 1969.* San Francisco: Jossey-Bass, 1969.

LANGER, S. *Feeling and Form.* New York: Scribner, 1953.

LAWTON, M. P., and L. NAHEMOW. "Ecology and the Aging Process." In C. Eisdorfer and M. P. Lawton, eds., *The Psychology of Adult Development and Aging.* Washington, D.C.: American Psychological Association, 1973.

LITTLE, J. T., et al. *The Contemporary Neighborhood Succession Process.* Report by the Institute for Urban and Regional Studies, Washington University, St. Louis, Mo., 1975.

LITWAK, E. "Voluntary Associations and Neighborhood Cohesion." In R. Gutman and D. Popenoe, eds., *Neighborhood, City, and Metropolis.* New York: Random House, 1970.

LULOFF, A. E., and K. P. WILKINSON. "Is Community Alive and Well in the Inner City?" *American Sociological Review,* 1977, *42,* 828–29.

MARRETT, C. B. "Social Stratification in Urban Areas." In A. H. Hawley and V. P. Rock, eds., *Segregation in Residential Areas: Papers on Racial and Socioeconomic Factors in Choice of Housing.* Washington, D.C.: National Academy of Sciences, 1973.

MAXWELL, A. E., and L. G. HUMPHREYS. "Factor Analysis." In D. L. Sills, ed., *International Encyclopedia of the Social Sciences*, Vol. 5. New York: Macmillan, 1968.

McCARTHY, D., and S. SAEGERT. "Residential Density, Social Control, and Social Withdrawal." Doctoral dissertation, Environmental Psychology Program, City University of New York, 1976.

McENTIRE, D. *Residence and Race.* Berkeley: University of California Press, 1960.

McFALL, T. P. "Racially and Economically Integrated Housing. Unpublished manuscript. Metropolitan Council, St. Paul, Minn., 1974.

MERTON, R. K. "The Social Psychology of Housing." In W. Dennis, ed., *Current Trends in Social Psychology.* Pittsburgh: University of Pittsburgh Press, 1948.

MICHELSON, W. H. *Man and His Urban Environment.* Reading, Mass.: Addison-Wesley, 1970.

———. "The Reconciliation of Subjective and Objective Data on Physical Environment in the Community." In M. P. Effrat, ed., *The Community: Appraoches and Applications.* New York: Free Press, 1974.

MILGRAM, S. "The Experience of Living in Cities." *Cities*, 1970, *67*, 1461–68.

MILLEN, J. S. "Factors Affecting Racial Mixing in Residential Areas." In A. H. Hawley and V. P. Rock, eds., *Segregation in Residential Areas: Papers on Racial and Socioeconomic Factors in Choice of Housing.* Washington, D.C.: National Academy of Sciences, 1973.

MOORE, W. *The Vertical Ghetto.* New York: Random House, 1969.

NAVASKY, V. S. "The Benevolent Housing Quota." *Howard Law Journal* (1960), *6*, 30, 46–47, 53.

NEWMAN, O. *Architectural Design for Crime Prevention.* Washington, D.C.: U. S. Department of Justice, Law Enforcement Assistance Administration, and National Institute of Law Enforcement and Criminal Justice, 1973.

———. "The Crime and Vandalism Problems in Two Indianapolis Public Housing Projects (Raymond Villa and Hawthorne) and Recommendations for Remedial Action." Unpublished Final report to Indianapolis Department of Metropolitan Development, Division of Planning and Zoning, 1975.

———. *Defensible Space.* New York: Macmillan, 1972.

———. *Defensible Space Modifications to Eight Jersey City Housing Projects.* Final report to the Jersey City Office of Criminal Justice Planning, 1973.

———. *Design Guidelines for Creating Defensible Space.* Washington, D. C.: Law Enforcement Assistance Administration, National Institute of Law Enforcement and Criminal Justice, 1976.

————, ed., *New Frontiers in Architecture: CIAM '59 in Otterlo.* New York: Universe Books, 1961.

NISBET, R. *The Quest for Community.* New York: Oxford University Press, 1953.

————. "Moral Values and Community." In R. Gutman and D. Popenoe, eds., *Neighborhood, City, and Metropolis.* New York: Random House, 1970.

NOHARA, S. "Social Context and Neighborliness: The Negro in St. Louis." In S. Greer et al., eds., *The New Urbanization.* New York: St. Martin's Press, 1968.

NORBERG-SCHULZ, C. *Existence, Space and Architecture.* New York: Praeger, 1971.

PARK, R. *Human Communities.* Glencoe, Ill: Free Press, 1952.

PETTIGREW, T. F., "Attitudes on Race and Housing: A Social-psychological View." In A. H. Hawley and V. P. Rock, eds., *Segregation in Residential Areas: Papers on Racial and Socioeconomic Factors in Choice of Housing.* Washington, D.C.: National Academy of Sciences, 1973.

POTOMAC INSTITUTE, *Housing Guide to Equal Opportunity.* Washington, D.C.: Potomac Institute, 1968.

RAINWATER, L. "Fear and the House as Haven in the Lower Class." *Journal of American Institute of Planners,* 1966, *32,* 23–30.

RAPKIN, C., and W. G. GRIGSBY. *The Demand for Housing in Racially Mixed Neighborhoods.* Berkeley: University of California Press, 1960.

REISS, A. J. "The Sociological Study of Communities." In R. Gutman and D. Popenoe, eds., *Neighborhood, City, and Metropolis.* New York: Random House, 1970.

REPPETTO, T., *Residential Crime.* Cambridge, Mass.: Ballinger, 1974.

ROSS, H. L. "The Local Community: A Survey Approach." In S. Greer and A. L. Greer, eds., *Neighborhood and Ghetto.* New York: Basic Books, 1974.

RYAN, W., et al. *All in Together: An Evaluation of Mixed Income Multi-family Housing.* Boston: Massachusetts Housing Finance Agency, 1974.

SADACCA, R., and M. ISLER. *Management Performance in Multi-family Housing Developments.* Working Paper No. 209-4. Washington, D.C.: Urban Institute, 1972.

————, M. DRURY, and M. ISLER. *Ownership Form and Management Success in Private, Publicly Assisted Housing.* Working Paper No. 209-3. Washington, D.C.: Urban Institute, 1972.

SCHMID, C. "Urban Crime Areas: Part I." *American Sociological Review,* 1960, *25,* 527–42.

————. "Urban Crime Areas: Part II." *American Sociological Review,* 1960, *25,* 655–78.

SCHULZ, D. A. *Coming Up Black: Patterns of Ghetto Socialization.* Englewood Cliffs, N.J.: Prentice-Hall, 1969.

SMITHSON, A., and P. SMITHSON. "An Urban Project." In T. Danatt, ed., *Architects' Year Book 5.* London: Elek Books, 1953.

————. "Criteria for Mass Housing." *Forum,* 1960, 16–17.

SMITHSON, A., ed. *Team 10 Primer.* Cambridge, Mass.: MIT Press, 1968.

STARR, R. "Which of the Poor Shall Live in Public Housing?" *The Public Interest* (Spring 1971).

STEIN, M. *The Eclipse of Community*. Princeton: Princeton University Press, 1960.

STEPHAN, F. F., and P. J. MCCARTHY. *Sampling Opinions: An Analysis of Survey Procedures*. New York: Wiley, 1958.

STERNLIEB, G., et al. "Housing Abandonment in the Urban Core." *Journal of the American Institute of Planners* (Sept. 1974).

SUDMAN, S., and N. BRADBURN. *Social-psychological Factors in Inter-group Housing*. Chicago: National Opinion Research Center, 1966.

SUDMAN, S., N. M. BRADBURN, and G. GOCKEL. "The Extent and Characteristics of Racially Integrated Housing in the United States." *Journal of Business*, 1969, *42*, 50–92.

SUTTLES, G. D. *The Social Order of the Slum*. Chicago: University of Chicago Press, 1968.

———. *The Social Construction of Communities*. Chicago: University of Chicago Press, 1972.

TAEUBER, K. E., and A. F. TAEUBER. *Negroes in Cities*. Chicago: Aldine Press, 1965.

TEUT, A. *Architektur im Dritten Reich (1933–45)*. Berlin: Bauwelt F.B. 19, 1967.

THE PRESIDENT'S COMMISSION ON LAW ENFORCEMENT AND ADMINISTRATION OF JUSTICE. *Task Force Report: Crime and Its Impact—An Assessment*. Wasington, D.C.: U. S. Government Printing Office, 1967.

———. *The Challenge of Crime in a Free Society*. Washington, D.C.: U. S. Government Printing Office, 1967.

TILLY, C. "Do Communities Act?" In M. P. Effrat, ed., *The Community: Approaches and Applications*. New York: Free Press, 1974.

VAN EYCK, A. "The Medicine of Reciprocity Tentatively Illustrated." *Forum*, 1961, *6*, 237–391.

VIDICH, A. J., and J. BENSMAN. *Small Town in Mass Society*. Princeton: Princeton University Press, 1958.

WEBBER, M. "The Urban Place and the Nonplace Urban Realm." In M. Webber, ed. *Explorations into Urban Structure*. Philadelphia: University of Pennsylvania Press, 1964.

———. "Order in Diversity: Community Without Propinquity." In R. Gutman and D. Popenoe, eds., *Neighborhood, City, and Metropolis*. New York: Random House, 1970.

WILKS, J. A. "Ecological correlates of crime and delinquency." In The President's Commission on Law Enforcement and Administration of Justice, *Task Force Report: Crime and Its Impact—an Assessment*. Washington, D.C.: U. S. Government Printing Office, 1967.

WILNER, D. M., R. WALKLEY, and S. W. COOK. *Human Relations in Interracial Housing: A Study of the Contact Hypothesis*. Minneapolis: University of Minnesota Press, 1955.

WIRTH, L. "Urbanism as a Way of Life." In P. Hatt and A. Reiss, eds, *Cities and Society*. Glencoe, Ill.: Free Press, 1957.

WOLF, E. P. "The Tipping Point in Racially Changing Neighborhoods." *American Institute of Planners Journal,* 1963, *29,* 217.

———. "The Baxter Area: A New Trend in Neighborhood Change?" *Phylon 26* (Winter 1965), 344–53.

———, and C. N. LEBEAUX. "Class and Race in the Changing City." In L. F. Schnore, ed., *Social Science and the City.* New York: Praeger, 1967.

———, and C. N. LEBEAUX. *Change and Renewal in an Urban Community.* New York: Praeger, 1969.

YANCEY, W. L. "Architecture, Interaction, and Social Control: The Case of a Large-scale Public Housing Project." In J. Helmer and N. A. Eddington, eds., *Urbanman: The Psychology of Urban Survival.* New York: Free Press, 1973.

ZALD, M. "Sociology and Community Organization Practice." In M. Zald, ed., *Organizing for Community Welfare.* Chicago: Quandrangle, 1967.

ZIMMER, B. G., and A. H. HAWLEY. "The Significance of Membership in Associations." *American Journal of Sociology,* 1959, *65,* 196–201.

Index

OSCAR NEWMAN is president and founder of the Institute for Community Design Analysis, a nonprofit research corporation engaged in the study of the effects of environmental design on human behavior. An architect and urban planner, Newman also serves as a consultant to many government housing development agencies in this country and abroad. He has prepared plans for the design and rehabilitation of housing projects in most of the major cities in the United States. His research on the ways in which design can be used to help control crime was the basis of his book *Defensible Space*.